*To the spirit of John Muir,
father of our national parks*

ACKNOWLEDGMENTS

If I Don't Do This, I'll Never Do Anything is the title of Chuck Herring's book about self publishing. It helped inspire this book, as did Chuck himself. To Chuck I owe the greatest debt of all. He not only was a gold mine of information about self publishing, but he also came up with the idea for this book. Its growth and my motivation fed on his enthusiasm, encouragement, and advice from beginning to end—which I suspect is only another beginning.

I owe another great debt to Don Sherwood. Most of the park histories and individual park maps were distilled from the abundantly detailed histories and maps he compiled during his years with the park department. I am also grateful to Don for reading and making needed changes in the original manuscript.

Many thanks also to the members of the Seattle Park Department—particularly Lou Anne Kirby, who put up with more than her fair share of trivial phone calls and went through the manuscript with a fine-tooth comb; and to John Bierlein, Ranger-Naturalist at Discovery Park. Thanks also to Betsy Fulwiler for editing the manuscript; to Eleanor Mathews for her cartographic and design talents; to Stephen Strelecki for his patience and production skills; and to my sister Pierr for the special spirit I knew her illustrations would add to the project.

I would also like to thank those in the local publishing industry who gave me so much helpful advice, and the many friends who provided ideas and encouragement—particularly Judy Herring, Charlie Johnson, Rose Ann Cattolico, and John Williams.

And finally, a warm thanks to Sally Bryan, who sparked an interest in writing years ago; and to my parents and my great aunt, Ruth McEvoy, who instilled and nourished an early love of wild places.

ENJOYING SEATTLE'S PARKS

BRANDT MORGAN

P. 25

ZOO P. 66
75 + 76

DISCOVERY PARK
P. 102

625-4636

Design and cartography by Eleanor Mathews

Illustrated maps by Pierr Morgan Leitz

Typesetting by Western Photon Typesetting, Seattle, Wash.

Printed by Snohomish Publishing Company, Snohomish, Wash.

Library of Congress Catalog Card No. 79—63074

ISBN: 0—933576—01—3

GREENWOOD PUBLICATIONS
P.O. Box 70106
Seattle, Wash., 98107

INTRODUCTION

When my brother and I were growing up in Seattle, we were lucky enough to live next to a wooded vacant lot, where we could lose ourselves in leafy explorations, clamber up tree trunks, and dig in the dirt to our hearts' content. "The woods" was only a few blocks square, but from an eye level of four feet it seemed like an impenetrable wilderness, enticing and forbidding at the same time, challenging us to strike out to the far side.

When one day we actually *did* dare—armed with sticks—to blaze through to the other side, we found another dead end street just like our own. "The woods," in fact, was an island surrounded by concrete. And yet it was enough to give us a feeling of excitement and adventure that I will never forget. Now it is gone completely, bulldozed away for new houses.

Wild lands and half-wild pockets like the one my brother and I enjoyed so much have been disappearing all over the country at an alarming rate, to be replaced by civilized streets and buildings. Urban parks are precious today in a way that our ancestors could not have forseen. Almost everyone who lives in the city relies on parks in some way for the refreshment of strength and spirits. All year long, both children and adults who have been contained in cramped environments flock to the parks to let their spirits unravel and soar like kites in a brisk wind. This is urban renewal at its best.

And urban parks are rapidly becoming even more vital. Today, over seventy percent of all Americans are living in cities. Over fifty-four million families do not own automobiles. Inflation and energy costs continue to increase. Not surprisingly, the federal government has been actively reassessing the importance of urban recreation, and it seems certain that park money which was once destined for wilderness areas will soon be funneled into the cities.

With the new focus on urban recreation, it seemed a good idea to let people know where Seattle's parks are and what they have to offer. That is primarily what this book tries to do. It also tries to give an historical perspective on the development of Seattle's park system and glimpses into the making of many of the parks themselves.

I have been pleasantly surprised to discover how extensive and exciting Seattle's park system really is. It includes literally hundreds of green patches scattered all over the city, with related programs and activities ranging from athletics to the visual and performing arts. The entire system spans about 5,000 acres. Many of these acres are especially wild ones, bottled up by pioneers and early park planners before it was too late. Others are tame and well manicured, popping up in new places with baffling frequency. Long after I thought my own list was complete, someone would point out a park I had missed, or I would read about a new one to be dedicated in some hidden corner of the city. I finally gave up trying to find them all, realizing that the system is constantly changing and expanding.

This I see as a hopeful sign, and a confirmation of my belief that parks spring from something in the human spirit that cannot do without wildness and greenery. It is no coincidence that some of the most attractive and intriguing parks in the city have been built over once decaying or dying concerns: a former garbage dump, an old gas plant, a surplused Army base, an abandoned railroad. Parks are an intimate part of the cycle of decay and renewal that ultimately nourishes something intangible but important in all of us. Even the mini parks, tucked like oases among businesses, warehouses, apartment buildings, and street ends, offer crucial breathing spaces for crowded residents, and often bring new horizons and possibilities into view.

No one can deny that parks have their problems. They suffer from vandalism, crime, and many of the other urban ills one can think of. Not the least of their problems is that there is not even enough money to maintain them. But I am not going to advocate parks reform here or elsewhere in this book. *Enjoyment* of Seattle's parks is what I am pushing, because that is what I think parks are all about. And, of course, the more people get from these fountains of renewal, the more they may be inspired to give back.

HOW TO USE THIS BOOK

Enjoying Seattle's Parks begins with a short history of Seattle's park system and an alphabetical listing of park programs and activities. The rest of the book is divided into eight sections, each corresponding to a geographical section of the city. Use the city map on the inside front cover to locate the page number of the desired section. On that page you will find an enlarged map showing locations of the parks and playgrounds in that section. Park areas shown in dark gray are discussed alphabetically on the pages immediately following the maps. Most playgrounds and playfields are shown in light gray and are not discussed in the text. (Playgrounds usually feature play areas for children, usually including swings, slide, and climbing apparatus; the maps in the "Programs and Activities" chapter will give you a good idea of what the playfields have to offer.) If you want to find a specific park, simply look it up in the index at the back of the book.

In some cases, nonmunicipal facilities such as the University of Washington have been included as parks because of the many parklike experiences they have to offer. Some playgrounds and playfields have also been treated as parks. This is the result of a complicated set of criteria involving everything from federal funding to community attitudes. In general, the park department defines a park as passive open space that may include children's play areas or sports facilities. A playground is an area of five or more acres that includes organized games and play apparatus for children. A playfield is an open area devoted to athletics such as softball, football, and soccer. The definitions, however, are not rigid, and frequently overlap and become hazy. If, for example, a neighborhood *perceives* a playground or playfield as a park, the city sometimes classifies it as a park. This book then treats it as a park also.

Inherent in this perception, I think, is the notion that parks are special in some way; that they provide a focal point for a community, helping to give it identity and cohesiveness. No doubt there will be some disappointment to find a favorite "park" treated here as a playground or playfield. I offer only one small consolation: it speaks well for Seattle's park system that it was impossible to discuss them all in one volume.

CONTENTS

History of Seattle's Parks

Seattle will rank foremost with the leading cities of the United States in the matter of parks and parkways.

—Board of Park Commissioners, 1909

In some ways, Seattle's parks can be enjoyed in the mind. One way is by simply reading about them. Just as one can travel back in time to unravel the history of the city—to see where it came from and to speculate on where it might be going—one can also trace the parallel development of the parks. And in the process, the interdependence of the two becomes more clear: the needs of the city give rise to the parks, while the parks in turn give the city new vitality. This chapter is an attempt to outline the important events in the unfolding of Seattle's park system, and serves as a framework for the histories that go along with many of the park descriptions in later pages.

About 15,000 years ago, the raw material for Seattle's parks was buried under glacial ice so thick that it would have taken four Seattle Space Needles stacked on top of one another to reach the surface. The tremendous pressure of this ice—several tons per square inch—sculpted the channels and elongate hills that are characteristic of the Puget Sound area today. Then, as it melted away, the glacier left the rocky rubble and underlying layers of sand and clay on which most of Seattle's parks are built.

Parks as such were unknown to the native Americans who first inhabited the shores of the *Whulge*, as they called Puget Sound. However, the Indians did have their favorite recreation areas. The Duwamish and Shilshoh tribes of the Seattle area enjoyed wrestling matches, footraces, lacrosse, and a variety of other games on the beaches. Periodically, they also met with other tribes for *potlatches*, which included much feasting and celebration. One of their favorite meeting grounds was called "Potlatch Meadows," the present site of the Seattle Center. The Indians also used Licton Springs (in north central Seattle) as a healing ground, and several other areas—notably Leschi and Alki—as campsites. Chief Seattle, the Indian for whom the city was eventually named, was on hand to greet the first white settlers at Alki Point.

After the pioneer settlement of Seattle began in 1851, Henry Yesler's sawmill on Elliott Bay became the town's first community center, and a sawdust-covered Occidental Square (now Pioneer Square) became the first ballfield and recreation area. During the early years, settlers were too preoccupied with clearing the wilderness to be much interested in creating a city park system. However, in 1884, some thirty-three years after he built the first log cabin at Alki Point, David Denny and his wife Mary donated five acres of land—a cemetery—for Seattle's first park. The pioneers pooled resources to relocate graves and convert the area into a place of beauty in the wilderness. The city was then nineteen years old, and still Denny Park was a long way by wagon trail from Occidental Square. Today, it is a five-acre oasis in the midst of a sea of concrete and rushing traffic a few blocks east of the Seattle Center.

Other parks were scarce in the 1880s. They included only Volunteer (then called City Park), Kinnear, and a few smaller tracts. But the 1890's put a new emphasis on park development. And surprisingly, that emphasis sprang from the urge to sell real estate.

The first homesteaders in the Seattle area had each been given 320 acres of land by the federal government. Those who had settled on or near Elliott Bay had no trouble subdividing and selling their land—for substantial profits—to later arrivals. However, would-be realtors who owned land in the wilderness areas of Lake Washington and Green Lake and across the tideflats near Duwamish Head for years had had no effective means of getting large numbers of buyers out to see their property.

Their problem was solved by the invention of the trolley and cable car in the late 1880s. Some realtors, such as John J. McGilvra on his Madison Park estate, quickly developed their own cable car companies and laid track straight through the woods into town. Others, such as Guy Phinney on his Woodland Park estate to the north, commissioned companies to lay track to their homestead sites. As an added incentive to prospective buyers, they developed elaborate amusement parks. Thrilling excursions on paddle wheel steamers and newfangled horseless carriages eventually helped to lure families into the country to picnic grounds, dance pavilions, sports fields, zoos, beaches, and beer halls. And while they were there, real estate agents were always on hand to point out the beauties of country living. These "Sunday Outings" were the birth of

Seattle's park system. Not only did they expand the city and instill a tradition of "getting away from it all," but many of these private amusement parks also became city parks after they had served the realtors' purposes.

By 1890 Seattle had established itself as a city; its harbor teemed with sailing ships and its streets cut farther into the wilds each year as forests were leveled for timber. Native Americans had been pushed off the land with guns and treaties, and some of their former campgrounds had become private parks. In the face of this simultaneous growth and destruction, a few visionaries began talking seriously about preservation.

The first of these was City Parks Superintendent E. O. Schwagerl, who in 1892 proposed the first comprehensive plan for a system of parks and boulevards. Schwagerl warned of the rapid ravagement of the forests and emphasized the natural beauty of the Seattle environs. He proposed a system to include major green spaces in all four corners of the city. His vision included boulevards linking the already popular private parks on Lake Washington— Leschi, Madison, and Madrona—with a large southeast peninsular park, later to become Seward. On Puget Sound he suggested the same: two major parks with a boulevard jutting inland to connect with Woodland Park, Ravenna, and the new University of Washington grounds.

As the years went by, a few others shared Schwagerl's views, while most did not. In 1900, for instance, Seattleites were outraged when the city paid Guy Phinney $100,000 for his Woodland Park estate. They were convinced it was too far outside the city to be of such value. That same year, Assistant City Engineer George F. Cotterill published a map of bicycle paths for Seattle's 55,000 citizens—10,000 of whom already owned bicycles. And it was also during the year 1900 that the first automobile puttered down the muddy streets of town.

Times were changing fast. Gold had been discovered in Alaska. Seattle was getting rich outfitting and entertaining northbound miners, and by producing timber for a growing nation. People had more leisure time. All over the country, cities were establishing park systems. And many of them were drafted by a famed parks fanatic and landscape architect named Frederick Law Olmsted. Olmsted designed New York's Central Park, and was soon in demand throughout the country.

In 1903, Olmsted's equally talented and fanatic sons were hired to design a detailed system of parks and boulevards for Seattle. Their firm, Olmsted Brothers Landscape Architects of Brookline, Massachusetts, expanded on Schwagerl's plan and used Cotterill's bike paths as the basis for an extended boulevard system. They swung boulevard loops west to Golden Gardens, east to Green Lake,

Ravenna, and the university, then south along Lake Washington to the Bailey Peninsula and Rainier Beach. From there they branched north to Jefferson Park, then to West Seattle and Alki.

In this scheme, the eager brothers envisioned various side branches connecting with still other parks, still to be created. They also recommended annexing a great many new park and playground areas, including Seward, Mount Baker, Colman, Frink, Gas Works, Edward, Westcrest, Fauntleroy, Lincoln, and Alki. In the end it would be a grand system allowing Seattleites to travel by horse, car or bike throughout the city without ever leaving a beautiful corridor of green.

Of course, the Olmsted Plan was not adopted all at once. But the brothers inflamed a growing public awareness and appreciation for parks. Their efforts were fueled considerably by the 1909 Alaska-Yukon-Pacific Exposition, a world's fair celebrating the gold rush and the city's coming of age. Just two years prior to the plan, Seattle citizens approved the city's first park bond, for a total of $500,000. In 1908, the year of the plan's publication, voters were willing to up the ante to twice that figure. And just two years later, fired by the fair and by the city's recent acquisition of West Seattle, Ballard, Columbia, and South Seattle, they were willing to double it again, to $2 million. These were years of intense growth for the city, years of planning in which there was room for the grand schemes of far-seeing men like Schwagerl and the Olmsteds.

Then came the greatest visionary of them all—Virgil R. Bogue. In 1910, this former engineer of railroads was asked to prepare an all-encompassing Seattle Plan. As if to outdo the brothers themselves, Bogue proposed a grand extension of the Olmsted Plan throughout the northwest corner of Washington State. He intended to expand the area's park space from a little over 1,000 acres to an astronomical 58,000 acres capable of serving a population of a million or more.

On the Seattle map Bogue drew in enormous chunks of parkland and more miles of boulevards. When he had finished with Seattle, he began encircling choice acreage elsewhere: 185 acres on the north end of Mercer Island; sixty-five acres at Bitter Lake; 200 acres on Lake Washington between Bothell and Juanita Bay. No doubt intoxicated by his railroad planning in the wilds of Alaska and South America, Bogue let his pencil run wild. He traced boulevards to Kirkland, Newcastle, Kent, Sunnydale, and Black River Junction. He spun around Lake Sammamish to Snoqualmie Falls, south to Tacoma along the bluffs overlooking the sound, on to Mount Rainier, around the Olympic Peninsula—and beyond. If Bogue had been handed a map of the world, who can say what he might have proposed in his Seattle Plan?

But Bogue was inspired by more than his own grandiosity. "The groves were God's first temple," he wrote in the preface to his plan. "The grand scene of Mount Rainier, hoary with its thousand ages, is awe inspiring, and the beholder is deeply impressed with a sense of the Infinite Presence and begins to understand why the native Indian had but one God—the Great Spirit."

Unfortunately, Bogue and the city fathers made a fatal error by presenting their Seattle Plan to the voters as a single package, which was defeated. It was killed, however, not because Bogue was considered a wild-eyed radical, but because of specific proposals— relatively small things, such as moving the civic center from Pioneer Square to the south end of Lake Union. It was a tragic mistake. Despite its defeat, city, county, and regional planners have returned to the Bogue Plan again and again. And gradually, piece by piece, much of the engineer's dream has become a reality.

For two decades after the Bogue Plan, Seattle's park system grew steadily with the city's rising fortunes. Even the Depression was not lost on Seattle's parks. Two years after the bottom dropped out of the stock market, Park Engineer E. R. Hoffman began public works projects to help combat unemployment and refuel the economy. This marked the city's first real cooperation with the federal government for parks improvement. With over $1 million in federal dollars from the Works Progress Administration, Hoffman had scouts and troops working on projects all over the city: recreational facilities at Camp Long, fish rearing ponds at Seward Park, a sea wall at Lincoln Park, animal cages at the Woodland Park Zoo, and a citywide supply of tennis courts and restrooms.

In the 1940s, with the system fairly well established, park development grew more complex. More millions were voted for parks. The city's planning commission, now with its own budget and staff, was asked to hammer out another comprehensive plan. The city began a new program combining park and school facilities.

In the 1950s, voters became lukewarm about park development, turning down bonds on three separate occasions. The park department also found it increasingly difficult to plan ahead while depending yearly on the whims of the city council at budget time.

The 1960s ushered in still more changes and complications. The solution to long-term planning came when the city council approved a six-year Capital Improvement Program allowing for yearly revision to meet changing conditions. More federal money flowed in through the Open Space Program, the Department of Housing and Urban Development, and the Bureau of Outdoor Recreation. In a few short years, the job of park development, which had formerly employed only a few far-seeing individuals and generous pioneers, had turned into a game of grantsmanship involving hundreds of bureaucrats and politicians all over the country.

Fortunately, Seattle played the game well. The city bureaucracy swelled with planners. Under the leadership of attorney James Ellis, who had spearheaded Seattle's successful effort to clean up the city's polluted waters a few years earlier, a "Committee of 200" hammered out a park plan ultimately called Forward Thrust.

The committee was determined not to make the same mistake made with the Bogue Plan in 1910. Instead of a single scheme, they split the overall plan into thirteen separate packages. In 1968, King County voters approved six of the plans for a total of $118 million. About $65 million went to Seattle. It was the largest park appropriation in the city's history. Matching federal money expanded the total to more than double its original amount, and even more money poured in from bond investments, Model Cities programs, and businesses and individuals. As the Forward Thrust plan was carried out over the next twelve years, the park department grew even larger and more complex.

The accomplishments of Forward Thrust are too numerous to list. Its greatest achievement is that it secured major new park space at a time when Seattle most needed it. Included are the city's new Waterfront Park and Aquarium, Discovery Park, the Freeway Park, the Burke-Gilman bicycle trail, and numerous neighborhood parks and playgrounds.

The 1970's have been some of the most exciting and productive in the entire ninety-five year history of Seattle's parks. With the acquisition of over 500 wild acres surplused by the Army at Fort Lawton and over 200 not-so-wild acres given by the Navy at Sand Point, the Seattle cityscape is beginning to fulfill the dreams first proposed by the early visionaries. If E. O. Schwagerl, the Olmsted Brothers, and Virgil Bogue could peruse a map of the city now, with over 5,000 acres of park patches and boulevards, they might be quite pleased that so many of their proposals had come to fruition.

On the other hand, they might say Seattle has not gone far enough. If they were to walk the city streets during rush hour some smoggy afternoon, they might even storm down to city hall, choking in outrage, saying, "This is not what we intended at all!"

And if Chief Seattle could testify, he would probably speak much as he did nearly one hundred years ago when asked to give up his land to the white settlers: "Our dead never forget the beautiful world that gave them being. They still love its verdant valleys, its murmuring rivers, its magnificent mountains, sequestered vales, and tree-rimmed lakes . . . . Every part of this soil is sacred to my people." It is not difficult to imagine this great Indian, unable to turn the tide back to simpler times, joining in chorus with the parks visionaries, saying, "Not enough, not enough! More parks! More wildness, more green!"

Park Activities and Programs

Time spent fishing is not deducted from life span.

—Anonymous

The activities and organized programs associated with Seattle's parks are too important to leave unmentioned. What goes on in the parks is, after all, the source of half the fun. And you can double your enjoyment by knowing what's happening where and when. The following pages are an alphabetical listing of most of the formal and informal activities that make Seattle's parks what they are. This section also includes maps and charts for your convenience in locating specialized park facilities throughout the city.

Art in the Parks

City parks are popular places to put up monuments, statues, and miscellaneous objects that may or may not pass for works of art. There is no way to list them all, but perhaps they are best discovered on your own as added surprises (or disappointments) in the total park experience.

The greatest concentration of art is in Volunteer Park's **Seattle Art Museum,** with permanent exhibits of Asian and European classical work, as well as exclusive shows and traveling exhibits from all over the world. The museum is open from noon to 5 p.m. Sundays, 10 a.m. to 5 p.m. Tuesday through Saturday, and from 7 to 10 p.m. Thursday evenings. Admission is $1 for adults, $.50 for students and seniors, and free for everyone Thursdays.

Just as a sampling, here are some other locations of artworks that may perk your interest:

Alki Beach. Bartholdi's bronze interpretation of the Statue of Liberty.

Belvedere Viewpoint. A replica of a Haida Indian totem pole.

Discovery Park. Home of the Daybreak Star Arts Center, with many displays of native American art, from John Hoover's carved and painted cedar "Spirit Boards" to Nathan Jackson's "Man and the Killer Whales" series done in acrylic on western red cedar.

Freeway Park. Naramore Fountain, designed by George Tsutakawa. The towerlike arrangement of bronze pieces is taken from the *Obos,* a Japanese expression of gratitude to nature.

Gas Works Park. A twenty-seven-foot sundial, designed by Charles Greening and Kim Lazare, unveiled in 1978.

Kerry Viewpoint. A massive steel sculpture entitled "Changing Form," by Doris Chase.

Licton Springs Park. Cedar carvings of birds and children by Fred Anderson.

Louisa Boren Viewpoint. Massive blocks of Rusted Cor-Ten steel in an untitled sculpture by Lee Kelly.

Mount Baker Park. A six-ton reproduction of an ancient stone lantern from Yokohama, 1923.

Myrtle Edwards Park. Michael Heizer's massive concrete and granite sculpture entitled "Adjacent, Against, Upon."

Pioneer Square. A bronze bust of Chief Seattle by sculptor James A. Wehn; also a replica of a Tlingit Indian totem pole.

Seattle Aquarium. Diane Katsiaficas' "Imprisoning Chair," oil on paper.

Seattle Center. Tony Smith's fabricated steel construction of Moses, between the Opera House and the International Fountain.

Seward Park. Japanese Torii Gate of Welcome; a seven-ton Japanese stone lantern; three smaller Japanese lanterns and a granite monument given by American organizations and the Japanese Consulate for the U.S. Bicentennial; and a carved pole by sculptor Rick Byers.

Tilicum Place. A fountain with James A. Wehn's bronze sculpture of Chief Seattle greeting pioneers at Alki.

Volunteer Park. Even aside from the Art Museum, this park contains probably the greatest number of statues, plaques, and monuments of any in the city. Among them are Richard Brooks' bronze figure of William Seward (in front of the Conservatory); a cedar sculpture by Dudley Carter called "Rivalry of the Winds" (east of the Art Museum); pairs of marble rams, camels, tigers, and warriors from the fifteenth to eighteenth centuries (in front of the Art Museum); and the doughnut-shaped "Black Sun," a sculpture done in Brazilian marble by Isamu Noguchi in 1969 (overlooking the water reservoir).

For locations of other works of art in public places, get the Seattle Public Library's series of five urban walking tours by calling the Central Library at 625-4969. Or order a copy of the city's leaflet entitled "Art and the Urban Experience" by calling 625-4534.

VISUAL AND PERFORMING ARTS (See map on page 29.)
The park department also operates five centers of visual and performing arts which offer courses and/or performances in art, ceramics, dance, and theatre. These include the Poncho and Bathhouse Theatres (see "Theatre in the Parks" in this section), the Madrona Dance Studio (see "Madrona Park"), the Seward Park Art Studio (see "Seward Park"), and the Pratt Fine Arts Center (see "Edwin Pratt Park").

Athletics

In pioneer days, there was a single informal ball field located in Occidental Square, near Henry Yesler's sawmill. Now there are nearly 200 athletic fields scattered all over the city. Throughout the year, almost all of them resound with the crack of baseballs, the bootings and scufflings of soccer players, and the roar of football fans along the sidelines.

Listed below are places where you can find baseball, football, and soccer fields. (Jogging, swimming, and tennis are covered in separate sections). Fields can be rented for a nominal fee by signing up *in person* a week in advance at the Scheduling Office (5201 Green Lake Way N., 625-4673). Sign-up hours are 11 a.m. to 1 p.m. and 4 to 6 p.m. Monday through Friday, and 8 to 9 a.m. Monday.

Alki Playground	58th S.W. and S.W. Stevens
Ballard Playground	N.W. 60th and 28th N.W.
Bar-S Playground	65th S.W. and S.W. Hanford

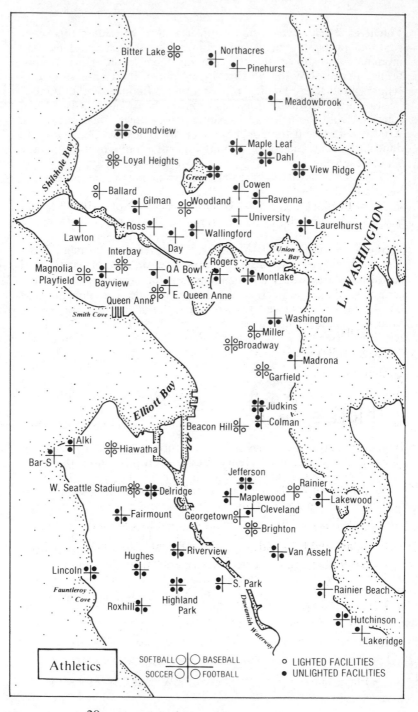

Athletics

SOFTBALL ⦾|⦿ BASEBALL
SOCCER ⦾|⦿ FOOTBALL

○ LIGHTED FACILITIES
● UNLIGHTED FACILITIES

Bitter Lake
Northacres
Pinehurst
Meadowbrook
Soundview
Maple Leaf
Dahl
Loyal Heights
View Ridge
Green L.
Ballard
Cowen
Gilman
Woodland
Ravenna
Ross
University
Laurelhurst
Lawton
Wallingford
Interbay
Day
Union Bay
Magnolia
Playfield
Rogers
L. WASHINGTON
Bayview
Q A Bowl
Montlake
Queen Anne
E. Queen Anne
Smith Cove
Washington
Miller
Broadway
Madrona
Garfield
Elliott Bay
Judkins
Colman
Beacon Hill
Alki
Hiawatha
Bar-S
Jefferson
W. Seattle Stadium
Rainier
Delridge
Maplewood
Lakewood
Fairmount
Georgetown
Cleveland
Brighton
Hughes
Riverview
Van Asselt
Lincoln
Fauntleroy Cove
S. Park
Rainier Beach
Roxhill
Highland Park
Duwamish Waterway
Hutchinson
Lakeridge
Shilshole Bay

Bayview Playground	24th W. and W. Raye
Beacon Hill Playground	14th S. and S. Holgate
Bitter Lake Playground	N. 130th and Linden N.
Brighton Playfield	42nd S. and Juneau
Broadway Playfield	11th E. and E. Pine
Cleveland Playground	13th S. and S. Lucille
Colman Playground	23rd S. and S. Grand
Cowen Park	University Way and N.E. Ravenna Boulevard
Dahl Playfield	25th N.E. and N.E. 77th
Day Playground	Fremont N. and N. 41st
Delridge Playfield	S.W. Oregon and Delridge Way S.W.
E. Queen Anne Playground	2nd N. and Howe
Fairmount Playground	Fauntleroy S.W. and S.W. Brandon
Garfield Playfield	23rd E. and E. Cherry
Georgetown Playground	Corson S. and S. Homer
Gilman Playground	11th N.W. and N.W. 54th
Green Lake Playfield	E. Green Lake Drive N. and Latona N.E.
Hiawatha Playfield	California S.W. and S.W. Lander
Highland Park Playground	11th S.W. and S.W. Thistle
Hughes Playground	29th S.W. and S.W. Holden
Hutchinson Playground	59th S.W. and S. Pilgrim
Interbay Athletic Field	17th W. and W. Dravus
Jefferson Playfield	16th S. and S. Dakota
Judkins Park and Playfield	22nd S. and S. Norman
Lakeridge Playground	Rainier S. between 68th and Cornell
Lakewood Playground	50th S. and S. Angeline
Laurelhurst Playfield	N.E. 41st and 48th N.E.
Lawton Park	26th W. and W. Thurman
Lincoln Park	Fauntleroy S.W. and S.W. Webster

Lower Woodland Park	N. 50th and Green Lake Way N.
Loyal Heights Playfield	N.W. 75th and 22nd N.W.
Madrona Playground	34th E. and E. Spring
Magnolia Playfield	34th W. and W. Smith
Maple Leaf Playground	N.E. 82nd and Roosevelt Way N.E.
Maple Wood Playground	Corson S. and S. Angeline
Meadowbrook Playfield	30th N.E. and N.E. 107th
Miller Playfield	20th E. and E. Republican
Montlake Playfield	16th E. and E. Calhoun
Northacres Park	1st N.E. and N.E. 130th
Pinehurst Playground	14th N.E. between N.E. 120th and N.E. 123rd
Queen Anne Bowl	3rd W. and W. Fulton
Queen Anne Playfield	1st W. and W. Howe
Rainier Playfield	Rainier S. and S. Alaska
Rainier Beach Playfield	Rainier S. and S. Cloverdale
Ravenna Park	22nd N.E. and N.E. 54th
Riverview Playfield	12th S.W. and S.W. Othello
Rogers Playground	Eastlake E. and E. Roanoke
Ross Playground	3rd N.W. and N.W. 43rd
Roxhill Park	29th S.W. and S.W. Roxbury
Soundview Playfield	15th N.W. and N.W. 90th
South Park Playground	8th S. and S. Sullivan
University Playground	9th N.E. and N.E. 50th
Van Asselt Playground	32nd S. and S. Myrtle
View Ridge Playfield	N.E. 70th and 45th N.E.
Wallingford Playfield	N. 43rd and Wallingford N.
Washington Park/Arboretum	Lake Washington Blvd. E. and E. Madison
West Seattle Stadium	35th S.W. and S.W. Snoqualmie

Bicycling

Bicycling has been a popular sport in Seattle since the 1890s, well before the arrival of the automobile. The first map of bike paths, published by the city in 1900, marked dusty buggy trails for pedaling through the woods on primitive one-speeders. Today the city offers a variety of asphalt and concrete bike routes, most of them conveniently connecting with Seattle parks.

BICYCLE ROUTES (See map on page 36.)

Alki Beach to Lincoln Park. About six miles one way. The bikeway is marked only along Alki Beach, from Duwamish Head south.

Burke-Gilman Trail. From the Gas Works Park north to Logboom Park in Kenmore, about 12.5 miles one way. This is the best in the city for family biking—away from traffic, with many eating and rest spots nearby. Among them are the University Village at 25th N.E., Albertson's Food Center at 40th N.E., Sand Point Park off N.E. 65th, and Matthews Beach Park off N.E. 93rd. There is also a food concession at the Gas Works Park in the summer and on sunny weekends throughout the year; and a restaurant and deli across the street.

Discovery Park. Several miles of old roadways.

Discovery Park to Magnolia Park. About three miles one way, along Magnolia Boulevard.

Discovery Park to Golden Gardens Park. About three miles one way. Ride to Commodore Park, walk your bike across the Ship Canal at the locks to Seaview N.W., and pedal north.

Elliott Bay Bikeway (Myrtle Edwards Park). 1.25 miles of asphalt from Pier 70 to Pier 86. Start from the north end off W. Galer. There are plenty of eats and waterfront surprises from Pier 70 south.

Green Lake. 2.8 miles of circular walkway/bikeway, often crowded on sunny weekends.

Green Lake to the University of Washington. About two miles along Ravenna Boulevard and 17th N.E.

Interlaken Boulevard. About two miles from Roanoke Park to the Arboretum. Good coasting downhill, easy pedaling uphill.

Lake Washington Boulevard. About six miles from the south end of the Arboretum to Seward Park, and seven miles from Seward Park to Madison Park along McGilvra Boulevard. This one loops down and runs along the lake, turning into a safe asphalt path for the last three miles. Food and restrooms can be found at Leschi Park.

Seward Park. About 2.5 miles along the lakeshore around the peninsula. There is a food concession here in the summer.

BICYCLE SHOPS

Alki Bikes 'n' Boats (2722 Alki S.W., 938-3322). Near the Alki Bikeway. Rents one- to ten-speeds for $1 to $2.50 per hour. They are closed on Sundays.

Aurora Cycle Shop (7401 Aurora N., 783-1000). On the northwest side of Green Lake. Has sales and service, but no rentals. They are closed on Sundays.

The Bicycle Center (4529 Sand Point Way N.E., 523-8300). Near the Burke-Gilman Trail rents ten-speeds for $2.50 an hour on up to $25 per week.

Gregg's Greenlake Cycle (7007 Woodlawn N.E., 523-1822). On the east side of Green Lake. Rents one- to ten-speeds, tandems, and child carriers for $1 to $2 per hour and up to $25 per week.

Magnolia Alpine Hut (2215 15th W., 284-3575). At Interbay. Rents one- to ten-speeds for $7.50 a day. They are open Sundays from May to mid-August only.

Velocipede Bike Shop (1301 E. Madison, 325-3292). Just south of the Arboretum. Has sales and excellent service, but no rentals.

SPECIAL EVENTS

On the third or fourth Sunday of the month from May through September, bikers meet at the Mount Baker Bathing Beach for the **Bicycle Sunday** tour south to Seward Park and around the peninsula. City signs discourage car traffic from 10 a.m. to 5 p.m. First aid stations with biking literature are set up along the route, and there is often a pottery show at the Seward Park Art Studio. **Bicycle Week**, celebrated the third week in May, features open riding on the freeway express lanes on Sunday. For answers to almost any biking question, call the **Bicycle Hot Line** at 522-BIKE.

Birdwatching

Parks are great places to get to know the city's winged residents. Seattle's woods and meadows are natural homes for an abundance of land birds, from robins and chickadees to warblers and woodpeckers. The city is also located along the Pacific Flyway, which makes it a popular stopping spot for migrating waterfowl both in spring and fall.

Over 150 species of birds have been sighted in Discovery Park, and over 200 on the University of Washington campus and Arboretum. Lists of these birds are available at the Discovery Park Visitor Center and the Burke Museum on the UW campus. Migrating and wintering waterfowl are quite abundant on Green Lake—and even moreso on Union Bay, where you can sometimes see thousands of ducks at a time bobbing, feeding, and preening on the water. For sea birds, any of the Puget Sound Parks will provide an eyeful, especially in the early morning.

To get started in this sport, all you need is a pair of binoculars, a keen eye, and a good bird guide. One of the best is *Birds of North America*, a Golden Field Guide. It includes range maps and excellent color paintings of some 700 species, plus useful tips for the beginner. For group involvement, with monthly meetings and frequent outings, call the **Seattle Audubon Society** (622-6695). The **Audubon Hotline** (455-9722) will give you up-to-date recorded information on unusual bird sightings throughout the state. And for classes on bird identification, you'll get more than your money's worth at **Discovery Park** (625-4636).

Boating

Seattle's many shoreline parks offer endless opportunities to row, paddle, sail, sputter, and ski on both fresh and saltwater. If it's a moorage you're after, call *now,* since the city has a long waiting list. But you should have no trouble finding boat ramps or renting a craft to fit your purpose.

BOAT RAMPS (See map on page 44.)

Freshwater boat ramps on Lake Washington (from north to south) are located at Sand Point (N.W. 65th off Sand Point Way), S. Day and Lakeside S. (under the old Lake Washington Floating Bridge), Sayres Memorial Park (Lake Washington Boulevard S. and 46th S., just north of Genesee Park), S. Ferdinand and Lake Washington Boulevard S. (just north of Seward Park), and Atlantic City (S. Henderson and Seward Park S., at Rainier Beach).

Saltwater boat ramps on Puget Sound (from north to south) are Eddie Vine (north end of Seaview N.W. near Golden Gardens), Don Armeni (Harbor S.W. off S.W. Maryland, at the north end of Alki Beach), and Seacrest Marina (Harbor S.W. and S.W. Georgia, near the Don Armeni Ramp).

Other boat ramps (small ones) are the Canal Ramp located at 14th N.W. and Shilshole N.W. (on the north side of the Lake Washington Ship Canal), the Northlake Ramp at N. 36th and Northlake Way (northeast of the Gas Works Park on Lake Union), and the Duwamish Ramp at 1st S. and S. River (on the Duwamish Waterway).

BOAT MOORAGES

Boat moorages on Lake Washington are under the jurisdiction of the city, with monthly rates from about $1.50 a foot, or $45 a month for a thirty-foot slip. The Lakewood Moorage (Lake Washington Boulevard S. and S. Genesee, north of Seward Park) is operated by a concessionaire. (Call 722-3887 for information.) The city operates the North and South Leschi Moorages (Lakeside S. off E. Alder, near Leschi Park). If you want moorage space, call 625-4671 right away, since they're booked up several years in advance.

Boat moorages on Puget Sound include the day moorage at the foot of S. Washington Street (a twenty-four-hour limit here, but no fee) and Shilshole Bay Marina (7001 Seaview N.W., 587-4900). The latter, operated by the Port of Seattle, charges $.20 per foot per day for large sailboats on a first come, first served basis. Their long-term rates are about $2 a foot, or $60 per month for an average-sized slip. Right now they're booked up for several years, with a $50 reservation fee.

BOAT RENTALS

The Boathouse (9812 17th S.W., 763-0688). At White Center. Has canoes with paddles and preservers from $11.50 a day to $23.50 for four days. They also rent rowboats, car racks, and trailers. Be sure to bring a car, though, since there's no water near White Center.

Greenlake Boat Rentals (Latona N.E. and Green Lake Drive N., 527-0171 or 362-3151). Has rowboats, paddleboats, and canoes from $2.50 per hour—May through late fall, depending on the weather.

Kelly's Landing (1401 N.E. Boat Street, 634-3470. At the foot of University Way on Portage Bay). Rents canoes with car racks and a variety of sailboats from twelve to twenty-eight feet. Their rates are $3 to $8 per hour, but no overnight rentals.

Ledger Marine Charters (101 W. Nickerson, 283-6160). On the south side of the Lake Washington Ship Canal. Offers boat charters for a minimum of one week. Here you can get sailboats twenty-seven to forty-seven feet long from $330 a week, power boats twenty-six to fifty-five feet long, yachts up to 110 feet with skippers provided, and even cruisers for groups of up to seventy-five people.

Lloyd's Boat House (1660 Harbor S.W., 932-1050). Near Alki beach. Especially good for salmon fishing in Elliott Bay. They rent fourteen-foot boats at $7.50 per day, and they also have outboard motors, bait, and fishing gear.

The Old Boathouse (2770 Westlake N., 283-9166). On Lake Union. Rents rowboats at $2.50 per hour, and sailboats from $4 per hour. They also rent canoes and give sailing lessons.

Ray's Boathouse (6049 Seaview N.W., 783-9779). At Shilshole. Has aluminum boats fourteen to sixteen feet long from $9 per day. They also have outboard engines, fishing gear, and bait. This is a good one for salmon fishing off Shilshole.

Recreational Equipment, Incorporated (1525 11th Avenue, 323-8333). On Capitol Hill. Rents only canoes, $12 a day or $21 for three days.

University of Washington Waterfront Activities Center (543-2217). Just east of the UW football stadium. Rents canoes and rowboats, outfitted with paddles and preservers for $1.50 an hour.

White Water Sports (307) N.E. 71st, 523-5150). Near Green Lake. Rents durable canoes, kayaks, and wind surfers for $18 a day. These come fully equipped with paddles, floats, helmets, and lifejackets, and are suitable for use on the roughest of Northwest waters.

Wind Works Sailing School and Charters (7001 Seaview N.W., 784-9386). At Shilshole Bay Marina. Rents sailboats twenty-five to fifty-seven feet long, from $50 per day. They also give sailing lessons, excursions, and waterfront tours.

Clam Digging

Horse clams, butter clams, striped cockles—even the king of clams, called the geoduck—you can find all of them on or under Seattle's Puget Sound Beaches. (Alki, Carkeek, Golden Gardens, and Lincoln offer the best spots.) All you need is a bucket, a shovel or rake, and a minus tide. Most of the clams are about three to five inches beneath the rocks or sand. One of the most successful ways of digging is simply to scrape down with a short, four-pronged garden rake. Then gather up the cream-shelled beauties and plunk them in saltwater for a while—usually overnight, depending on how anxious you are for steamed clams—giving them time to extrude any sand or mud they may have taken in at low tide.

It's easy to get overzealous about clams, so watch yourself. The limit is seven pounds per person. If you're going for geoducks, the limit is three clams apiece. Remember also that clam digging is not permitted at Discovery Park.

Also remember that *clams may not always be safe to eat. Check with the park department before digging.*

You can get more information about clam digging or collecting other wild saltwater edibles such as sea urchins and seaweed by consulting Euell Gibbons' book, *Stalking the Blue-Eyed Scallop.*

Community Centers, etc.

Classes, gatherings, sports, special events—community centers, studios, theatres, and museums are located all over the city to make life more interesting for you. Here they are, with asterisks beside the ones geared for the physically disabled.

Alki	59th S.W. and S.W. Stevens	932-5504
Ballard	26th N.W. and N.W. 60th	784-0654
Bathhouse Theatre	W. Green Lake Way N.	524-9110
Bitter Lake	N. 130th and Greenwood N.	363-4152
Burke Museum	N.E. 45th and 17th N.E.	543-5590
Delridge	Delridge Way S.W. and S.W. Alaska	935-4685
Garfield	23rd and Jefferson	625-4178
Green Lake	Latona N.E. and E. Green Lake N.	625-4259
Hiawatha	California S.W. and S.W. Lander	932-3294
Henry Gallery	15th N.E. and N.E. 41st	543-2880
High Point	S.W. Graham and Sylvan Way	935-7130
*Jefferson	Beacon and Spokane	625-4681
Langston Hughes	17th S. and E. Yesler Way	329-0115
Laurelhurst	N.E. 41st and 47th N.E.	523-5350
Loyal Heights	21st N.W. and N.W. 77th	782-1819
Madrona Dance Studio	Lake Washington Boulevard S. south of Madrona Drive	625-4303
Magnolia	W. Raye and 34th W.	625-4035
*Meadowbrook	30th N.E. and N.E. 107th	362-2922

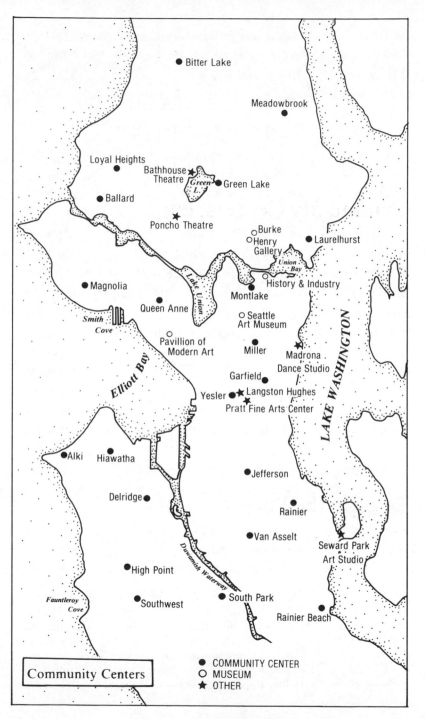

Bitter Lake

Meadowbrook

Loyal Heights

Bathhouse Theatre
Green L. Green Lake

Ballard

Poncho Theatre

Burke
Henry Gallery

Laurelhurst

Lake Union

Union Bay

Magnolia

History & Industry

Queen Anne

Montlake

Smith Cove

Seattle Art Museum

Pavillion of Modern Art

Miller

Madrona Dance Studio

LAKE WASHINGTON

Elliott Bay

Garfield

Yesler   Langston Hughes

Pratt Fine Arts Center

Alki   Hiawatha

Jefferson

Delridge

Rainier

Van Asselt

Seward Park Art Studio

High Point

Duwamish Waterway

Fauntleroy Cove

Southwest

South Park

Rainier Beach

Community Centers

● COMMUNITY CENTER
○ MUSEUM
★ OTHER

Activities and Programs 29

Miller	20th E. and E. Republican	323-9181
Montlake	E. Calhoun and 16th E.	625-4036
Museum of History and Industry	2161 E. Hamlin	324-1125
Pavilion of Modern Art	Seattle Center, 5th and Thomas	447-4795
Poncho Theatre	N. 50th and Fremont N.	633-4567
Pratt Fine Arts Center	19th S. and S. Main	323-0144
Queen Anne	1st W. and W. Howe	625-4040
Rainier	Rainier S. and S. Oregon	722-2150
Rainier Beach	Rainier S. and S. Henderson	723-5900
Seattle Art Museum	Volunteer Park, 14th and E. Prospect	447-4670
Seward Park Art Studio	Lake Washington Boulevard S. and S. Orcas	723-5780
South Park	8th S. and S. Thistle	763-0890
*Southwest	28th S.W. and S.W. Thistle	935-1866
*Van Asselt	Beacon S. and S. Myrtle	723-5060
Yesler	E. Yesler Way and Broadway	625-4677

Dogs in the Park

Where can you legally take your dog without a leash? Unfortunately, nowhere except your own backyard. Time and again our city officials have considered loosening the leash law, but each time they have come to the same conclusion: people first in city parks. So, if you're thinking about running your dog without a leash (hundreds do), know the penalties: unleashed dog within the city limits, $15 for the first four offenses and $75 plus mandatory court appearance for the fifth offense; dog without a license, $20; dog loose in city park, $30; dog in public lake, pond, fountain, or stream, $30.

It's also good to know that the city has no tolerance policy on loose dogs. If yours has not been picked up yet, it may be just a matter of time. Yes, the pound has been short on personnel; but beware, they have just added another seven members to the force, along with a few extra trucks!

On the bright side, city officials have considered a park for dogs, but the suggestion was lost under greater priorities. They may reconsider if they get enough public input—especially petitions based on valid and specific suggestions.

Fishing

Trout, crappies, salmon, catfish, chub, perch, bass, flounder, red snapper—you name it, you can catch it in waters off Seattle's parks. If you need a vessel to take you to deep waters, you'll find what you need in the "Boating" section of this book. If you are content to cast or dangle a line from the shore, try the marsh channels and bridges at the north end of the Arboretum. These are especially good for catfish, perch, and bass; and kids catch many a crawfish in cages from the first bridge on the Waterfront Trail behind the Museum of History and Industry. If you prefer a pier, the city has plenty of public ones, both saltwater and fresh, just waiting for your baiting.

FISHING PIERS (See map on page 44.)

Freshwater fishing piers include three at Green Lake (a juvenile pier on the east side, a casting pier on the west, and one near the Aqua Theatre), which are stocked each year with small trout. Some old lunkers are still caught occasionally, too, both from the banks and from boats. On Lake Washington you'll find piers at Madison Park, North Leschi Moorage, Mount Baker Bathing Beach, and Seward Park.

Saltwater fishing piers can be found at Golden Gardens, Commodore Park by the Locks, and the Waterfront Park on Pier 57. The saltwater fishing is also excellent from the bulkhead at Duwamish Head in Alki Park.

If you're after salmon, various species are coming in through Puget Sound to their spawning grounds all year long. For information and boat rentals, call either Lloyd's Boat House (932-1050) or Ray's Boat House (783-9779). And whatever fishing you plan to do, be sure to pick up a copy of the Washington State Sport Fishing Regulations, available at most sporting goods stores. Another help is Dot's Fishing Guide, which will tell you about everything from tides to knot tying.

Foraging for Food

Stalking wild edibles is even better in the lowlands than in the mountains—and especially good in Puget Sound country. Seattle's parks and pathways are chock-full of berries, flowers, mushrooms, and greens rich in vitamins and minerals, many of them more nutritious than you can buy in the store. And most of them are yours for the picking—if you know how to identify them. Naturalists at Discovery Park and Camp Long give periodic introductions to wild edibles with walks and identification tips. If you want to try it yourself, the best local books are *Why Wild Edibles?* by Russ Mohney, and *Northwest Foraging* by Doug Benoliel. Once you really get into this delectable sport and you get tired of that same old plate of cattail roots, you may want to try some creative gourmet dishes—like lasagna stuffed with stinging nettle greens, served with dandelion wine!

Blackberry picking time in Seattle is July and August. Some people spontaneously take to the brambles with little more than a free hand and a watering mouth. Others, with visions of pies, cobblers, tarts, and cereal toppings, go forth supplied for battle with everything from canes and crooked sticks to ladders, planks, and wide-bottomed buckets. Any container—berry basket, fruit juice pitcher, or wire-handled coffee can—will do. But if it's a big one, don't fill it too full, or the accumulated weight of the fruit will make juice of the berries on the bottom.

Most of the city's undeveloped parks are havens for blackberries. Discovery Park (especially the North Bluff area), the Burke-Gilman Trail, and Licton Springs are especially succulent spots.

Mushroom hunting is a subspecialty of foraging that has caught on hard and fast in Seattle, and with good reason. Mushrooms are both beautiful and delectable, so searching for them is a little like a treasure hunt. About fifty species of them grow in Seattle's parks. The common meadow mushroom and the fairy ring can be found in almost all the parks with mowed areas (try Lincoln, for example). Schmitz Park offers a variety of species common to older growth forests, and if you're lucky you may even come across a rare chanterelle there. Lincoln and Woodland parks produce tremendous quantities of honey mushrooms and boletes at the bases of trees. And Discovery Park, which is one of the best for blackberries and mushrooms, offers classes in mushroom identification during the peak months of October and November. *Some mushrooms are poisonous, so be sure to get well acquainted with them before picking and eating!*

Frisbee Throwing

"It's a sport that's still in its infancy, but it's indeed a sport," says Doug Newland, a regional director of the International Fisbee Association. And he's right. Colorful plastic platters are spinning and soaring through the air in almost every city park these days. For people who take these flying saucers seriously, there are two clubs in Seattle: The **International Frisbee Association** and the **Olympic Windjammers** (P.O. Box 5312, Seattle, 98105, 527-0150) jointly sponsor a number of exciting events the year around.

For example, **Ultimate Frisbee** is a game played much like soccer, but with seven members to a team. Players advance the Frisbee down a forty-by-sixty-yard field to the goal by throwing instead of kicking. Games start at noon on Saturdays. Meet at the Lower Woodland Park soccer field at N.E. 50th. Another interesting game is **Frisbee Golf,** in which Frisbees are used instead of golf balls and trees take the place of holes. The first tee in Seattle's unmarked eighteen-hole course starts at the top of Lower Woodland's Soap Box Derby Ramp on N.E. 50th. Meet other club members there for an introduction Sundays at 3 p.m.

In addition to these regular events, the Frisbee associations also sponsor special events—for example, **State Championships** with competitions for distance, accuracy, freestyle, boomerang throw, and maximum time aloft. (The world's record for distance is 444 feet; for time aloft, fifteen seconds.) They have also organized a **Senior Citizens' Frisbee,** with picnics, demonstrations, and instruction; and a **Special Olympics Frisbee** for the handicapped.

Incidentally, the best Frisbee brands are Wham-O and World Class, with the 119-, 141-, and 165-gram models being the most popular among the experts.

Golfing

Whack! Another small white sphere goes sailing into the air. Whether it lands on the green or in the rough, its pursuer is in for a good day's exercise and relaxation.

Seattle has three eighteen-hole municipal golf courses and three practice ranges, all of which are excellent, but they get increasingly crowded as the day wears on. Tee time is between 5 a.m. and 6 a.m. in spring and summer. The rate for eighteen holes is $4.50 on weekdays and $5 on weekends and holidays. For a short nine course you will pay about $2.50. There is also a half rate for players eighteen and under, and for seniors over sixty-five. All three municipal courses have golf shops and restaurants and are usually open from 6 a.m. to 4 p.m.

Eighteen-hole golf courses include Jackson Park (10th N.E. and N.E. 135th, 363-4747), just off Interstate 5; Jefferson Park (S. Spokane and Beacon S., 762-9949), off the Columbian Way Exit from Interstate 5; and West Seattle (35th S.W. and S.W. Snoqualmie, 932-9792), just off Fauntleroy Avenue. **Jackson** has a Pacific Northwest Golf Association (PNGA) rating of 67 for 6,000 yards and is a fast course over rolling terrain with stands of conifers. **Jefferson** has a PNGA rating of 70 for 6,225 yards and includes lots of hills with fine views of the city. **West Seattle** has a PNGA rating of 68 for 6,054 yards, with ravines and rolling hills near the Duwamish River.

Green Lake Pitch and Putt at the south end of Green Lake (632-8084) is a nine-hole par three course for pitching and putting only. The green fee here is $1.58, plus $.26 for rental of iron and putter. It is open every day, weather permitting, from 8 a.m. to 8 p.m. You can get candy bars and pop from the machines.

Interbay Golf Park (15th W. and W. Wheeler, 625-2820) between Queen Anne and Magnolia includes a driving range, a nine-hole par three course and a small putting green. Rates for the driving range are $2 for a large bucket of balls, $1.70 for a small bucket. And for the course the fee is $2 for nine holes and $2.65 for eighteen. It is open daily from 10 a.m. to 7:30 p.m. during the spring and summer.

The West Seattle Driving Range (35th S.W. and S.W. Snoqualmie, 935-8212) just off Fauntleroy Avenue includes nineteen tees. Rates are $2 for a large bucket and $1.50 for a small bucket.

Handicapped Programs

Seattle's parks do not yet have braille signs for the blind, but more and more of their facilities are being constructed with the handicapped in mind. A good example is the city's new Commodore Park, with easy ramps leading down to the Ballard Locks and fish ladder. Other city parks that are relatively barrier free include the Seattle Center, the Aquarium, the Arboretum, the Burke-Gilman Trail, Gas Works Park, Freeway Park, Golden Gardens and Shilshole, Green Lake, Lincoln Park, Seward Park, Volunteer Park, Waterfront Park, and the Woodland Park Zoo. Discovery Park's Ranger-Naturalists also offer wilderness tours for the blind, using touch and smell to transmit the beauties of nature.

As for particular programs, the park department's **Special Populations Office** (625-2989) has many things planned for the handicapped of all ages. Varied sports and social programs are geared to specific disabilities. And in the summer there are day and overnight camping experiences, plus a Tiny Tots Program, which concentrates on creating an atmosphere of understanding and acceptance among kids.

Some community centers also offer programs for the handicapped. Those that are relatively barrier free include Green Lake, Jefferson, Loyal Heights, Meadowbrook, Montlake, Queen Anne, Rainier Beach, Southwest, and Van Asselt. All of the city's public swimming pools have adjacent parking and easily accessible restrooms. Those that are barrier free include Ballard, Helene Madison, Medgar Evers, Queen Anne, Rainier Beach, and Southwest. The Fine Arts Center in Edwin T. Pratt Park and the Poncho Theatre in Woodland Park are also geared for the physically disabled.

The best local guidebook for the physically disabled is *Access Seattle,* published by the Junior League and available at the park department offices at 100 Dexter Avenue N. (625-2989).

Jogging

With its varied terrain and energetic outdoor spirit, Seattle has become a jogging city in recent years. On sunny afternoons and weekends, the city's popular runways are jammed with joggers, and on race days you can see human specks strung out for miles along boulevards and city streets. For the latest information on equipment and training, call Super Jock and Jill (7210 E. Greenlake Drive N. 522-7711), just east of Green Lake. They can put you in touch with running clubs, too. If you're a really hard core runner, you may even want to get ahold of the diehard racers at Club Northwest (325-3167). Once you're off and running, though, you'll find the perfect place somewhere in Seattle's parks, whether you're gregarious, competitive, or the lonely long-distance type.

PARK AND PLAYFIELD JOGGING

Alki Beach. A two-mile strip along the sound, or on sand at low tide.

Carkeek Park. Primitive trails, gravel piper's Creek Trail, or beach at low tide.

Discovery Park. 2.8-mile loop trail through forest, meadows, and sand dunes and a half-mile fitness course at the south end of the park.

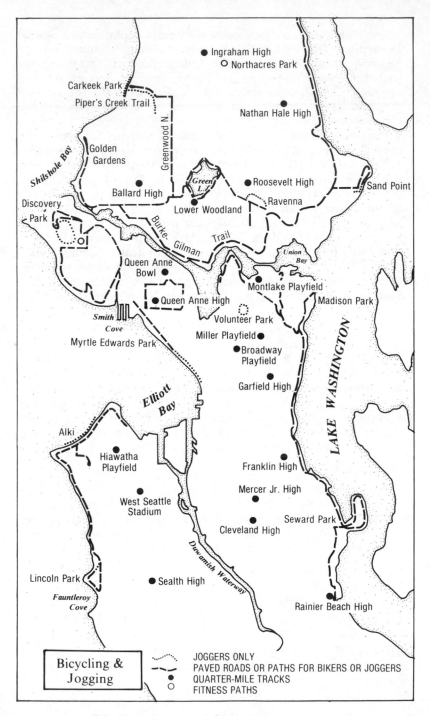

Ingraham High
○ Northacres Park

Carkeek Park
Piper's Creek Trail

Greenwood N.

Nathan Hale High

Shilshole Bay

Golden Gardens

Green L.

Ballard High

Roosevelt High

Sand Point

Discovery Park

Lower Woodland

Ravenna

Burke- Gilman   Trail

Union Bay

Queen Anne Bowl

Montlake Playfield

Madison Park

Queen Anne High

Volunteer Park

Smith Cove

Miller Playfield

Myrtle Edwards Park

Broadway Playfield

Garfield High

Elliott Bay

LAKE WASHINGTON

Alki

Hiawatha Playfield

Franklin High

West Seattle Stadium

Mercer Jr. High

Cleveland High

Seward Park

Duwamish Waterway

Lincoln Park

Sealth High

Fauntleroy Cove

Rainier Beach High

Bicycling & Jogging	

JOGGERS ONLY
PAVED ROADS OR PATHS FOR BIKERS OR JOGGERS
● QUARTER-MILE TRACKS
○ FITNESS PATHS

Green Lake. 2.8-mile paved pathway around the lake, often very crowded.

Lincoln Park. Several miles of dirt paths along the bluff and through the woods, plus a mile of paved beach pathway.

Lower Woodland Park. Wooded hills with paths and trails. This area is used for the two-mile high school cross country course.

Myrtle Edwards Park. 1.25 miles of asphalt pathway from Pier 70 to Pier 86. A popular lunch-hour and after-work runway for downtown business people.

Northacres Park. A half-mile fitness course through woods.

Ravenna/Cowen Park. Dirt pathways through a wooded ravine.

Seward Park. 2.5 mile loop path and roadway encircling the peninsula beside Lake Washington.

Washington Park/Arboretum. Many miles of dirt and gravel paths through plantings of trees and shrubs.

Volunteer Park. About 0.7 mile around the perimeter of the park on paths, grass, and quiet roadways.

ROADRUNNING

Burke-Gilman Trail. A 12.5-mile asphalt pathway with gravel side path much of the way, from Gas Works Park north to Kirkland.

Fairview Avenue. Quiet roadway running along the east side of Lake Union from Newton Street to the University Bridge. For more good roadrunning, continue south from the University Bridge along Fuhrman and Boyer Avenues beside Portage Bay.

Interlaken Boulevard. About two miles of winding, quiet hillside roadway through forest and woods, from Roanoke Park to Washington Park/Arboretum.

Lake Union. Almost exactly 10,000 meters (6.2 miles) around the lake. Start at Gas Works Park and cross the Ship Canal on the University and Fremont bridges.

Gas Works to Golden Gardens. About six miles along the Lake Washington Ship Canal and Shilshole Bay.

Lake Washington Boulevard. About six miles from Seward Park to the Arboretum and seven miles from Seward Park to Madison Park via McGilvra Boulevard. The first three are along an asphalt pathway.

Queen Anne Hill. 4.3 miles of Scenic Drive loop with paved road, parking strips, and fantastic city views.

Ravenna Boulevard. About two miles of grassy corridor (with several stoplights at busy intersections) following the bike route from the University of Washington to Green Lake.

Waterfront. Sidewalk running along Elliott Bay to Pier 70 and beyond. This is a lunch break favorite for downtowners, since there are no traffic signals to stop for.

PLAYFIELD AND SCHOOL TRACKS

Ballard High School	14th N.W. and N.W. 65th
Broadway Playfield	11th E. and E. Pine
Cleveland High School	S. Lucille and 15th S.
Franklin High School	30th S. and S. Mt. Baker Boulevard
Garfield High School	23rd and E. Jefferson
Hiawatha Playfield	California S.W. and S.W. Lander
Ingraham High School	Burke N. and N. 135th
Lower Woodland Park	N. 50th and Green Lake Way N.
Mercer Junior High	16th S. and S. Columbian Way
Miller Playfield	20th E. and E. Republican
Montlake Playfield	16th E. and E. Calhoun
Nathan Hale High School	N.E. 107th and 30th N.E.
Queen Anne Bowl	3rd W. and W. Fulton
Queen Anne High School	2nd W. and W. Galer
Rainier Beach High School	Seward Park S. and S. Henderson
Roosevelt High School	14th N.E. and N.E. 66th
Sealth High School	26th S.W. and S.W. Thistle
West Seattle Stadium	35th S.W. and S.W. Snoqualmie

Kite Flying

From the first blustery winds of March all through the summer you can see them fluttering up in the sky. Kites of all colors, kites of all sizes, from tiny wafers to long trailing centipedes—bright expressions of the human spirit. The best parks in Seattle for flying kites are the Gas Works, Golden Gardens, Sand Point, Myrtle Edwards, and Sayres Memorial. Probably the most popular of all is the Gas Works, with its sixty-foot mound picking up winds off Lake Union.

For kiting equipment and information, the best place in town is the **Great Winds Kite Shop** (116 S. Jackson Street, 624-6866). The folks there offer advice, kite classes, demonstrations, and will direct you to the Washington Kite Fliers' Association, which schedules "flies" every Sunday of the year in the above mentioned parks. If you can't reach them, try Jack van Gilder at 938-0550. He'll give you a hand—if he's not out somewhere grappling with his 800-foot centipede.

Lawn Bowling

Most lawn bowlers are dapper-looking people, dressed in snappy sweaters and scotch-plaid berets. Some bring whole suitcases of clothing and equipment to roll shiny black balls across a manicured green. But this is as it should be, since the game was imported from England. And underneath the calm you will find they have a keen eye and a dedication that keeps them practicing almost every day of the year—as evidenced by the fact that some locals have made it to national championships.

Lawn bowling is rapidly growing in popularity here, particularly among senior citizens. To get started, all you need is flat-bottomed shoes and contact with one of the city's two clubs: the **Jefferson Park Lawn Bowling Club** (S. Dakota and Beacon Avenue S., 762-9728), near the Jefferson Park Golf Course; and the **Queen City Lawn Bowling Club** (N. 63rd and Whitman N., 782-1515), at the north end of Lower Woodland.

Metal Detecting

In almost any city park you may see what appear to be misplaced astronauts outfitted with earphones, coiled wires, and satchels of different sized screwdrivers sweeping electronic vacuum cleaners over the grass. These are metal detectors, and their use can be a profitable hobby if you don't get addicted to buying the machines themselves. The good ones cost between $150 and $400. Devotees of metal detecting have formed clubs and found coins dating back to early pioneer days. With a little library research and some mental archaeology, you can locate the old homesteads and meeting halls that are likely to yield the most interesting finds.

If you're interested in getting started, or in learning more about this hobby, call **Pearl Electronics** (1300 1st Avenue S., 622-6200). You will also need a permit to dig in a park, and you will be expected to restore any turf you disturb. Call 625-4673 for permit information.

Music in the Parks

The first music (in Seattle's only park) was organized by George Frye, who in 1860 put together a brass band to liven up meetings at Yesler Hall and the sawdust-covered spot that later became Pioneer Square. By 1890, Madison Park on Lake Washington had become the scene of spectacular water shows and operettas on offshore barges. The traditional Music in the Parks program began in 1896, and reached a zenith of popularity in 1910, when seventy-nine concerts were performed around the city.

Today, the park department offers two series of varied music performances, ranging from soloists to thirteen-piece orchestrations. Throughout the year you can enjoy concerts at the Poncho Theatre on Sunday evenings from 7 to 9. And a summer Music in the Parks series offers free performances Tuesday, Thursday, Saturday and Sunday afternoons in various parks from 2 to 4 p.m. For a listing of schedules, write Doug Dillon, Seattle Parks and Recreation, 100 Dexter Avenue N., Seattle 98109.

Picnicking

Lawns, beaches, tables, benches, trees—almost any place in the parks is a good spot for a picnic. Just pack your lunch and head on out. Or for a more fancy affair, such as a barbecue or a large group gathering, you may want to do a little advance planning.

The best parks for group picnics are Carkeek, Discovery, Gas Works, Lincoln, Seward, and Lower Woodland. In all these and many others you can find picnic shelters with wood stoves and running water. These can be reserved at $5 a day for each fifty persons by calling the Scheduling Office at 625-4671. Be sure to bring your own fuel—wood or charcoal briquets. Beach fires are allowed at Alki, Carkeek, Golden Gardens, and Seward Parks.

Sailing

If you've seen the cheery-looking sailboats gliding over the waters of Green Lake, Lake Washington, and Puget Sound and have felt an urge to try your hand at the tiller, there are several places that will help you get started.

The Seattle Sailing Association (SSA) offers springtime courses for beginners starting in May, including twelve hours of sailing theory with the Red Cross and twelve hours on Green Lake for a cost of $25. The SSA uses eight-foot El Toro boats, which are ideal for beginners, and Green Lake's calm waters are very forgiving if you should happen to get dumped. For $10 you can join the SSA and use the boats anytime. For registration, call 323-2345.

The Corinthian Yacht Club (122 Lakeside S., 322-7877) at Leschi offers both beginning and intermediate sailing classes on Lake Washington. The beginning class includes six hours of theory and a sailing demonstration on the water using various types of boats owned by Corinthian members. They charge $7 per person and $10 per couple. Beginning classes usually start in May. Intermediate classes, which include eighteen hours of instruction for $50, usually begin in the summer.

The Wind Works Sailing School (7001 Seaview N.W., 784-9386) at Shilshole Bay Marina offers beginning courses in saltwater sailing, with four hours of instruction for $10. Intermediate and advanced courses in twenty-five-foot to thirty-foot sloops include nine hours of instruction for $35, or thirty-six hours for $100. After six of the three-hour sessions, you can rent a twenty-five-foot sloop and take it out on your own—$30 for half a day, $55 for a day, and $75 for a weekend.

Scuba Diving

Diving is great sport in Puget Sound waters, and often you will see web-footed, wet-suited humanoids walking or bobbing along the beaches at Alki or Golden Gardens, or descending among the pilings near the Don Armeni Boat Ramp northeast of Alki. After a half hour finning among schools of fish, and watching the sunlight stream down from the surface while bubbles tumble skyward, you'll bob up again, awed by the wonder of this topsy-turvy environment.

Whether skin or scuba diving, though, you had better know what you're doing. The park department occasionally offers scuba courses through its municipal pools (call the one nearest you to find out), and there are several good dive shops that can help you get certified and dive safely. Convenient ones are **Underwater Sports** (10545 Aurora N., 362-3310), **New England Divers** (11009 1st Avenue S., 246-8156), and the **Lighthouse Diving Center** (8215 Lake City Way, 524-1633).

Senior Programs

The park department has many programs geared especially for seniors. **Golf courses** have a special rate most weekdays (about half price), and a semi-annual golf card sells for $66.24. In the fall there is an all-city golf tournament for seniors, and you can also get golfing instruction in five half-hour sessions for a total of $5. Call 625-2981 or 762-4513. **Lawn bowling** is another popular sport among seniors, with two clubs eager for new members. In the North End call 782-2906, in the South End call 937-4640. **Adult Swims** are programmed at all of the city's municipal swimming pools, and there are a limited number of free swim tickets available for seniors at Ballard, Evans, Medgar Evers, Rainier Beach, and Southwest. **Free film series** (633-4567) and stage performances (524-4834) are also available.

Special events for seniors include such things as an Old Timers' Picnic, trips to Longacres to watch the horseraces, and tours that may take you as far away as Crater Lake and Harrison Hot Springs. There is also a Senior Camping Program, with boating, fishing, nature walks, and other outdoor enjoyment at the park department's forty-acre **Red Barn Ranch** in Auburn. You can go on similar adventures even closer to home, with overnight camping or group picnics at Camp Long (935-0370) and free nature walks with Ranger-Naturalists at Discovery Park (625-4636). For more information on any of these specials, call 625-2981.

Community Centers that offer programs year around for senior adults include Alki (932-5504), Bitter Lake (363-4152), Green Lake (625-4259), High Point (935-5444), Langston Hughes (329-0115), Laurelhurst (523-5350), Loyal Heights (782-1819), Magnolia (625-4035), Rainier (722-2150), and Rainier Beach (723-5900).

Swimming

You don't have to go far to find a swimming hole in Seattle. If Puget Sound's saltwater is too nippy for you (forty-six to fifty-six degrees

Fahrenheit), there are always Lake Washington and Green Lake, with summertime temperatures in the seventies and wintertime temperatures bearable for quick dips. On really chilly days, you can choose from eight indoor heated pools.

SALTWATER SWIMMING
There are three major saltwater beaches, all with lifeguards. They are located off Carkeek Park, Alki Beach Park, and Lincoln Park. Alki has the best sandy beach of the three, and is also the most crowded. Lincoln Park includes the city's only saltwater pool, open daily in the summer only.

FRESHWATER SWIMMING
Seattle has nine public beaches—two on Green Lake and seven on Lake Washington. They are open and staffed with lifeguards from 11 a.m. to 8 p.m. from the last day of public school to mid-August, and 11 a.m. to 7 p.m. from mid-August through Labor Day, weather permitting. Most beaches include a bathhouse with restrooms, a float with diving boards, and shallow roped-off swim areas for small children. Some also offer rentals of Frisbees, volleyballs, and other athletic equipment. These swimming spots include:

Green Lake	E. Green Lake Drive N. and W. Green Lake Drive. N.
Madison Beach	E. Madison and Lake Washington Boulevard E.
Madrona Beach	Lake Washington Boulevard and Madrona Drive
Matthews Beach	N.E. 93rd off Sand Point Way N.E.
Mount Baker Beach	Lake Washington Boulevard and Lake Park Drive S.
Pritchard Beach	55th S. and S. Grattan
Sand Point Beach	N.E. 65th off Sand Point Way N.E.
Seward Beach	Lake Washington Boulevard S. and S. Juneau

PUBLIC POOL PROGRAMS
Seattle's eight indoor heated pools have something to offer everybody. Each of the pools schedules separate **"Swims"** for adults, families, seniors, and the general public. Admission to the swims is $.50 for kids eighteen and under, $1.00 for adults, and $.50 for seniors and handicapped. **Swim lessons** with beginning and intermediate instruction for all ages are offered at most pools. Costs

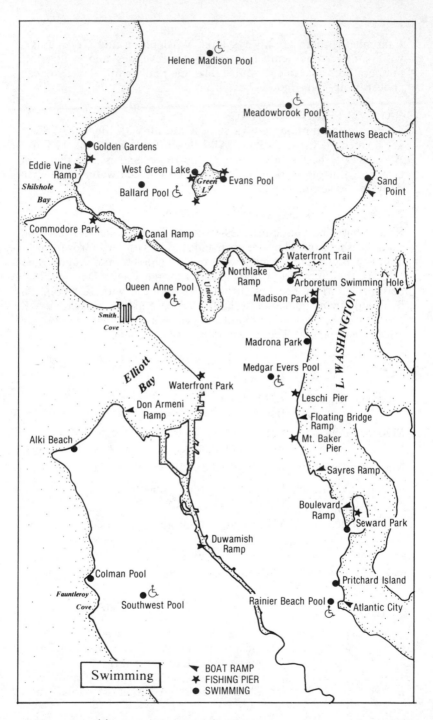

Swimming

BOAT RAMP
FISHING PIER
SWIMMING

range from $7.50 to $12.50 for ten sessions of thirty-five minutes to one and one-half hours. Instructors say the "Kinder" category, ages three to six, is the most popular time to introduce children to the water. **Pool rentals** can be arranged by sending a letter requesting a specific date and time. Rental rates are from $25 to $60 an hour depending on time and number of people. **Special programs** at the pools include everything from Red Cross lifesaving and scuba diving to drownproofing and small-craft safety. "The safety course doesn't necessarily qualify you for shooting the rapids," says one instructor, "but for that you can take our whitewater canoeing course."

Ballard Pool (1471 N.W. 67th, 782-0282) has a Jacuzzi and a heated wading pool and is geared for the handicapped. It is closed on Saturdays. **Colman Pool** (Lincoln Park, 625-4673) is an outdoor saltwater pool open in summer only. **Evans Pool** (Green Lake, 625-4258) is often crowded, and closed on Sundays. **Helene Madison Pool** (134th and Meridian N., 362-5344) is closed on Saturdays. **Meadowbrook Pool** (105th and 35th N.W., 365-9933) is closed Sundays. **Medgar Evers Pool** (23rd and E. Cherry, 324-2560) is excellent and uncrowded, closed on Sundays. **Queen Anne Pool** (1st W. and W. Howe, 625-2282) is the city's newest pool, closed Sundays. **Rainier Beach Pool** (Rainier S. and S. Henderson, 723-5919) is closed on Sundays. **Southwest Pool** (28th S.W. and S.W. Thistle, 935-6006) includes a free sauna, and is closed Saturdays.

Tennis

There are some 200 tennis courts available to the public in Seattle. The largest complex is at the University of Washington, including twenty-six courts—twelve of them lighted. The City of Seattle and Seattle Public Schools maintain over 170 more. The largest centers for outdoor courts are the complex at Lower Woodland, with ten lighted and four unlighted courts; the Lincoln Park complex, with six lighted courts just east of Fauntleroy Avenue; and the six lighted courts at Meadowbrook in Northeast Seattle.

The Seattle Tennis Center near the former Sick's Seattle Stadium has ten indoor courts and four outdoor courts, all lighted. The center is open from 7 a.m. to 11:15 p.m. daily. For an hour and fifteen minutes of play, you pay $4.50 for singles and $6 for doubles. Make reservations up to a week in advance by calling 324-2980.

Eight of the city's tennis courts are reservable. These include the courts at Ballard, Bitter Lake, Broadway, Lower Woodland, Meadowbrook, and Mount Baker. Sign up *in person* at the city's

Scheduling Office, 5201 Greenlake Way, between 8 a.m. and 6 p.m. Monday through Friday. Rates are $2 for one and a half hours, or $1 per hour per court for tournament play. Courts may also be scheduled for lessons, tournaments, and other special events. Call 625-4673.

A few of the city's courts are presently in a state of disrepair. These include courts at Franklin High, Kinnear, Oak Lake, and Ravenna Boulevard. Hopefully they will be reconditioned soon.

The best way to get a court is to *get there early*. The lighted courts are usually packed after sundown. If you don't find an open court, you can get one without too much trouble if you know the rules. Put your racket up against the net of the court. Then wait quietly for one set or one hour for singles, two sets or one and a half hours for doubles, including warmup time. Then politely assert your rights.

TENNIS COURT LOCATIONS

Alki Playground	58th S.W. and S.W. Stevens
Ballard High	15th N.W. and N.W. 67th
Ballard Playground	28th N.W. and N.W. 60th
Beacon Hill Playground	14th S. and S. Holgate
Bitter Lake Playground	N. 130th and Greenwood N.
Brighton Playfield	S. Juneau and 42nd S.
Broadview Elementary	N. 125th and Greenwood N.
Broadway Playfield	11th and E. Pine
Bryant Playground	N.E. 65th and 40th N.E.
Cleveland Playground	13th S. and S. Lucille
Cowen Park	N.E. 58th and 15th N.E.
Delridge Playfield	Delridge S.W. and S.W. Alaska
Discovery Park	36th W. and W. Government Way.
Franklin High	30th S. and S. Mount Baker Boulevard
Froula Playground	12th N.E. and N.E. 72nd
Garfield Playfield	23rd and E. Cherry
Genesee Park	S. Genesee and 43rd S.
Georgetown Playground	Corson S. and S. Homer
Gilman Playground	N.W. 54th and 11th N.W.
Green Lake	N.E. 72nd and E. Green Lake Drive N., West Green Lake Drive N.

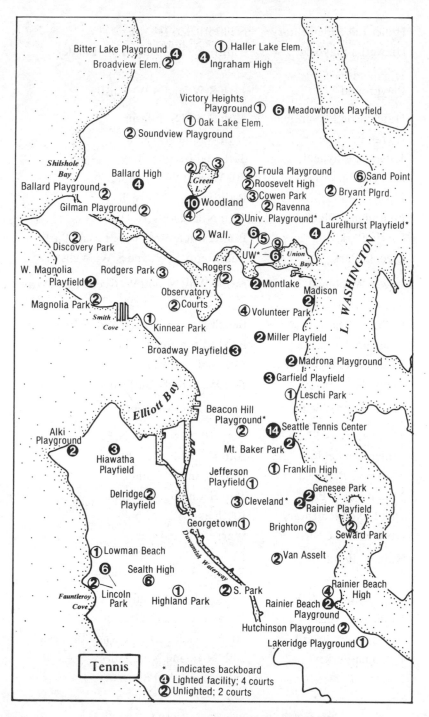

Bitter Lake Playground ④
Broadview Elem. ②   ④ ① Haller Lake Elem.
                      ④ Ingraham High

Victory Heights
Playground ①   ⑥ Meadowbrook Playfield
① Oak Lake Elem.
② Soundview Playground

Shilshole
Bay   Ballard High
Ballard Playground ② *   ④   ② Froula Playground
                   Green   ② Roosevelt High   ⑥ Sand Point
Gilman Playground ②   *L.*   ③ Cowen Park   ② Bryant Plgrd.
                   ⑩ Woodland ② Ravenna
                   ④   ② Univ. Playground *   Laurelhurst Playfield *
② Discovery Park   ② Wall.   ⑥ ⑤ ④
                            ⑨
W. Magnolia   Rodgers Park ③   UW * ⑥ *Union*
Playfield ②   Rogers   ② *Bay*
Magnolia Park ②   Observatory Montlake Madison
      Smith   ② Courts   ④ Volunteer Park ②
      Cove   ① Kinnear Park
              Broadway Playfield ③   ② Miller Playfield

Elliott Bay   ② Madrona Playground
                            ③ Garfield Playfield
                            ① Leschi Park

Alki   Beacon Hill
Playground   Playground *   ⑭ Seattle Tennis Center
②   ③   ②   ②
    Hiawatha   Mt. Baker Park
    Playfield   Jefferson   ① Franklin High
    Delridge ②   Playfield ①   Genesee Park
    Playfield   ③ Cleveland * ② ② Rainier Playfield
              Georgetown ①   Brighton ②   ② Seward Park
① Lowman Beach   ② Van Asselt
⑥   Sealth High
②   ⑥   ④ Rainier Beach
Fauntleroy Lincoln ① Highland Park   Rainier Beach ② High
Cove   Park   ② S. Park   Playground
                                    Hutchinson Playground ②
                            Lakeridge Playground ①

┌─────────┐
│ Tennis │   * indicates backboard
└─────────┘   ④ Lighted facility; 4 courts
               ② Unlighted; 2 courts

Haller Lake Elementary	N. 135th and 1st N.E.
Hiawatha Playfield	California S.W. and S.W. Lander
Highland Park Playground	11th S.W. and S.W. Thistle
Hutchinson Playground	59th S. and S. Pilgrim
Ingraham High	18th N. and N. 135th
Jefferson Playfield	38th and Beacon S.
Kinnear Park	7th W. and W. Olympic
Lakeridge Playground	Rainier S. and Cornell
Laurelhurst Playfield	45th N.E. and N.E. 41st
Leschi Park	Blaine Boulevard above Leschi Park
Lincoln Park	Fauntleroy S.W. and S.W. Webster
Lower Woodland	Stone Way N. and W. Green Lake Way N., N. 50th and Woodland Park Avenue
Lowman Beach	Beach Drive S.W. and 48th S.W.
Madison Park	E. Madison and 42nd E.
Madrona Playground	34th and E. Spring
Magnolia Park	31st W. and W. Garfield
Magnolia Playfield	34th W. and W. Smith
Meadowbrook Playfield	N.E. 107th and 30th N.E.
Miller Playfield	20th E. and E. Republican
Montlake Playfield	16th E. and E. Calhoun
Mount Baker Park	35th S. and S. McClellan
Oak Lake Elementary	100th and Aurora N.
Observatory Courts	Warren N. and Lee
Rainier Beach Playfield	Rainier S. and S. Henderson
Rainier Beach High	Seward Park S. and S. Henderson
Rainier Playfield	Rainier S. and S. Oregon
Ravenna Boulevard	5th N.E. and N.E. Ravenna Boulevard
Ravenna Park	20th N.E. and N.E. 58th
Rodgers Park	3rd W. and W. Fulton

Rogers Playground	Eastlake E. and E. Roanoke
Roosevelt High	N.E. 67th and 14th N.E.
Sand Point Park	N.E. 65th and Sand Point Way
Sealth High	26th S.W. and S.W. Thistle
Seattle Tennis Center	Empire Way and S. Holgate (324-2980)
Seward Park	S. Juneau and Lake Washington Boulevard S.
Soundview Playfield	15th N.W. and N.W. 90th
South Park Playground	8th S. and S. Thistle
University of Washington	N.E. 45th and 17th N.E.; Montlake Boulevard N.E.
University Playground	N.E. 50th and 9th N.E.
Van Asselt Playground	Beacon S. and S. Myrtle
Victory Heights Playground	N.E. 107th and 19th N.E.
Volunteer Park	15th E. and E. Prospect
Wallingford Playfield	N. 43rd and Wallingford N.
West Green Lake	N. 73rd and W. Green Lake Drive N.

Theatre in the Parks

Rowdy, ribald, melodramatic plays performed in the open air! These are traditionally as much fun for the actors as for the family members of all ages who go to see them. During the months of July and August the **Empty Space Theatre** performs on Saturday and Sunday afternoons in Volunteer Park. For specific dates and times, call 325-4443. Throughout the month of August, gifted high school actors under professional directorship present from twenty to thirty performances in parks, community centers, and playfields all over the city. For dates and times, call the **Bathhouse Theatre** at 524-9110.

Regular indoor performances are also offered at the Bathhouse, located on the west shore of Green Lake, and children's productions at the **Poncho Theatre** (700 N. 50th, 633-4567) at the south entrance to Woodland Park.

Viewpoints

Thanks to the Ice Age glaciers that gouged and contoured the Puget Sound countryside into beautiful hills and waterways, Seattle has been graced with spectacular views. For the best in the city, try these:

Alki Point Lighthouse	Alki Avenue and Point Place S.W.
Bagley Viewpoint	10th E. and E. Roanoke
Banner Place	N.E. Banner Place off N.E. 75th
Beach Drive Viewpoint	Beach Drive and 60th S.W.
Beacon Hill Viewpoint	12th S. and S. McClellan
Belvedere Viewpoint	S.W. Admiral Way and S.W. Olga
Bonnie Viewpoint	N.W. 120th and 6th N.W.
Carkeek Park	N.W. 110th off N. Greenwood
Discovery Park	36th W. and W Government Way
Duwamish Head	North end of Alki Avenue S.W.
Emma Schmitz Overlook	Beach S.W. and S.W. Alaska
Floating Bridge Viewpoint	Lake Washington Boulevard S. and S. Day
Foster's Island	East end of Waterfront Trail Arboretum
Four Columns Viewpoint	Pike and Boren at Interstate 5
Freeway Park	6th and Seneca
Gas Works Park	N. Northlake Way and Meridian N.
Golden Gardens	North end of Seaview N.W.
Green Lake	Green Lake Way
Hamilton Viewpoint	California S.W. and S.W. Donald
Harborview Viewpoint	8th and Jefferson behind hospital
High Point	35th S.W. and S.W. Willow
Jose Rizal Park	12th S. and S. Judkins
Kerry Viewpoint	W. Highland Drive and 2nd W.
Lincoln Park	Fauntleroy S.W. and S.W. Webster
Louisa Boren Lookout	15th E. and E. Garfield

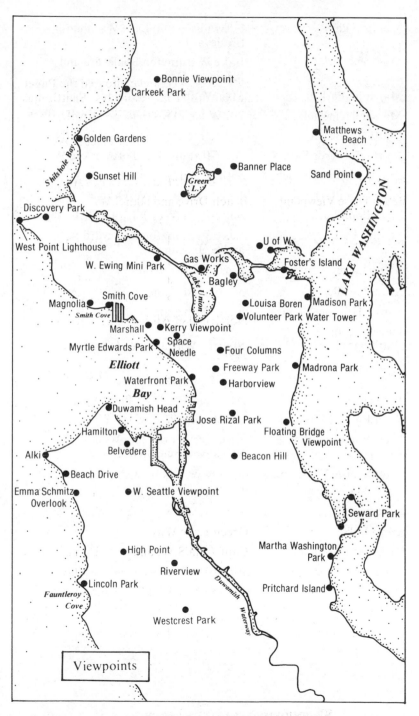

Viewpoints

Madison Park	E. Madison and Lake Washington Boulevard E.
Madrona Park	Lake Washington Boulevard and Madrona Drive
Magnolia Park	31st W. and W. Garfield
Marshall Viewpoint	7th W. and W. Highland Drive
Matthews Beach	N.E. 93rd and Sand Point Way N.E.
Myrtle Edwards Park	Pier 70 at north end of Alaskan Way
Pritchard Island Beach	55th S. and S. Grattan
Riverview Playfield	12th S.W. and S.W. Othello
Sand Point Park	Sand Point Way N.E. and N.E. 65th
Seward Park	Lake Washington Boulevard S. and S. Juneau
Smith Cove	Port of Seattle, Pier 91
Space Needle	5th N. and Thomas (Seattle Center)
Sunset Hill Viewpoint	N.W. 77th and 34th N.W.
University of Washington	Stevens Way and Pend Oreille Road
Volunteer Park Water Tower	14th E. and E. Prospect
Waterfront Park	Alaskan Way from Pier 57 to 59
West Ewing Mini Park	3rd W. and W. Ewing
West Point Lighthouse	Discovery Park (36th W. and W. Government Way)
West Seattle Viewpoint	35th S.W. and S.W. Alaska

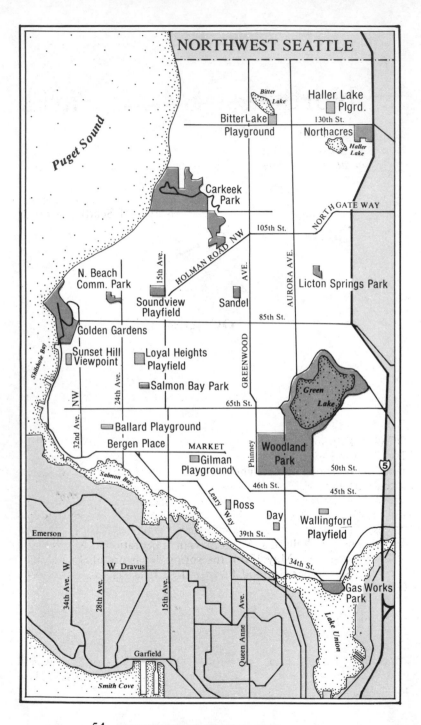

NORTHWEST SEATTLE

Puget Sound

Bitter Lake

Haller Lake Plgrd.

Bitter Lake Playground

130th St.

Northacres

Haller Lake

Carkeek Park

NORTH GATE WAY

105th St.

HOLMAN ROAD NW

AURORA AVE.

15th Ave.

AVE.

N. Beach Comm. Park

Licton Springs Park

Soundview Playfield

Sandel

85th St.

Shilshole Bay

Golden Gardens

Sunset Hill Viewpoint

Loyal Heights Playfield

GREENWOOD

Salmon Bay Park

Green Lake

NW

24th Ave.

65th St.

32nd Ave.

Ballard Playground

Phinney

Bergen Place

MARKET

Woodland Park

50th St.

5

Gilman Playground

Salmon Bay

Leary Way

Ross

46th St.

45th St.

Day

Wallingford Playfield

Emerson

39th St.

34th St.

34th Ave. W

28th Ave.

W Dravus

15th Ave.

Queen Anne Ave.

Gas Works Park

Lake Union

Garfield

Smith Cove

1
Northwest Seattle Parks

*Parks are the breathing lungs and beating hearts of
great cities... and in them are whispers of peace and joy.*

—J. T. Ronald
Mayor of Seattle, 1892—3

Bergen Place

22nd N.W and N.W. Market
Size: 0.2 acre
Buses: 17, 18, 43
Major use: community square

DESCRIPTION

This bustling, colorful square is a fine place to stop for a rest or
snack while shopping or sightseeing in downtown Ballard. A huge
blue awning protects you from rain and sun while you sit on concrete
stools or spread a sack lunch out on picnic tables. The square is
within easy walking distance of many shops and entertainment
places, waterside restaurants, and historical points of interest. Try it
during one of Ballard's Scandinavian celebrations: Norwegian
Independence Day (May 17th); the spring departure of the halibut
fleet; the September Seafood Fest; or Leif Ericksen Day (October
14th).

NEARBY ATTRACTIONS

From Bergen Place it's an easy few blocks west on N.W. Market
Street to the Carl S. English Gardens and the fish and ship ladders at
the Ballard Locks. For more information on where to go in Ballard,
call 625-4534 and ask for a copy of the city's walking tour, "The
Heart of Old Ballard."

HISTORY

It is not surprising that the Scandinavians took such a liking to the Puget Sound area—particularly to the land around Salmon Bay—for in many ways it resembled their own water-washed homelands. One of the first developers in this area was an Ohio-born Englishman named William Ballard, who, like most other ambitious young men of his time, went into real estate. As the Scandinavians arrived, Ballard subdivided and sold his land, and the area soon became known as "Little Sweden." In 1907, this industrious community of lumbermen, fishermen, and shipbuilders was annexed to Seattle as the Ballard neighborhood.

Bergen Place is named after Seattle's sister city in Norway. The city, located among Norway's fjords and founded by King Olav Kyrre in 1070, is distinguished as the home of composer Edvard Grieg. Norway's modern-day King Olav was on hand to dedicate the park in 1975.

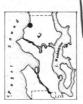

Carkeek Park

N.W. 110th off Greenwood N.
Size: 216 acres (23 acres tidelands)
Buses: 5, 28
Major uses: hiking, picnics, nature study

DESCRIPTION

Plunge down the road into this large wilderness park on the northwest shore of the city, following Piper's Creek to the beach and then looping back out. Here you can experience wild, wooded pathways and wide-open saltwater beaches, streams rushing down forested hillsides, picnic feasts and soccer games on a field overlooking the sound.

For easy access to the park, turn west onto N.W. 110th from Greenwood N. and wind down the hillside about three fourths of a mile to the entrance. A parking lot to your right borders on an archery range with six straw backings for paper targets (you bring the targets).

About a quarter mile farther on (drive slowly—police are often waiting for hotrodders), you will pass a small sewage treatment plant on your left. The wide, graveled Piper's Creek Trail runs behind the plant. If you go left, it will take you a half mile upstream over footbridges and quiet, woodsy spots to a small parking lot at 100th Place and 6th N.W., just across the street from a major shopping

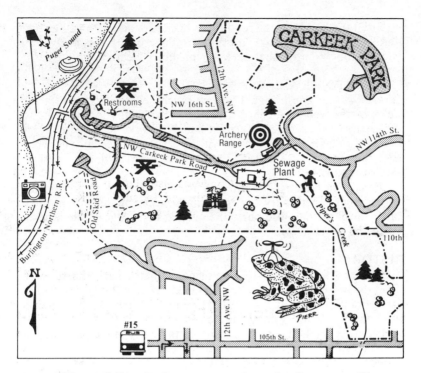

center. If you follow it downstream along the flat, you will soon
come to the beach parking lot. A third alternative is to cross the
footbridge about fifty yards below the sewage plant. This path curves
and switches back up through leafy, fern-infested woods to a maze of
confusing trials—including an old skid road. If you keep your
westward bearings, you will come out on a bluff overlooking the
sound. From here you can descend to a model airplane/softball field
with four picnic tables. Or, if you like, cross the railroad tracks to
the beach, where you can build a fire in one of the permanent pits or
on the beach itself.

Now, back to the fork in the road. The one-way fork to the right
leads on to the beach parking lot with adjacent restrooms, a playing
field, two large stove shelters (one grand old shelter made of stone),
lots of picnic tables, a play area, and another maze of forest trails.

After crossing over a high overpass, you will find yourself on the
beach, which is listed as covering twenty-three acres. But with the
view to the north, west and south it becomes much larger. In the
distance you can see the south end of Whidbey Island, the cliffs of
the Kitsap Peninsula, Bainbridge Island, and beyond; and in the far
distance, the misty outlines of the Olympics—Constance, Jupiter,
the Brothers, and their neighbors.

From the beach lot the road loops back around to Piper's Creek. Here you can go right, over a bridge, to the model airplane/softball field, or follow on up the creek for picnics beneath willow trees.

THINGS TO REMEMBER
Carkeek can be confusing. If you go much beyond the road, picnic areas, or the well-established Piper's Creek Trail, you are likely to find yourself in a maze of trails and pathways leading in every direction imaginable. The map will give you an idea of where the better beaten ones are, but it's easy to get sidetracked, so be sure to watch the kids.

Be careful crossing the railroad tracks. Trains roar around the Carkeek curve with nary a warning, and accidents have happened. Particularly for the little ones, the overpass is a much safer way to get to the beach.

HISTORY
If Carkeek's forest trails are confusing, so is the park's history. In 1918, the original "Carkeek Park" was at Pontiac Bay, just north of Sand Point. It was the gift of Morgan J. Carkeek, an English building contractor who came to Seattle in 1875. Carkeek left Seattle a legacy that includes many of the early stone buildings in Pioneer Square and the Army barracks at Fort Lawton. He also organized Seattle's first street railway.

Carkeek's twenty-three-acre park on Pontiac Bay was used primarily as an overnight camping facility from 1918 until 1926, when it was converted, along with the rest of Sand Point, into a naval air station. Then, in 1928, Carkeek donated the park's $25,000 sale price to help purchase a new park site across town. The city paid a total of $125,000 for this "Piper's Canyon" land, the present site of the park.

Piper's Creek is named after A.W. Piper, a candy manufacturer who lived in the southwest portion of the ravine. In the early days, a single dusty road wound along the ravine past Piper's place and over the railroad tracks to a sawmill near what is now the park's southwest shore. The mill finished chewing up the forest's original timber in the 1920s. It was replaced by the Whiz Company fish trap, which caught salmon there until 1932.

Carkeek was slow to catch on as a major park. It was first used to grow vegetables for Woodland Park Zoo animals, and as a rented pasturage for grazing animals. Its popularity among humans increased as works projects during the Depression created camp buildings and forest trails. But even so, it was a dubious popularity. In 1938, the resident caretaker was commissioned as a sheriff's deputy to help curtail the "rowdy orgies" that had become prevalent there.

In later years, the park experienced a brief Army encampment (1942) and a variety of new construction: a sewage plant in 1949; a loop road, shelter, and picnic area in 1953; and a model airplane field in 1959.

The park is still the scene of some rowdyism. Like Alki and Golden Gardens, Carkeek is a place for teenagers and hotrods during certain seasons. But it is a contained wilderness, and there seems to be room for everybody.

Gas Works Park

N. Northlake Way and Meridian N.
Size: 21 acres
Bus: 26
Major uses: playbarn, views, kites, picnics

DESCRIPTION

This is one of the most exotic, action-packed parks in the city. A peninsular knob at the north end of Lake Union, it is easily identified by the stark skeletons of the old gas plant and undulating grassy hills. A waterside promenade and a sixty-foot "mound" with an enormous sundial on top give wide-open views of Lake Union and the Seattle cityscape. Breezes race across the lake, pushing sailboats and seaplanes and lifting kites into the sky.

Some days the air is literally dancing with multicolored kites and streamers, visible for miles away and truly symbols of the joy and festivity permeating this park. Children run through grasses and along winding pathways to hilltop and play areas. Couples spread blankets for waterside picnics, bathers swim and swelter on parched grasses in summer, and rock bands occasionally blare out music to happy throngs.

The mood is emphasized by the facilities: a large covered playbarn packed with gaily colored gasworks artifacts—engines, cogs, wheels, pipes, and tanks for all ages to climb on; a large play area with ropes, poles, slides, and towers; a concession stand; restrooms; and an enormous picnic shelter with loft, electrical outlets, barbecues, and eating space for up to 500! Be sure to call the park department (625-4671) in advance to make reservations for space here.

The Gas Works Park is also the graveyard for some fascinating artifacts, among them a half dozen fenced-in oxygen gas generator towers, which used to convert crude oil for heating Seattle homes.

The park department has enshrined these temporarily with cyclone'
fencing to prevent climbing accidents. But these relics are constantly
being photographed, and before long they will be fitted with safety
skyways and brightened up as a celestial adjunct to the already
existing playbarn.

THINGS TO REMEMBER
Keep an eye on the children. It's easy to lose sight of them,
especially on crowded weekends when they can get swept away by
the roving spirit of the place.

NEARBY ATTRACTIONS
There are a number of good eating spots along N. Northlake Way,
between the park and the University Bridge. They include the
America's Cup right across the street (1900 N. Northlake Way, 633-
0161) with Sunday brunches, lunches, and dinners as well as an art
gallery and boating shops; the **Gasworks Restaurant** (2501 N.
Northlake Way, 632-7666), especially good for Sunday brunch with
the kids; **Ivar's Indian Salmon House** (401 N.E. Northlake Way, 632-
0767), a fine spot for the whole family; and the **Northlake Tavern and
Pizza House** (660 N.E. Northlake Way, 633-5317).

    Seattle Police Harbor and Air Patrol (625-2051). While you're
at the Gas Works, you might see an occasional helicopter whirl into
the air or set down for a landing just west of the "mound." If you
want to take a closer look at these air and boat operations, make
arrangements by calling first.

    Burke-Gilman Trail. The city's new walking, jogging, and biking
path begins by the Gas Works parking lot and follows the abandoned
bed of the Burlington-Northern Railroad 12.5 miles north to
Kirkland's Log Boom Park. Except at intersections, it is completely
isolated from traffic, making it especially safe for children. And in
July and August its brambles offer blackberry picking par excel-
lence.

HISTORY
Like most of Seattle's oblong hills and waters, Lake Union was
formed by the grinding of the glacier that plowed its way over the
Puget Sound area about 15,000 years ago. It owes its name to
pioneer Thomas Mercer, who in 1854 predicted that someday it
would form the "union" between Lake Washington and Puget
Sound.

    Before the Lake Washington Ship Canal was dug in 1917, Lake
Union was connected to Salmon and Shilshole bays by a small
stream (now the site of the Ballard Locks), and was cut off from
Lake Washington by a narrow stretch of land now sliced through by
the Montlake Cut. The Indians first used Lake Union, which they

called *Tenas Chuck* or "Little Water" (*Hyas Chuck* or "Big Water" being Lake Washington), as a canoe portage between Shilshole Bay and Lake Washington. Pioneer loggers later used Lake Union as a repository for timber floated through a narrow man-made channel from lake Washington. This channel was dug by Judge Thomas Burke's Improvement Company in 1885.

Today's conglomeration of industrial artifacts and derelict ships crowding the shoreline hints at the abuses that were heaped on the lake starting around the turn of the century. Part of the craze was coal and railroads. Seattleites were angered that Tacoma was chosen as the western terminus for the Transcontinental Railroad. In 1887, again led by Judge Thomas Burke, a citizens' group started laying tracks for the Seattle Lakeshore and Eastern Railroad to connect with the transcontinental trunk and to exploit coal and timber to the north and east. Eventually the tracks wound all the way around the shoreline and north toward Canada.

It was alongside these tracks at the north end of Lake Union that the Seattle Lighting Company constructed a gas plant in 1906. (The company was one of the many pioneering enterprises of Arthur Denny and Dexter Horton. It had started out at 6th and Jackson with forty-two customers and five street lamps in 1873.) For the next twenty years it spewed smoke, soot, and cinders as trainloads of coal were heaped into its ovens. Even after the plant's conversion to oil-gas burners in 1937, it continued pouring out billows of white steam and throwing great flashes of flame against the clouds. Nearby residents remember these flashes sometimes lighting up the whole lake at night, while sludge and tar accumulated on the ground like lava from a volcanic eruption.

The plant heated Seattle homes until 1956, when the last of the company's customers turned to natural gas. The city acquired the site for a park in 1962.

One of those who worked hardest to make the park a reality was City Council member Myrtle Edwards. The park was named in her honor shortly after she died in an auto accident in 1969, but relatives withdrew her name because of the park's association with the old, unattractive artifacts.

Now much of the park has been recycled. It took a considerable amount of dirt and sawdust to produce a topsoil that would grow even grass on top of the sludge-tar base surrounding the plant. But today thousands of people revel in and run over this grass every week, never sensing the wasteland that lies beneath. And what about the big "mound," that most entrancing of hills, where skateboarders slalom down pathways and kite fliers watch the lake for telltale puffs of wind? It was heaped up there by dump trucks carrying dirt from the foundations of buildings being constructed in other parts of the city!

Golden Gardens Park

North end of Seaview Avenue N.W.
Size: 95 acres
Bus: 17
Major uses: sunbathing, picnics, boating, hiking

DESCRIPTION

The Burlington Northern Railroad neatly slices Golden Gardens into two very different sections: an upper, forested hillside sloping west from the Loyal Heights neighborhood, and a long stretch of sandy beach along the north end of Shilshole Bay.

Most people pass right by the hillside facilities about halfway down Golden Gardens Drive in their eagerness to get to the beach. A small parking lot gives access to a stove shelter, picnic areas, and forest trails. Wide concrete stairs beside a rushing stream lead down toward the beach from here, too. You can reach it by taking the pedestrian underpass from the parking lot at the foot of the hill, or by following the road around the fence to Seaview Avenue.

Hit the beach on a hot weekend and you'll be bowled over by teeming humanity alternately baking on the sand and plunging into the fifty-degree waters of Puget Sound. The strand is a teen haven most summer afternoons and evenings, but it's irresistible for many reasons: a wide, sandy beach (no lifeguard), grassy areas with picnic tables, stove shelter, a shady play area with swings and balance beams, a bathhouse, a concession stand, bike racks, pits for beach fires, and choice clam-digging spots off Meadow Point at low tide. This is also a favorite haunt for scuba divers, and for bikers who use it as the terminus for freewheeling trips along Seaview Avenue.

At the far south end of the strand you will find a public fishing dock, a 120-foot-wide public boat ramp, and parking for about 100 cars with trailers. Beach parking for cars without trailers is in long strips going north from here and on the east side of the railroad tracks.

NEARBY ATTRACTIONS

For food, try **Little Coney** right next to the boat ramp. You can get anything here—from hamburgers to clam chowder to hot pastrami—for very reasonable prices. You'll find plenty of fancier eating farther south at restaurants along Seaview Avenue. And while you're at it, enjoy a leisurely stroll beside a forest of waving masts along Shilshole Bay.

While you are in the Golden Gardens area, be sure to experience the view from **Sunset Hill**. Drive back up Golden Gardens Drive and follow 32nd N.W. southward to a Scenic Drive sign at N.W. 77th.

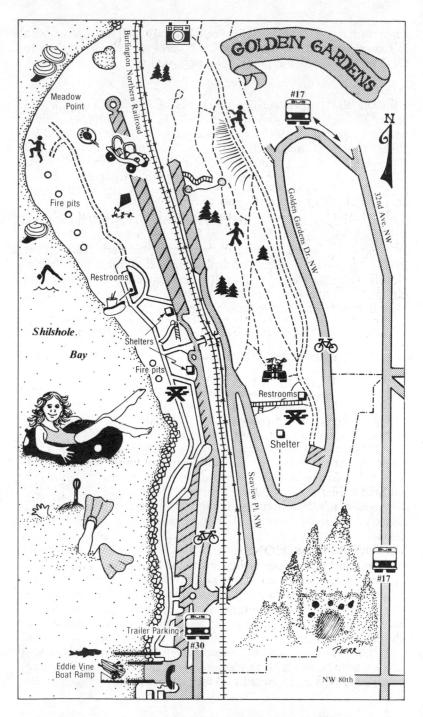

GOLDEN GARDENS

#17

N

Burlington Northern Railroad

Meadow Point

Fire pits

Restrooms

Shilshole Bay

Shelters

Fire pits

Golden Gardens Dr. NW

32nd Ave. NW

Restrooms

Shelter

Seaview Pl. NW

Trailer Parking

#30

Eddie Vine Boat Ramp

#17

PIERR

NW 80th

Then turn right to the viewpoint. The bay below is alive with sailboats, and you can smell the salt breezes as you gaze far out to the Puget isles and the craggy Olympic skyline.

HISTORY
Shilshole Bay, which washes the sands of Golden Gardens, was named for the Indians who once inhabited the area. Golden Gardens itself was named in 1907 by its original owners, Harry and Olive Treat. Typical of most such real estate "gold mines" at the turn of the century, Golden Gardens became the terminus of a trolley line built to lure families on Sunday outings from the central city— ostensibly to have a good time, but more practically to be "made aware" of the real estate.

The northern half of Meadow Point was a shipyard until 1913. Ten years later the city bought the land, and it quickly overflowed with cars as it became Ballard's most popular park. Despite (or maybe because of) the acres of asphalt devoted to the automobile at Golden Gardens today, it is still often congested with steel and chrome. And the first "tin lizzies" that puttered down the dusty hillside road to the beach are now only dim memories.

Green Lake

Latona N.E. and E. Green Lake Drive N.
Size: 342 acres (water included)
Buses: 6, 16, 26, 48, 306
Major uses: biking, jogging, swimming, boating

DESCRIPTION
Green Lake is a shimmering patch of blue and green in the midst of a densely populated residential district just west of the freeway. Rimmed by trees and gently sloping grass and encircled by a meandering asphalt pathway, it is the most popular year-round walking, jogging, and bicycling park in the city.

The lake has many moods. On early spring mornings its banks are lined with fishermen casting for rainbow trout. On hot summer days its shores teem with sunbathers, swimmers, picnickers, Frisbees, dogs, ducks, and geese; and the pathway is jammed with churning bodies and bicycles. In winter the trees look stark and empty and the lake bobs with wind-driven waterfowl, heads tucked low against the storms. During foul weather the path is sometimes nearly empty—but never quite. Always there is the lone jogger, the pensive walker, the couple arm in arm. And toward evening the multicolored lights of the city stab long reflections off the water.

A QUICK TOUR OF THE LAKE

Northeast. This side of the lake is the most popular takeoff point for joggers and bikers. Here they unload their two-wheelers from car racks and stretch a few muscles before starting on their three-mile loop trip. This area is also the most packed with facilities: playground and soccer/football fields, three tennis courts; community center with public swimming pool, gym, snack bar, restrooms, and public telephone; sandy beach with lifeguards in summer; rowboat and canoe rentals ($2.50 per hour); and children's pier.

North to Northwest. Spinning around the lake with the crowd—counterclockwise—the asphalt pathway (half for pedestrians, half for bikers) passes groves of big cottonwood trees, a wading pool, restrooms, and stately sequoias at the far north end of the lake. Then it winds past another bathing beach, sometimes called West Green Lake, and the Bathhouse Theatre (524-9110). The theatre offers indoor stage productions throughout the year.

West. Just past another fishing pier and two tennis courts, you will enjoy feeding ducks and geese that make their homes in the nearby Waldo Waterfowl Sanctuary ("Keep Off"). These birds are quite gregarious—even pushy—as they gab and shuffle and gaggle and honk in the scuffle for flying bread crumbs. Among them, little children sometimes seem joyously lost in a flutter of feathers.

From here the path winds past marshy fishing spots (the lake is stocked yearly with 15,000 to 20,000 legal-sized trout) to the Aqua Theatre and the Clarence Massart Shellhouse at the south end of the lake.

South. Here you'll find another large collection of facilities, including restrooms, snack bar, and public telephone. The area is a spectator site for a variety of aquatic events, from water skiing to boat racing (see "Special Events" below). The shellhouse is used by members of the women's Green Lake Crew for early morning and afternoon workouts. The Aqua Theatre has fallen into disuse in recent years because of the unpredictability of the weather. But the Seattle Sailing Association (323-2345) launches beginning sailors in eight-foot El Toro boats from its docks. And you can easily launch your own small wind or muscle-powered craft from the shellhouse pier.

South to Northeast. Just south of the Aqua Theatre you'll see the fields and picnic grounds of Lower Woodland Park. The pathway starts on its northward stretch by passing between another pier and the nine-hole Pitch 'n' Putt Golf Course. Then it's a fairly flat mile past more restrooms and fishing and sunbathing spots on the east side back to the recreation center.

THINGS TO REMEMBER
Green Lake is often crowded. The most popular parking lot is on the northeast side near the recreation center, and it is often jammed to overflowing. Parking is usually easier at the south lot, and the west lot is almost never full.

NEARBY ATTRACTIONS
Most of the food spots are clustered at the north end of Ravenna Boulevard, near the northeast side of the lake. A real summertime favorite is **Spud Fish and Chips** (6860 E. Green Lake Way N., 524-0565). Other gastronomic attractions here include **Albertson's Food Center** (6900 E. Green Lake Way N.), for picnic fixings; **Baskin and Robbins** (N.E. 71st and Green Lake Drive N., 524-2555), for umpteen flavors of ice cream; the **Green Lake Grill** (N.E. 71st and Green Lake Way), for more fish and chips, etc.; and the **Green Lake Bowl Cafe** (401 N.E. Ravenna Boulevard, 525-0120), where you can down bowling pins along with your food. For sweet-tooths, **Boehm's Candy Kitchen** (559 N.E. Ravenna Boulevard, 523-9380) is just a few blocks south.

Then at the far north end of the lake there's **Green Lake Jake's** (7918 E. Green Lake Drive N., 523-4747), serving delicious charbroiled burgers, fresh cut fries, and shakes made with hard ice cream. Next door is the **Cantonesia Restaurant** (7850 Green Lake Drive N., 524-2720 for Chinese-food connoisseurs.

Woodland Park and the Zoo. On the hills just above the Aqua Theatre and south parking lot you will find some prime picnic areas. You may also want to trek up there to watch the lawn bowling or to pitch a few horseshoes. The Lower Woodland Park track and playfields are just south of the lake. You can reach the zoo by walking uphill from the Aqua Theatre and crossing Aurora Avenue on the overpass, or by driving around to the entrance at N.E. 50th and Fremont Avenue N. or N. 59th and Evanston N.

SPECIAL EVENTS
Crew Races. Local, regional, and national competitions, with viewing from the shellhouse at the south end of the lake. Call 625-2975 or 625-4010 for schedules.

Seafair Events. Water skiing competitions, limited hydro races, and the annual Milk Carton Derby. Call 625-4673.

Fireworks Displays. Green Lake is usually one site for this annual gala event on the Fourth of July, with rockets, bombs, and brilliant explosions lighting up the whole sky.

Ice Skating. This is a *very* special event, occurring only once in a generation or so, when the ice on the lake is at least six inches thick.

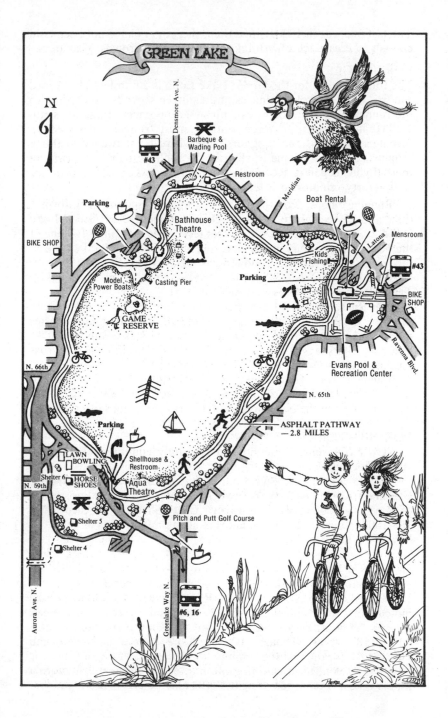

GREEN LAKE

N

Densmore Ave. N.

#43

Barbeque & Wading Pool

Restroom

Meridian

Boat Rental

Parking

Bathhouse Theatre

BIKE SHOP

Kids' Fishing

Latona

Mensroom

#43

Parking

BIKE SHOP

Model Power Boats

Casting Pier

GAME RESERVE

Ravenna Blvd.

N. 66th

Evans Pool & Recreation Center

N. 65th

ASPHALT PATHWAY — 2.8 MILES

Parking

LAWN BOWLING

Shelter 6

N. 59th

HORSE SHOES

Shellhouse & Restroom

Aqua Theatre

Shelter 5

Pitch and Putt Golf Course

Shelter 4

Aurora Ave. N.

Greenlake Way N.

#6, 16

The last one was in 1930. Since then, the winters have not been cold enough to create ice of a thickness to support crowds of skaters.

FOR JOGGERS

The total distance for the Green Lake Loop is 2.8 miles. The record run was done in twelve minutes and eighteen seconds. According to the runners at Club Northwest, most serious racers these days run the lake in thirteen to fourteen minutes, most "runners" in sixteen to seventeen minutes, and "joggers" anywhere from twenty to thirty minutes. If you are none of the above, don't despair—you can get there if you keep at it. Remember that Green Lake is also a pleasant walk—forty minutes to a leisurely hour.

Running Shops. For the latest in running equipment, information, and advice, go to **Super Jock and Jill** (7210 E. Green Lake Drive N., 522-7711, in the old Masonic Temple Building). It's one of the best running shops in the city, and the people there take time to talk with you. Another good one is **Green Lake Sports** (7902 E. Green Lake Drive N., 525-1400, at the far north end of the lake). They also have sailboats and hot tubs.

Fun Runs. If you want somebody to time you for a lap around the lake, the people from Super Jock and Jill have their stopwatches ready near the recreation center at East Green Lake, Sundays at 11 a.m. and Thursdays at 6 p.m. They'll call out your time as you cross the finish line—no matter how long you take.

Racing Events. Green Lake has races from informal to national competitions, the year around. For information and entry blanks on races throughout the Northwest, call either of the shops listed above.

FOR BICYCLERS

Avoid Smashups. Be sure to ride only counterclockwise and stay in the bike lane.

For sales, service, and rentals, the nearest shop is **Gregg's Greenlake Cycle** (7007 Woodlawn N.E. 523-1822, at the north end of Ravenna Boulevard). **The Aurora Cycle Shop** (7401 Aurora N., 783-1000, a block west of the lake) is open daily except Sundays but has no rentals.

HISTORY

Green Lake was formed by the gougings of a glacier during the last Ice Age, about 15,000 years ago. Recent dredgings from the lake indicate that the Indians must have been on hand to see Glacier Peak shower the Seattle area with volcanic ash about 6,700 years ago.

By 1870, when Erhart ("Green Lake John") Saifried began felling trees for the first log cabin on its northwest shore, much of the lake had been filled in with organic matter. In places it was more a marsh than a lake—abounding with the aquatic plants and algae that inspired its name. The lake was also much wider and longer then, extending southward as far as N. 54th Street.

The first major change came when A. L. Parker built a sawmill on the northeast shore, at the present site of the recreation center. In 1888, Green Lake John sold out to Realtor W. D. Wood and his partner E. C. Killbourne, an electrical engineer. These two men pooled their talents, circling the east side of the lake with trolley tracks and building a picnic park on the western shore. Then they ran the trolley line south to Fremont, where it connected with the Lake Union ferry—and finally with the trolley bringing prospective buyers from Pioneer Square.

Meanwhile, an eccentric country gentleman named Guy Phinney was busy establishing his Woodland Park country estate to the southwest, complete with a private trolley line to Fremont. Phinney's zoo, conservatory, picnic grounds, ballfield, and boating and swimming beach helped to lure even more settlers to the Green Lake area.

The lake was given to the city by the State of Washington in 1905, much to the dismay of W. D. Wood, who called it "an act of grand larceny," and much to the contentment of the green-thumbed Olmsted Brothers, who had included it in the city's comprehensive parks plan. Then began a long series of tamperings—with lake levels, contours, and water quality—that has not abated to this day.

In 1911, Green Lake was lowered seven feet to expose new lakeshore. Creek beds that fed the lake from the north were filled or diverted into sewer lines as new streets tore through the forest. The lake was alternately diked, dredged, and filled until, after twenty years, it had shrunk by 100 acres. The last of the fill, from the excavation for Aurora Avenue, was dumped at the south end of the lake in 1932.

Then came chronic stagnation and pollution, rampant algae growth, complaints of "swimmers' itch," copper sulfate treatments, sewer collapses, university studies, beach closings, public outcries, underwater chlorination, and more cries to "Clean up the lake!" All these things have been a periodic part of Green Lake's history since 1932.

The Waldo Waterfowl Sanctuary, named for former park commissioner Waldo Dahl, was built with planks and wheelbarrows as a WPA project in 1936. It was originally called Swan Island because its first purpose was to provide a sanctuary for a pair of swans from Victoria, British Columbia.

The Aqua Theatre was built in 1950. In its prime it seated some 5,000 people and was the scene of everything from aqua follies to Broadway specials. But Seattle's weather never cooperated enough for the theatre to make money, and now it is on the skids.

Green Lake used to abound with wildlife—bear, deer, salmon, beaver, raccoons, and birds of all kinds. Migrating wildfowl still drop down on its waters to rest and feed in fall and spring, but most of the other animals disappeared as the forests were sawed down and the lake became a more popular haunt for humans. With a note of irony, then, a local paper reported in 1960 that a pair of beaver had moved in, chewed down several trees near the Aqua Theatre, and begun constructing a den—"without a building permit!"

Even now Green Lake has a wild streak of sorts, though. The city has never managed to tame its algae blooms. When the "green tinge" of summer was last noticed, the park department wisely promised to harvest only what weeds it could. Hopefully, the city will find the "final solution" without having to convert the lake into an eighteen-hole golf course, as one misguided citizen once suggested. Meanwhile, Seattleites go on enjoying it with a passion they have for few other parks.

 # Licton Springs

N. 97th and Ashworth N.
Size: 6.3 acres
Bus: 16 to North Seattle Community College
Major uses: play area, walking, relaxing

DESCRIPTION
This park is well worth going out of your way to see. Just two blocks west of North Seattle Community College, a special freshness and a rustic, natural quality arise from its meandering pathways, bogs, trickling stream, pond, long grasses, and wooded glens. Even the play area at the northeast end of the park is rustically done, with some of the supports and planks carved gaily with gnomes and childlike figures. A sturdy climbing apparatus with an undulating slide towers like a two-story treehouse against a backdrop of woods—a favorite for children who love to climb its pipe ladders and railings to dangle their legs from high platforms. Another favorite is a cluster of tall pilings fitted with tires and a heavy log that rolls above the ground while hands grasp the rail above and feet churn below. There are also grasses for picnics, peripheral pathways with a few benches, and restrooms.

HISTORY
Perhaps the special spirit permeating this park is a remnant of the native Americans who were so devoted to it and who used it as a

healing center before the white man's arrival. Its "painted waters" contained minerals—iron, sulphur, and magnesium—that had powerful medicinal qualities. Here the Indians constructed sweat lodges. Medicine men, or *"Tamahnous,"* administered herbs and counseled the sick, who came to drink and bathe, to soothe aching bodies with red mud, and to dance in thankfulness to the Great Spirit.

The healing powers of the springs were also appreciated by the early settlers. Pioneer David Denny built a cabin there in 1870, and seven years later his brother Arthur bought the land for a summer home. Hundreds of settlers drove buggies for miles to immerse themselves and their ailing animals in the springs, and to cart back barrels of mineral water and mud.

In 1909, realtors platted the land and offered it for sale. "Six Hundred Choice Lots! Get Away from the Roar and Dust of Downtown Toil!" urged the ads in the *Seattle Post Intelligencer.* And many did.

But the springs site itself remained as a picnic area until 1935. The tract was then bought by E. A. Jensen, who built a two-story spa and advertised "relief from rheumatism, neuritis, arthritis, and asthma." Thousands flocked to gulp his bottles of renewing mineral water and to dunk themselves in thermal baths.

Another attempt to build a spa fell through in 1954, and in 1960 Seattle voters approved the area as a park site. The city bought the springs the following year, but Forward Thrust development did not get underway until 1975. Today Licton Springs still flows, although inconspicuously, from a concrete basin beside one of the pathways. From here its precious minerals trickle southward in pipes to mix with the city's sewer system.

Northacres Park

N. 130th and 1st Avenue N.E.
Size: 20.7 acres
Bus: 305
Major uses: picnics, play areas, walking

DESCRIPTION

This pleasant, fir-studded picnic and barbecue area borders on thick woods in a wild pocket between N. 130th and the freeway. Its chief civilized feature is a new half-mile health trail with eighteen exercise stations winding among alder, madrona, fir, salal, and flowering dogwood.

But the real attraction here is isolation. An out-of-the-way park, Northacres is rarely crowded, even on weekends and holidays. A few refugees from busy central city parks have discovered this special spot so close to the freeway, and come here regularly to walk their dogs, to sit in quite contemplation, or to follow the buzzings of insects through the woods.

For children, Northacres also includes a play area, complete with a large sandbox, a trestlelike climbing, balancing, and sliding contraption made out of ties from the former Burlington Northern Railroad (now the Burke-Gilman Trail), and an adjacent ballpark. And don't be dismayed if you run into a couple of unmarked buildings that look like concrete bomb bunkers. Those are the restrooms. (They're making them that way these days—windowless and without mirrors—because of the escalating cost of vandalism.)

North Beach Park

N.W. 90th and 24th N.W.
Size: 5 acres
Bus: 18
Major use: natural woods

DESCRIPTION

Almost every working day at noon for the past fifteen years, Conrad Gettman has parked his mail truck in a leafy nook on the dead end of N.E. 90th. There he relaxes, spreads a magazine out on the steering wheel, pours a cup of coffee, and listens to the sounds of birds resonating up from the ravine.

"It's the only open space on my route," he says. "I've gotten attached to it."

A primitive trail leads down into this natural ravine just to the left of where N.E. 90th leads up the hill and dead ends. It follows a creek through woods thick with alder and maple trees, salmonberries, skunk cabbage, delicate wildflowers, and stinging nettles. It is a beautiful place, but because of its inaccessibility, perhaps it is best left for the neighborhood kids—and the mail carriers.

Salmon Bay Park

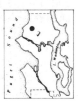

N.W. 70th between 19th and 21st N.W.
Size: 2.8 acres
Buses: 15, 18 to N.W. 70th
Major use: neighborhood picnic and play area

DESCRIPTION
Tall trees and picnic tables are scattered over the grassy hills of this little neighborhood park near Ballard High School and Monroe Junior High. On bright days crows harass squirrels in treetops, children scurry along pathways and expend boundless energies on swings, slides, bars, pipe tunnels, and springboards, while swallows skim the grass for flies.

NEARBY ATTRACTIONS
Two long blocks north is the Loyal Heights Playfield, and not far away, at N.W. 65th and 15th N.W., is Ballard High School, with four tennis courts and an indoor swimming pool (782-0282).

HISTORY
Salmon Bay Park was deeded to the city in 1890 by Elon W. Denton, a seaman and realtor, and was annexed to the city along with the rest of Ballard in 1907. It was named after a former tidal flat, which is now part of the Lake Washington Ship Canal. The bay was originally named in 1852 by pioneers William Bell and the Denny brothers, who found that salmon were abundant there. At that time, the bay area was inhabited by the Shilshole Indians, who loved to play and dig shellfish on its beaches. And for years after, a native affectionately known as "Indian Charlie" lived on its western shore.

Sandel Playground

1st N.W. and N.W. 90th
Size: 4.4 acres
Buses: 28, 48
Major Use: neighborhood play area

DESCRIPTION
Here's a gently sloping hill, with plantings of domestic trees, in the Greenwood neighborhood. At the upper end you'll find a wading

pool, a mini basketball court, swings, slide and restrooms. Then long concrete pathways pour down the hill, inviting skateboarders and bikers for a spin. At the bottom is a flat field suitable for romping and Frisbee throwing. Benches are provided for more sedate activities such as reading, loafing,and chewing on sandwiches.

Woodland Park

N. 55th and Phinney N. (west zoo entrance)
Size: 188 acres
Buses: 5 to west; 6 to east; 43 to south
Major uses: zoo, picnics, walking

DESCRIPTION

Woodland Park is an exciting rectangular complex just southwest of Green Lake and north of the Fremont district. Bisected by Aurora Avenue, it is really two parks in one.

West of Aurora. This half is devoted to zoo exhibits, some grassy picnic space, a formal rose garden, and an amusement park for small children. The zoo includes animals from all over the world—more than 1,100 in all, representing over 280 species of mammals, birds, amphibians, and reptiles. It is, of course, one of the city's most popular family park experiences and a grand educational outing for school groups from all over the Puget Sound area. Recent construction has also provided more natural environments for some of the animals and a more enjoyable and educational experience for visitors. (For zoo details, see map on page 76.)

East of Aurora. This half dovetails with the south end of Green Lake and extends south to N. 50th Street. It is largely an informal picnic park with pleasant grassy hills and pathways. At the far north end, on the hills just above Green Lake, you will find several picnic shelters with barbecue grills, horseshoe pits, and lawn bowling greens. (If you want to try this brand of bowling yourself, call the **Queen City Lawn Bowling Club,** 782-1515). The eastern flats (sometimes called Lower Woodland) include a nine-hole **Pitch 'n' Putt Golf Course** (632-8084), lighted tennis courts, a track and field area, and athletic fields extending all the way down to N. 50th Street. A soap box derby ramp runs north onto the flats from higher up on N. 50th. The upper south portion is devoted to woodsy pathways and picnic areas, including several more picnic shelters (call 625-4671 for reservations). Several other tennis courts are near the south entrance.

This area is worth a visit, if only for a walk among the trees. Such a variety of trunks—cedars, maples, firs. In the springtime their branches are the homes of chattering squirrels and crows, and the grass is hopping with robins and rabbits. The rabbits, which make their homes in protective piles of boulders and chunks of cement, rarely stray from this center except at early hours of the morning and later in the evening, when they are less likely to be pursued by eager dogs.

THINGS TO REMEMBER
Woodland Park is big and confusing, so study a map. If you're bound for the zoo, you can start from pay lots on the south, west, or north sides. If picnicking is your goal, enter either at N. 50th and Woodland Park N., or from the parking lot just above the Lower Woodland tennis courts. You can also cross over Aurora on pedestrian overpasses.

Zoo hours: 8:30 a.m. to sunset every day. Tropical and Nocturnal houses and Children's Zoo are open from 10 a.m. to 4 p.m.

Zoo admission: $1.50 for adults, $.50 for children and seniors. Children under six are admitted free if accompanied by a parent. Admission is free from 8:30 a.m. to 10 a.m. all day from October through March, and all day every Monday and Tuesday except holidays. The fifth day of every month and Christmas Day are also free. You can also cut costs with an annual pass: $5 for an individual, $10 for the family, including children and grandparents.

Zoo rules: no dogs or pets, skateboarding, bicycling, radio playing, or animal feeding. (They don't even sell peanuts anymore, due to many cases of animal indegestion.)

ZOO ATTRACTIONS FOR KIDS
Woodland Rides. This small amusement park offers rides on a merry-go-round, cars, boats, helicopters, fighter planes, caterpillars, and roller coasters. Price is $.25 per ride, $1 for a book of five, and $2.50 for a book of sixteen.

Pony Ring. Children weighing 115 pounds or less can ride around a ring on a Shetland pony for $.25, weather permitting, April through September from 10 a.m. to 3 p.m., and weekends only from October through March.

Children's Zoo and Farm. This is a place especially designed for young children. Here they can see and touch small animals, many of which are babies—ocelots, chimps, guinea pigs, and many others. A farmyard, with everything from chickens and turkeys to pigs and cows, creates a rural setting for city kids. The **Rural Crafts Center** is also here and features demonstrations of spinning, weaving, butter churning, and such—daily at 11 a.m. during the summer.

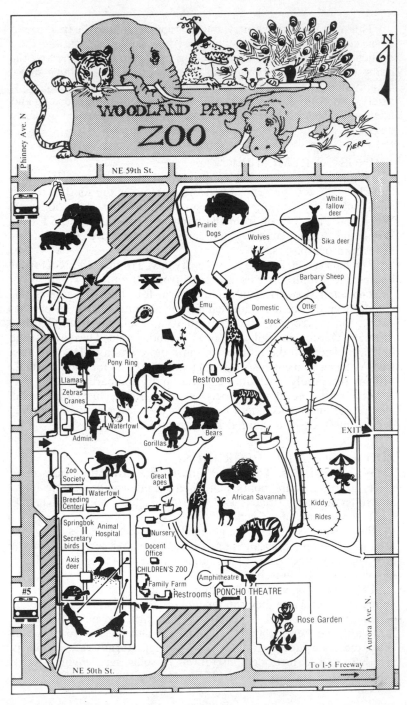

Poncho Theatre (zoo entrance at N. 50th and Fremont N., 633-4567). This small theatre offers children's productions, films, drama classes, and special events from festivals to mime. It also provides touring shows and workshops for schools and community centers. Call for more information.

OTHER ZOO ATTRACTIONS

Administration Building (just inside west entrance, 625-2244). Here you will find information about the zoo's latest exhibits and plans for the future, as well as first aid for minor cuts and bruises.

Seattle Zoological Society (just inside west entrance, 782-9455). The Society sells books, magazines, and pamphlets about wildlife. You can become a member by sending $9 to P.O. Box 30673, Seattle, 98103. Membership fees help provide money for educational programs, animal research and preservation of endangered species. They also entitle you to a year's subscription of *Pacific Search* (a magazine about Northwest nature and life), previews of new zoo exhibits, behind-the-scenes tours, and a ten percent discount on all gift shop items.

Tours (782-5045) Call the zoo docents to arrange tours for groups of ten or more. They will also bring small animals to such places as schools, churches, and retirement homes.

Rose Garden. Here you can walk through manicured lawns, hedges, and odd-looking trees interspersed with extensive plantings of magnificent roses: Grandiflora, Comanche, Pinocchio, Pillar of Fire, Golden Fleece, Red Ripple, Matterhorn, Summer Sunshine, Greenfire, Montezuma, and many more. This formal garden was originally laid out in the 1890's by Guy Phinney as part of his Woodland Park estate. The most colorful time to visit is late May through August.

HISTORY

Woodland Park owes its character to the visions of an eccentric Englishman named Guy Phinney. Phinney built and operated the first sawmill on Lake Washington, and it netted him a fortune. With his newly acquired money and his old dreams of the English aristocracy, he invested $40,000 in wilderness land just southwest of Green Lake and began creating a country estate in the grand old style.

Phinney installed a private trolley car along Fremont Avenue, and constructed an impressive stone entrance at N. 50th Street, a bandstand, a formal rose garden, a small zoo, and elaborate pathways. These paths wound down through the woods to the shores of Green Lake, where he built a pumphouse to supply his gardens. Further inspired by the beauties of the lake, he built a bathing beach, boathouse, picnic grounds, and two ballfields.

With all these trappings, Phinney's estate was ideal for a city park. The city bought it in 1900 for $100,000 in spite of vigorous protests that it was "too far out of town!" Three years later the famed Olmsted Brothers drafted plans to expand it into a full-fledged zoological garden.

Since the Olmsted philosophy of landscape architecture was itself an outgrowth of the English landscape tradition, the brothers must have found it a joy to pencil new plans around the formal gardens and pathways Phinney had left, creating great spaces with animal quarters on the periphery.

The Olmsted Plan called for eventual expansion of the zoo into Lower Woodland as well. In 1930 however, City Engineer W. B. Barkuff announced plans to bisect Woodland Park with a six-lane highway (Aurora Avenue). This plan enraged City Councilman George Hill, who already had taken Barkuff's predecessor, R. H. Thomson, on a tour through Europe "to cure him of the habit of putting roads through parks." But not even a public vote against Aurora Avenue was able to defeat it. In 1932 construction crews cut a deep, wide channel through Woodland Park, using the excavated earth to fill in the southernmost portion of Green Lake. The park has been bisected ever since, its eastern and western portions thinly connected by concrete overpasses.

Planners tried once to reunite the parks shortly after passage of the 1968 Forward Thrust Bond issue. With new millions allotted for Woodland Park improvement, architects presented a plan to "lid" Aurora Avenue with a 700-foot zoological conservatory, and create natural environments in Lower Woodland for such creatures as cheetahs, gazelles, elephants, and hippos. But this plan was defeated by a public initiative. The two parks remain separate, and the bond money is being spent to improve animal exhibits on the existing zoo grounds.

Zoo History. The zoo concept has come a long way since Stone Age people began keeping bears as pets some 30,000 years ago, and since kings and noblemen stocked their estates with live trophies of the hunt. Today, zoos are beginning to emphasize education, and as wild spaces continue to dwindle, are also serving as sanctuaries and breeding grounds for endangered species.

The first zoo in Seattle was built at Leschi by the Lake Washington Cable Railroad Company as part of an attempt to lure buyers out from Pioneer Square to see the real estate. The Leschi animals were given to Woodland Park in 1903, and were fed largely on vegetables grown at Carkeek Park.

Most recently the zoo has been undergoing a major facelift, aimed at taking many animals out of their glassed-in or barred cages and placing them in more natural environments. Such new exhibits include an African Savannah, with antelope and zebra roaming freely; a Tropical Forest Island Complex, with primates swinging through leafy skyways above a river; a Temperate Deciduous Forest, with native waterfowl wading and flying through marshlands; and the first exhibit in the world that allows gorillas to live together in a natural setting modeled after their native jungle environment.

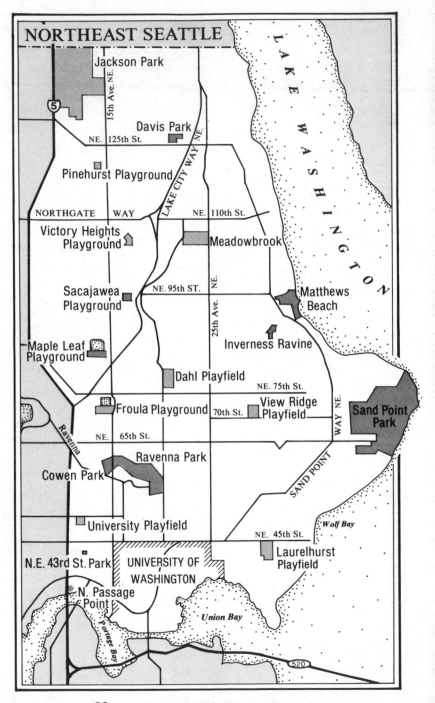

NORTHEAST SEATTLE

Jackson Park

15th Ave. NE.

5

Davis Park

NE. 125th St.

Pinehurst Playground

LAKE CITY WAY NE.

LAKE WASHINGTON

NORTHGATE WAY

NE. 110th St.

Victory Heights
Playground

Meadowbrook

Sacajawea
Playground

NE. 95th ST.

NE. 25th Ave.

Matthews
Beach

Inverness Ravine

Maple Leaf
Playground

Dahl Playfield

NE. 75th St.

Froula Playground

70th St.

View Ridge
Playfield

SAND POINT WAY NE.

Sand Point
Park

Ravenna

NE. 65th St.

Ravenna Park

Cowen Park

SAND POINT

University Playfield

NE. 45th St.

Wolf Bay

N.E. 43rd St. Park

UNIVERSITY OF
WASHINGTON

Laurelhurst
Playfield

N. Passage
Point

Portage Bay

Union Bay

520

2
Northeast Seattle Parks

*Trees and stones will teach you that which you can
never learn from masters.*

—St. Bernard de Clairvaux

Cowen Park

University Way N.E. and N.E. Ravenna Blvd.
Size: 8.4 acres
Buses: 7, 48
Major use: neighborhood play area

DESCRIPTION (See map on page 87.)
A generally quiet enclave north of the University of Washington, Cowen Park is tacked onto the west end of Ravenna Park, adding grassy play and picnic areas to the ravine that descends toward the southeast. Here you will find a softball field, a few picnic tables and barbecue pits, a play area with swings and climbing bars, and restrooms. Three tennis courts are located just east of the 15th Avenue Bridge. In the summer, Cowen is a popular sunbathing spot.

HISTORY
Cowen Park was originally part of the Ravenna creekbed, which flowed southeast from Green Lake through untouched forests, then rushed down the Ravenna ravine to empty into Lake Washington. As homes were built in the area, most of the creek was rechanneled into the North Trunk sewer line, which now runs below Ravenna Boulevard. In 1961, this section of the ravine was filled with 100,000 cubic yards of dirt from the freeway construction, and flattened into play areas.

The park is the legacy of a British-born realtor named Charles Cowen, who grew up among the South African diamond mines and later spent many years as a resident of Washington's San Juan Islands. Perhaps his early years among the glittering stones of Africa and those later spent among the gemlike islands north of Seattle helped to inspire the declaration accompanying his gift to the city: "Man shall not live by bread alone." The words are now inscribed on the gatepost at the entrance to the park.

A trolley began serving the park area during the Alaska-Yukon-Pacific Exposition of 1909. The tracks have been replaced by paved streets and boulevards, but the old pillared trolley shelter and bandstand still sit at the 15th Avenue entrance as a reminder of days gone by.

Davis Park

28th N.E. between N.E. 125th and 127th
Size: 1.2 acres
Buses: 8, 41, 72, 307
Major use: neighborhood playground

DESCRIPTION
This is actually the backyard of the Lake City Branch Public Library, just south of the Lake City Community Center. Sand box, slide, whirl, and sitting places make it a good spot to peruse your new books while the kids get some exercise. The park was given to the city in 1964. It is named after Albert Davis, a leading citizen in the Lake City community until his death in 1971.

Inverness Ravine

Inverness Drive N.E. off N.E. 85th
Size: 2.9 acres
Buses: 8, 41 along Sand Point Way
Major use: natural woods

DESCRIPTION
It's worth driving to the top of Inverness from Sand Point Way just for the views of Lake Washington and the forested countryside. The ravine is natural and inaccessible right now, and the park depart-

ment has no immediate plans for it. But some day it may have the isolated and rejuvenating flavor of the Ravenna gorge—thick with alder and brightened by birds and a gurgling stream. The park was given to the city by Crawford and Conover, Inc., realtors, in 1972. It takes its name from the neighborhood, whose topography is suggestive of the Inverness highlands of Scotland.

Maple Leaf Playground

N.E. 82nd and Roosevelt Way N.E.
Size: 5.4 acres
Buses: 7, 22
Major use: neighborhood play area

DESCRIPTION

Wrapped around the south end of the water reservoir in the Maple Leaf neighborhood, this huge grassy area is perfect for Frisbee throwing. It has a big ballfield, swings, a whirl, and tetherball poles (bring your own tetherball).

Matthews Beach Park

N.E. 93rd off Sand Point Way N.E.
Size: 20.9 acres
Bus: 8
Major uses: swimming, picnics

DESCRIPTION

Seattle's largest freshwater bathing beach is spread out below a grassy, tree-studded knoll about a mile north of Sand Point Park. On hot summer days (lifeguard on duty), it overflows with swimmers and sunbathers. At more quiet times of the year, you can enjoy maples, firs, and giant cottonwoods, and share the expansive grassy areas with ducks and swooping swallows. You might also try a walk over the footbridge above Thornton Creek to the little wildlife refuge at the south end of the park.

Matthews Beach is an ideal stopover for bicyclers on the Burke-Gilman Trail. Facilities include a stove shelter with large picnic tables at the top of the knoll, and a bathhouse with restrooms near the beach. Kids will enjoy rolling down the sloping knoll to the play area (complete with swings, climber, slide, whirl, giant turtle, and four gaping pipes) and climbing on nearby boulders. These are glacial erratics, carried on the back of a glacier from as far away perhaps as northern British Columbia, and left here as the ice melted away about 10,000 years ago.

HISTORY

The park is named for John G. Matthews, the pioneer who homesteaded on the property in the 1880s. A sawmill buzzed and whined on the north side of the cove in 1894, at which time the entire cove area was submerged beneath the waters of Lake Washington. The flats emerged in 1917, when the lake receded nine feet after the opening of the Chittenden Locks and the Lake Washington Ship Canal.

The ouline of the original cove is suggested now by the Burke-Gilman Trail, formerly the Northern Pacific and later the Burlington Northern Railroad. The first tracks were laid here by Seattle citizens as part of the Seattle Lake Shore and Eastern Railroad.

During the 1940s, the area just south of the main bathing beach was the site of the Pan American World Airways office and the dock for Pan American's "Clipper Ships," which carried seventy passengers and were the world's first amphibious commercial air transports over the ocean.

The city bought the first ten acres of Matthews Beach in 1951, for $70,000.

Northeast 43rd Street Park

9th N.E. and N.E. 43rd
Size: 0.1 acre
Buses: 7, 8, 30 to N.E. 45th
Major use: rest spot

DESCRIPTION

Careful, or you'll miss this one—even if you're looking for it! A rockeried, shrub-shrouded place to sit and take a breather on the fringe of the busy University District.

North Passage Point

N. Northlake Way and Meridian N.
Size: 0.7 acre
Bus: 26 to Wallingford and 35th
Major uses: picnics, views

DESCRIPTION

Parks sprout up in the strangest places! This little one, and its South Passage sister directly across the channel, sit between the pillars of the Freeway Bridge on the water passage between Lake Union and Portage Bay. Finished in 1977, it offers two small picnic tables on grass, and several benches on a concrete bulkhead at the water's edge. Stairs go into the water for wading, but because of heavy boat traffic, the area is not a spot for swimming. So be content with an unusual peek into both Lake Union and Portage Bay with their ships, rowing shells, sailboats and ducks—or crane your neck to see the roaring freeway in the sky with pigeons flapping among green girders.

NEARBY ATTRACTIONS

North Passage Point is a good stopping point on your way to the Gas Works Park along the Burke-Gilman Trail. While you're in the area, you might also want to go across the street to the **Northlake Tavern** (660 Northlake Way) for beer and pizza, or go down the way to **Ivar's Salmon House** (410 N.E. Northlake Way) for a mariner's meal.

HISTORY

In pioneer days, the narrow passage between Lake Union and Portage Bay was the site of a little town called Latona. Residents on the south shore could easily paddle across the channel to visit and get supplies.

In 1885, Judge Thomas Burke's Improvement Company dug the first primitive canal to connect Lake Union and Lake Washington, allowing small boats and timber to pour through the passage. Shortly afterwards. David Denny, who operated a sawmill at the south end of Lake Union, built a low timber bridge over the passage—directly beneath the present Freeway Bridge—for horses, wagons, and pedestrians. The opening of the Lake Washington Ship Canal in 1917 made the passage an industrial slough, and for years it steamed with coal barges and log booms bound for the shores of Elliott Bay.

The present University Bridge was built in 1933; the double-decker Freeway Bridge in 1962. North and South Passage Points were two of the many excess "patchwork" properties acquired by the highway department for the freeway. For over ten years these areas were littered with construction rubble, but Forward Thrust Bond money eventually funded their beautification.

Ravenna Park

20th N.E. and N.E. 58th
Size: 52.4 acres
Buses: 7, 8, 48
Major uses: hiking, jogging, picnics, playground

DESCRIPTION

Ravenna Park is a steep, half-mile wooded ravine connecting two large play and picnic areas just north of the University District. This place is sometimes almost a fantasyland, sunk away from the cares of the world like the woods of the hobbits. Standing quietly in Cowen Park at its upper end, you'll feel like you're between two worlds—the freeway roaring above, the woods offering silent solitude below.

Follow the path "down the rabbit hole" in this lush wild place, alive with streams and birds. Stroll or jog along the trails lacing the sloping sides of the gorge, far beneath arching bridges and city bombardments.

At the upper (west) end of the ravine, you'll come (puffing) up under the wide concrete arches of the 15th Avenue Bridge, where the woods open up into the play and picnic area of Cowen Park. As you approach the lower (east) end of the ravine, the woods spread out into even more spacious meadows, with picnic tables, barbecue pits, and a picnic shelter. The extreme eastern end has more amenities still: picnic tables, another shelter, swings, restrooms, a wading pool, and softball fields. Treelined Ravenna Boulevard on the south provides easy access to both picnic areas, and then continues from Cowen Park as a popular bikeway/runway leading out to Green Lake, about a mile to the northwest.

Another way to enjoy Ravena Park is to view it from above, looking down with a crow's eye view through the treetops to the bottom of the gorge. For the best view, try peering over the railings of the 20th Street Bridge, which is closed to all but bicycle and pedestrian traffic.

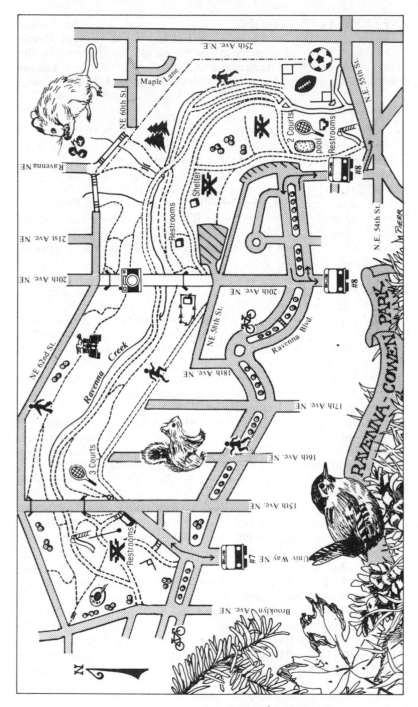

25th Ave. N.E.

Maple Lane

NE 60th St.

N.E. 55th St.

Ravenna NE

Restrooms

Shelter

2 Courts

pool

Restrooms

#8

21st Ave. NE

N.E. 54th St.

20th Ave. NE

#8

20th Ave. NE

NE 58th St.

Ravenna Blvd.

NE 62nd St.

Ravenna Creek

18th Ave. NE

17th Ave. NE

3 Courts

16th Ave. NE

15th Ave. NE

RAVENNA-COWEN PARK

Restrooms

#7

Univ Way NE

Brooklyn Ave. NE

N

M BEER

NEARBY ATTRACTIONS

You can go south from Cowen Park to a myriad of specialty shops, bookstores, and eating spots in the University District. From the lower (east) end of Ravenna you can also follow 25th N.E. south for several blocks to the University Village Shopping Center.

HISTORY

The special spirit of the Ravenna ravine may be partly the whisper of history. The ravine was originally part of a creekbed running from the northeast shore of Green Lake and emptying into Union Bay at about the present site of the University Village Shopping Center. Most of the creekbed has since been filled and replaced by the North Trunk sewer line, which now gurgles beneath Ravenna Boulevard. The lower section of Ravenna was filled in the 1920s along with an ever-expanding Lake Union shoreline, and the Cowen section was flattened in 1961 with 100,000 cubic yards of fill from the freeway excavations.

If Ravenna seems a leafy paradise now, it is only a weed patch compared with the magnificent forest it once was. Even after the original logging craze had leveled most of the virgin timber in the Seattle area, Ravenna had been saved as a haven for fir and cedar giants. Some of them were monarchs thousands of years old—cedars thirty to sixty feet around at the base, with topmost needles scraping the clouds 300 to 400 feet above the ravine.

W. W. Beck, the realtor who bought the land in 1887, was ecstatic when wandering among these trees. He named the place "Ravenna" after an Italian seacoast town that was famous for its pine trees, where poets, warriors, and statesmen once strolled in a state of euphoria similar to his own. He installed pavilions, benches, and pathways, and named the largest of the trees after famous people—Paderewski, Theodore Roosevelt, Robert E. Lee, and others. Ravenna became famous as the place to see "the trees that swept the stars."

Unfortunately, Beck's devotion to trees was not shared by the city, nor by lumberman Henry Yesler. Yesler had located a second sawmill on the shores of Union Bay near the mouth of Ravenna creek (in what is now Laurelhurst). No sooner had the city acquired the Ravenna land in 1911 than timber crews began clearing the woods, cutting up felled trees for cordwood, and finally even hacking away at the enshrined monarchs.

"Sacrifice for commerce!" came the cry from the outraged few; but it was only a feeble cry, muffled by the raging blades of Yesler's mill and the roar for more lumber and shingles from a growing Seattle. By 1930, the last of the great giants had crackled and thundered to the ground and been sliced into slabs, with the city's feeble justification that they were a danger to the public safety. And the famous park was no more.

Ravenna Park had many names while under Beck's green thumb: Ravenna Spring, Big Tree Park, Twin Maple Lane, and *Im Walde* (German for "In the Forest"). In 1919, the name was even changed to Roosevelt Park on a wave of sentiment after the former president's death. Beck's original name was restored in 1930 at the request of the community club.

Sacajawea Playground

N.E. 94th between 17th and 20th N.E.
Size: 2.6 acres
Bus: 7 to N.E. 95th
Major uses: neighborhood playground, picnics

DESCRIPTION

This is a small grassy field flanked by woods (maples, firs, cedars, cherries) just south of the Sacajawea Elementary School. Woodsy pathways lead to several picnic tables, a drinking fountain, and places for kids to climb. The park's name is taken from the adjacent school, which is named for the Shoshone Indian woman who accompanied Lewis and Clark on their famous expedition.

Sand Point (Warren Magnuson) Park

Sand Point Way N.E. and N.E. 65th
Size: 213 acres
Bus: 8
Major uses: boating, swimming, picnics, views

DESCRIPTION

Sand Point is an exciting new park-in-the-making just east of the View Ridge community on the shores of Lake Washington. Beaches, bluffs, sports fields, boating center, pathways, bikeways, 5,000 feet of shoreline, and fine views of the lake make it hard to imagine that it

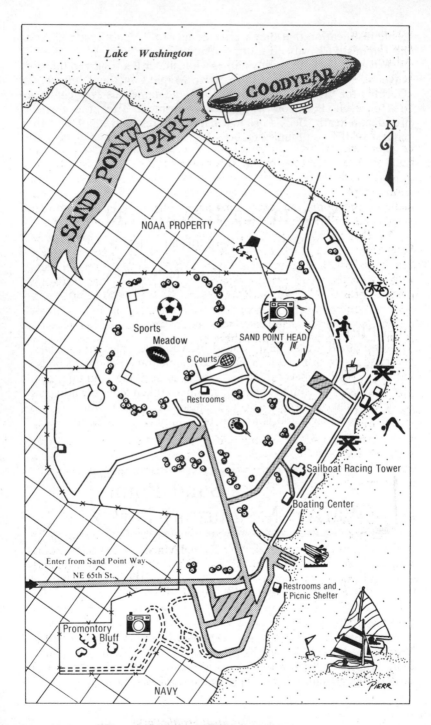

Lake Washington

N

SAND POINT PARK

GOODYEAR

NOAA PROPERTY

Sports
Meadow

SAND POINT HEAD

6 Courts

Restrooms

Sailboat Racing Tower

Boating Center

Enter from Sand Point Way
NE 65th St.

Restrooms and
Picnic Shelter

Promontory
Bluff

NAVY

PIERR

was once a naval air base. The park is bounded on the north by the new homesite of the National Oceanographic and Atmospheric Administration, and on the west by the remaining buildings of the U.S. Naval Air Station.

South Parking Area. Enter at N.E. 65th off Sand Point Way, driving past the Navy Commissary to the south parking area. From here you can dip your boat in the water at a three-piered, four-ramped launch, find private picnic spots, or take trails to viewpoints on Promontory Bluff, some of whose rocky glacial remains have been chewed away to provide fill for other areas of the park. If you saunter along trails here during quiet hours, you are sure to flush a quail or pheasant. The boating center just north of the launch includes restrooms, an operations area with a tower for sailboat races, and facilities for boating and water safety programs.

North Parking Area. Farther north, a parking lot just below Sand Point Head gives access to a swimming beach with restrooms, beach pavilion, lifeguard station, picnic shelter, and concession area with hot foods in the summer. From here you can take the loop road past tall grasses to the boundary fence and back to Sand Point Head, a broad knoll with excellent views of Lake Washington and Kirkland to the east. Here it's also fun to remember that you're standing on a mound of gravel and asphalt rubble, the remains of the old runways and parts of Promontory Bluff that were plowed up to recontour the old air base.

Central Parking Area. A central lot borders on a sports area with six tennis courts, a meadow with baseball, softball, and combination soccer/football fields, and restrooms.

As more money becomes available, Sand Point Park will grow even more interesting and enjoyable. One of the more remarkable developments will be the redredging of old Mud Lake to provide a unique fishing hole and rowing center, possibly with a teahouse restaurant on its northwest shore.

NEARBY ATTRACTIONS
You can get food (both cold and hot) at the park concession area. If you want a wider selection, **Landin's Food Market** (6224 Sand Point Way N.E., 523-2200) is a few blocks south of the park entrance, and a **Seven-Eleven Store** (7215 Sand Point Way N.E., 525-4260) is farther north, just opposite the Navy entrance.

National Oceanographic and Atmospheric Administration (NOAA). At this point it is still uncertain what NOAA facilities will be built north of the park. For the time being, though, NOAA's **Marine Mammal Division** (7500 Sand Point Way N.E., 442-4711) gives informal tours and a slide presentation to high school and college groups only. Call to make arrangements.

HISTORY

In 1875, when building contractor Morgan J. Carkeek bought twenty-three acres of land on Pontiac Bay, Sand Point was still a gently undulating, forested area. The point was alive with birds and animals. Frogs and herons croaked in the reeds. Pheasant and quail strutted through the grasses. Beaver, otter and muskrat built marshy dens near the shores of Mud Lake to the southeast of Carkeek's property. The little lake teemed with sunfish, crappies, catfish, squawfish, and chubs—and later with bass and perch introduced from the Midwest.

Then the area began to change. Eager to exploit coal and timber resources, Seattle citizens laid rails for the Seattle Lake Shore and Eastern Railroad. Pontiac Bay became the site of the Lake Washington Shipyards. Trains chugged along the lakeshore. The Maple Sawmill began buzzing at the present site of Matthews Beach. In 1916, the construction of the ship canal lowered the level of Lake Washington by eight to ten feet, creating a new shoreline. Two years later, the Carkeeks, who had lovingly watched Seattle spread outward from Pioneer Square, fulfilled a dream by deeding their land to the city for a park, in spite of the fact that Sand Point was still county land.

But almost from the beginning, Carkeek Park was competing with a new wave of change—air power. Already, the fledgling Boeing Airplane Company had begun turning out stick and cloth biplanes in the Rainier Valley, and the county hoped to build a major air station at Sand Point. In 1920, the county cleared a small landing field near Pontiac Bay. As the field grew longer and wider, eating its way toward Carkeek Park, an alarmed park department voiced the "growing need for city children to experience life in the green forests—an almost forgotten experience." Despite the lack of funds, a grassroots movement began to develop the park. Someone donated a dilapidated cart, someone else a bony old horse. Others gave plants and tools, and volunteers and children quickly hammered a camphouse together. During the next four summers, children from all over the city had their day and night in the camp.

But by 1924, the clamor for a federal air base was becoming louder than the Great Seattle Fire Bell that called the campers to dinner. An international race for air supremacy had been growing heated ever since Italian pilots had first peered onto World War I battlefields from reconnaissance planes, and in 1924, Sand Point was chosen as the takeoff point for an American attempt to make the first round-the-world flight.

The flight was not without mishaps. On April 26th, four pilots donned helmets and goggles, climbed into the open cockpits of four Douglas World Cruisers—the "Seattle," the "Chicago," the

"Boston," and the "New Orleans"—and whined off Lake Washington into the air. The "Seattle" crashed on a mountain in Alaska. The "Boston" was disabled over the Atlantic Ocean and replaced with the "Boston II." But on September 28th, more than five months after their departure, three tattered planes chugged to a landing at Sand Point after a globe-encircling flight of 26,345 miles.

In 1926, the Navy acquired all of Sand Point as an air base. The Carkeek's park gift was returned in the form of $25,000, which went to help purchase a new "Carkeek Park" in northwest Seattle. And the children's camp buildings were barged across the lake to O. O. Denny Park, the former country estate of pioneer Orion O. Denny.

Gradually, all of Sand Point was leveled. Woods were cleared, knolls were pushed flat, Mud Lake was filled, and the shoreline was expanded. From 1926 to 1949, the base grew from dirt field to cinder runway to a major naval air station and the headquarters of the Thirteenth Naval District.

Air activity around the point reached its peak during the 1940s. Pan American Airways built a dock, at the present site of Matthews Beach, for the first passenger air transport over the ocean. From here, pontooned Boeing Clippers came and went: double deck liners with sleeping accommodations for seventy-five; planes able to fly from Seattle to London in twelve hours. During World War II, Sand Point itself thronged with thousands of military and civilian personnel scurrying to keep the battlefields of the Pacific supplied with men and bombers.

Sand Point continued to resound with the roar of planes and the rattlings of helicopters during and after the Korean War. But beneath all the activity, old Mud Lake was not quite dead. Over the years, the runway had continually settled into the bog and had to be resurfaced again and again until the asphalt in places was many feet thick.

In 1969, the airstrip was resurfaced and extended from shore to shore, to a length of 4,800 feet, at a cost of half a million dollars. Then suddenly, in 1970 the base was deactivated. Major operations were transferred to Whidbey Island, and almost overnight Sand Point became a quiet Naval Support Center.

Then came the haggling over the surplus land. Seattle wanted a park. King County wanted an airstrip. NOAA wanted a new western headquarters. In 1973, the federal government suggested a three-way split for the land—park, airport, and NOAA. But for years, nearby residents had been complaining of airport noise, and NOAA, which as a federal agency had first priority at Sand Point, declared that an airport would be incompatible with its activities.

Largely through the efforts of U.S. Senator Warren G. Magnuson, with his clout as chairman of the Commerce Committee and his uncanny ability to tack restrictive amendments onto bills and budgets, the government was prohibited from surplusing the land for an airport. In 1974, Seattle voters also rejected the airfield-park idea, and the following year the government agreed it woud be just NOAA and the park.

On May 29, 1977, 196 acres of Sand Point were dedicated as Warren G. Magnuson Park. "Maggie" was presented a chunk of runway asphalt mounted on a wooden plaque—a symbol for the recycling of the old air base and the birth of the park. Since then—with $1,722,000 worth of Forward Thrust Bond money and matching federal and state grant dollars—Sand Point has begun to take its former shape. Bulldozers and dumptrucks have chewed up the runways and recontoured the old undulating terrain. Pheasant and quail have returned to the grasses. Boaters and swimmers are filtering back to the beaches. With time and more money, Mud Lake will be dredged out and resuscitated with fresh water, and before long, it will be alive once again with trout, frogs, and fishermen.

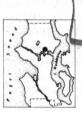

University of Washington

N.E. 45th and 17th N.E.
Size: 692 acres
Buses: 9, 30, 43, 48, 77, 212, 252
Major uses: museums, walking, picnics, wildlife

DESCRIPTION

The University of Washington is not a city park, but it's a lot like a park in the city, so we'll mention it here. The expansive grounds stretch from N.E. 45th to the Lake Washington Ship Canal and from 15th N.E. to Union Bay, with hundreds of buildings, boulevards, and semi-forested spots. It is a setting that often lures families and school groups for recreational and educational outings.

You can enter the campus on all four sides by car, and get the lay of the land with a fifteen minute drive-through pass and a free map. Try the university's walking tour, or plot your own course over the campus. The following are a few highlights.

Information Center (University Way N.E. and N.E. Campus Parkway, 543-9198). Stop here Monday through Friday, 8 a.m. to 5 p.m., to get a calendar of events and a walker's map.

Burke Museum (near 45th and 17th N.E., 543-5590). This is one of the favorite campus tour stops, because of its natural history and anthropological displays—rocks, butterflies, birds, bones (including

Allosaurus and Pleistocene crocodile skeletons!), and Northwest Coast Indian exhibits. Hours are Tuesday through Saturday, 10 a.m. to 4:30 p.m., and Sundays, 1 to 4 p.m. For self-guided tours, you can buy a guide book at the desk for $1.75. School groups can arrange for guided tours by giving a month's notice. The museum also has some traveling exhibits for $2.50 to $12.50, depending on the exhibit and the rental time.

Henry Gallery (15th N.E. and N.E. Campus Parkway, 543-2280) A popular place for Seattle art lovers, this art museum features nineteenth-century and older paintings, works of university students and faculty, and some traveling shows and tactile arts for the blind.

Theatres. You can see UW student and faculty productions ranging from classics to musicals in three local theatres: the Glenn Hughes Playhouse, (4045 University Way N.E., 543-5636); the Penthouse Theatre (543-5636 or 543-5638), America's first theatre-in-the-round; and the Showboat Theatre (543-5636), an old clunker resting on Portage Bay and fashioned after the turn-of-the-century floating showboat and proscenium stage.

Wildlife. If you like to stalk birds with binoculars or a camera, you can hardly find a more happy hunting ground than the Montlake Fill, just east of Montlake Boulevard and a sea of parking spaces. This area has gone from lake to lakeshore to garbage dump to wildlife refuge during the last sixty years. It is a special retreat for scores of meadow and marsh birds. If you're lucky, you may even see a muskrat or beaver.

Athletics. Fields and lots of lighted tennis courts are north of the football stadium and pavilion. For football, basketball, and other university athletic events, call the ticket office at 543-2200.

Just east of the stadium you can also rent canoes at the Waterfront Activities Center (543-2217). For $1.50 an hour, you can go for an afternoon of pleasant paddling on Union Bay or among the reedy channels and freeway pillars of the nearby marsh.

Food. Either bring your own or make a selection from hot and cold meals and goodies at the Student Union Building (HUB) on the central part of the campus.

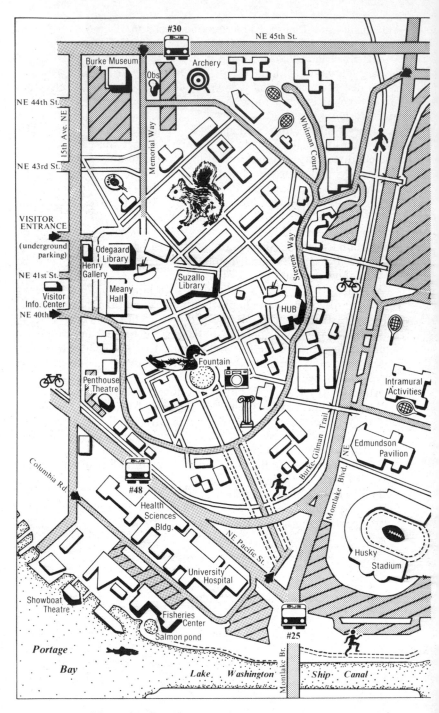

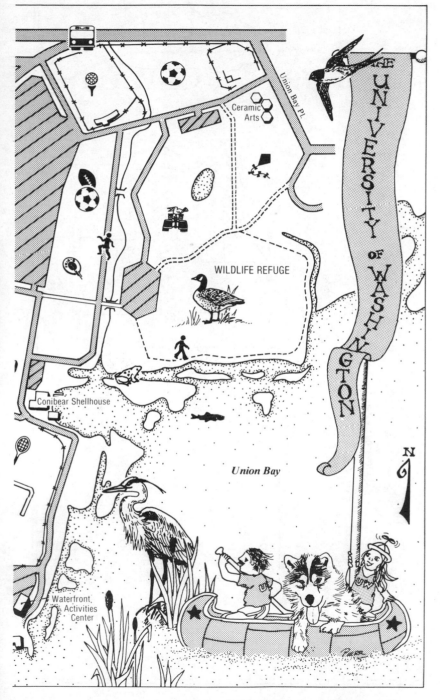

Ceramic Arts

Union Bay Pl.

THE UNIVERSITY OF WASHINGTON

WILDLIFE REFUGE

Conibear Shellhouse

Union Bay

N

Waterfront Activities Center

Northeast Seattle Parks 97

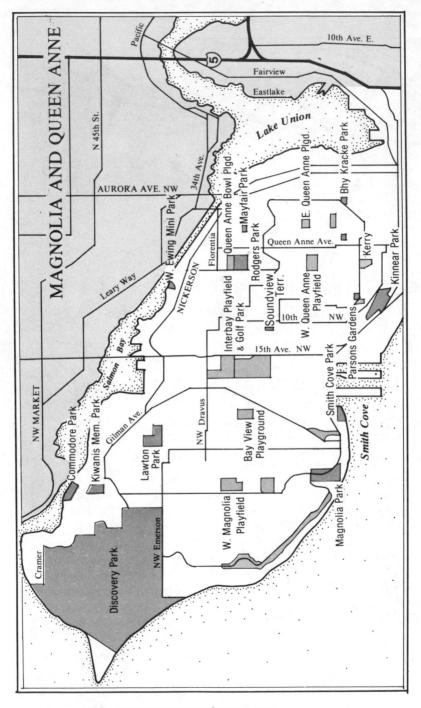

MAGNOLIA AND QUEEN ANNE

10th Ave. E.

Pacific

Fairview

Eastlake

Lake Union

N 45th St.

34th Ave.

AURORA AVE. NW

Queen Anne Bowl Plgd.

Mayfair Park

E. Queen Anne Plgd.

Bhy Kracke Park

W. Ewing Mini Park

Florentia

Rodgers Park

Queen Anne Ave.

Kerry

Kinnear Park

Leary Way

NICKERSON

Soundview Terr.

W. Queen Anne Playfield

Interbay Playfield & Golf Park

10th

NW

Parsons Gardens

Salmon Bay

15th Ave. NW

Smith Cove Park

Smith Cove

NW MARKET

Commodore Park

Kiwanis Mem. Park

Gilman Ave.

NW Dravus

Bay View Playground

Magnolia Park

Lawton Park

Cramer

NW Emerson

W. Magnolia Playfield

Discovery Park

3
Magnolia and Queen Anne Parks

In wildness is the preservation of the world.

—Henry David Thoreau

Bhy Kracke Park

Bigelow N. and Comstock Place
Size: 1.5 acres
Buses: 3, 4 to Comstock and Taylor
Major uses: views, walking

DESCRIPTION

This unusual park, neatly sandwiched into a steep residential area, makes ingenious use of "difficult" space. From the sloping hillside you have a great view of the central city, Lake Union, the freeway, and Capitol Hill, with benches, bike rack, and drinking fountain provided if you want to stay and gaze a while. Then you can walk down the steep, ivied hill—passing azaleas, rhododendrons, and more surprise views—to a patch of grass with a play area for kids and a pergola for parents.

The park was named, not without some humor, for Werner H. "Bhy" Kracke, a golf and gardening addict, world traveler, and bank auditor, who lived on the upper level and had a hand in its unique design.

Commodore Park

W. Commodore Way and Gilman W.
Size: 6 acres
Bus: 33 on Gilman W. to 26th W.
Major uses: locks, fish ladder, views

DESCRIPTION

Commodore Park is a pleasant entryway into several exciting environments. Follow concrete pathways on a landscaped hillside down to the Lake Washington Ship Canal, where water foams over spillways and ships glide through the government locks. Walk along the waterside promenade, provided with benches, shelters, restrooms, and fishing spots. Then leave the park and enter the world of the canal, with its fish ladder and locks.

THINGS TO REMEMBER

Facilities are specially disigned for the physically handicapped and include graded ramps that lead down to the canal.

If you're planning to fish in the canal, be sure to get a copy of the Washington Sport Fishing Regulations, available at most sporting goods stores. You can catch steelhead and sea run cutthroat at any time of the year, but there are special restrictions on the salmon species. To protect fish on their way to the spawning grounds, state regulations forbid fishing within 400 feet of the fish ladders. Signs indicate where fishing is not permitted.

NEARBY ATTRACTIONS

Fish ladder. Underwater viewing windows give you nose-to-nose encounters with salmon and trout, finning in stages from saltwater to fresh as they return to their spawning grounds. The most spectacular time to visit is mid-July, when the red sockeye are leaping in the air. About a third of a million fish pass through each year.

Government locks. Walk north across the spillways and watch the opening and closing of great gates as boats and ships are raised and lowered in massive water chambers. The locks are 825 feet long and 80 feet wide, with a maximum lift of 26 feet. They handle about 78,000 vessels a year—and numerous flotillas of ducks.

Visitor Center (3015 N.W. 54th, just north of the locks, 783-7059). Excellent slide shows here with exciting audio effects will propel you back to the turn of the century and the feverish days of logging and canal construction. Brochures about the fish ladder, the locks, canal history, and the gardens are available. For guided tours, call at least two weeks in advance.

Carl S. English Gardens (just west of the Visitor Center). Seven acres of gardens planted with flowers, shrubs, and trees from around the world make this a great picnic spot!

HISTORY

In 1852, when pioneers began taking soundings in Elliott Bay with clothesline and horseshoes, forests still blocked the passage between Puget Sound and Lake Washington. The idea of building a canal was first suggested in 1853 by Captain George B. McClellan (later a Union general in the Civil War). He suggested to Secretary of War Jefferson Davis that Seattle could be "the finest naval resort in the world."

The following year, pioneer Thomas Mercer made an eloquent Fourth of July speech about the eventual union of Puget Sound and Lake Washington—hence the name Lake Union—but the canal idea was mostly talk and no action. The closest anybody came to doing something in the early days was when Harvey L. Pike started digging the canal singlehandedly with pick and shovel. He gave up after a week.

The first primitive canal between Lake Union and Lake Washington was dug in 1885 by Judge Thomas Burke's Lake Washington Improvement Company. The first locks were between Union Bay and Portage Bay. The second locks were built at Fremont by Wa Chong and twenty-five Chinese laborers.

The ramrod behind the modern locks was Major Hiram M. Chittenden, head of the Northwest District Army Corps of Engineers. Through his efforts Congress gave its support to the canal project in 1910, and construction began the following year. For more than five years, giant steam shovels ate away at the earth. Thousands of workers poured hundreds of thousands of cubic yards of concrete, "stepping lively" to keep from sinking and getting stuck.

The new Hiram Chittenden Locks and Lake Washington Ship Canal were dedicated on the Fourth of July, 1917. Congratulations poured in from all over the country—even from President Teddy Roosevelt. Boats and ships paraded through the canal, and a biplane from the one-year-old Boeing Company sputtered overhead. The new ship canal, second largest in the world, opened the way for the industrialization of Lake Union.

Commodore Park itself is named for the street that runs in front of it, although it is not certain whom the street was intended to honor. Most likely it was Commodore Thomas Peary, who reached the North Pole during the Seattle's World's Fair of 1909.

The park first sprouted in the minds of local residents, who formed the Green Belt Association in 1966 to prevent the construction of an apartment building. Although they had no money, the determined residents took good advantage of the canal's golden anniversary. Their Fourth of July celebration—complete with parades, politicians, twenty thousand people, and a replica of the Boeing biplane—rivaled the original dedication celebration and netted $20,000 as "seed money" to buy the property. The resultant publicity helped to bring in over $1,000,000 more from federal and state governments and the Army Corps of Engineers.

The park was dedicated in 1978—predictably, during the Fourth of July weekend. It is another link in the Waterfront Trail, which will eventually allow pedestrians to walk the entire length of the canal from Ballard to Montlake and the Arboretum.

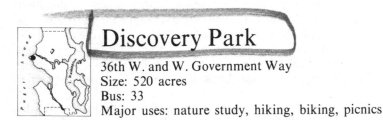

Discovery Park

36th W. and W. Government Way
Size: 520 acres
Bus: 33
Major uses: nature study, hiking, biking, picnics

DESCRIPTION

The spirit of nature thrives in this park, which is gradually reclaiming the old Fort Lawton Army base. Discovery Park encircles generous areas of woodland and beach, and offers mountain views and a variety of natural life zones to explore: meadows with deermice and shrews; forests with wildflowers and ferns; tidal beaches with barnacled rocks and smooth sands; and magnificent sea cliffs that tell 20,000 years of geologic history in colorfully stratified layers.

Wildlife also abounds in this nature park. Over 150 species of birds have been seen here, and whales and giant squid have been sighted off the beaches. Flying squirrels soar between tree branches. Rabbits hop down hidden pathways. Berries abound in summer, mushrooms in fall and spring. Discovery Park is a tranquil place away from the stress of the city—at once a wildlife sanctuary and an outdoor classroom for people to learn about the natural world.

Facilities and programs. Park facilities include a 2.8-mile loop trail, a self-guided nature trail, a fitness trail, a bicycle path, scenic picnic areas, and a visitor center with books and programs for environmental education. A full-time staff of Ranger-Naturalists offers lecture courses on mosses, mushrooms, trees, birds, beach life, and much more. Rangers also conduct weekend nature walks and programs for families and schools, including puppet shows and story telling around campfires. (See below for more details.)

THINGS TO REMEMBER

Discovery Park is large and confusing. Study the map first and decide where you want to go. The main entrance is the East Gate just inside 36th W. and W. Government Way. A rainbow-colored sign indicates the Visitor Center, one block ahead on your left. Here you can get information about tides, park policies, and nature programs. (The Fort Lawton grounds straight ahead are off limits unless you have made prior arrangements with the Army.)

If you turn right at the rainbow-colored sign, the road will lead you past a cemetery and Army equipment to the North Gate and the north parking lot. This entry gives best access to the self-guided nature trail, bicycle path, North Bluff picnic area, and the Indian Cultural Center. You can reach the south parking lot which allows access to south meadow and dunes, by driving around the outside of the park on 36th Avenue W. and W. Emerson.

Only the west end of the park has any access to the beach, which can be reached by hiking from either the north or south parking lots along the loop trail. Follow the signs to an asphalt road leading to the beach.

There is no food at Discovery Park, and no restaurants or stores nearby. If you have forgotten the picnic lunch, the nearest shopping area is Magnolia Village. From the East Gate turn south onto W. 34th (Bus 24) and go south about twelve blocks past the Magnolia Playfield to W. McGraw Street.

Discovery Park is a natural area. To protect wildlife, *keep dogs on leashes* and off the beach and self-guided nature trail. To protect the fragile bluffs (and yourself), stay off the steep cliffs below the sand dunes. Everything in the park is protected, so be sure to leave rocks, shells, bird nests, and everything else for others to enjoy. Sounds like a lot of restrictions, right? Don't worry—you'll feel more free at Discovery Park than almost anywhere in the city.

NATURAL AREAS

Forest. As you walk on trails that wind through alder, maple, and wild shrubs, you'll spot remnants of the once-mighty red cedar and hemlock that covered this area. Magnolia Bluff was logged in the 1880s and then again after Fort Lawton was established, so today you can see a mix of pioneer and climax species. For a better understanding of the forest and the interactions of its residents, you can buy a copy of "The Forest Community" for $1 at the Visitor Center.

South Meadow. The large open meadow in the southern part of the park used to be a sports area where soldiers batted baseballs during their free time. Now that the grass is growing back, you can find evidence of moles, shrews, and mice—and if you're lucky, you may even see a sparrow hawk plummet from the sky to capture one

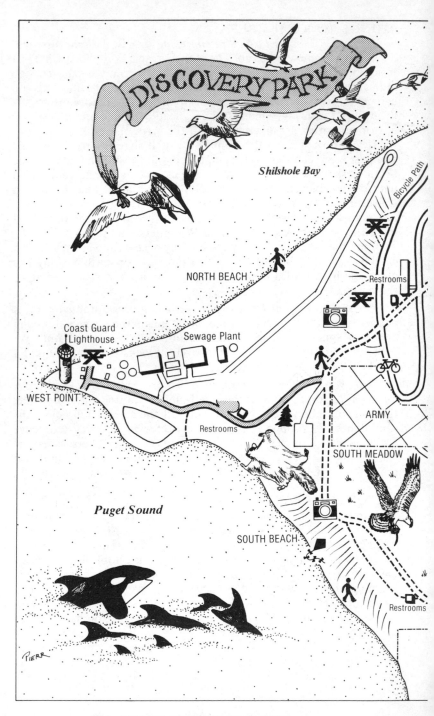

DISCOVERY PARK

Shilshole Bay

NORTH BEACH

Coast Guard
Lighthouse

Sewage Plant

WEST POINT

Restrooms

Restrooms

Bicycle Path

ARMY

SOUTH MEADOW

Puget Sound

SOUTH BEACH

Restrooms

PIERR

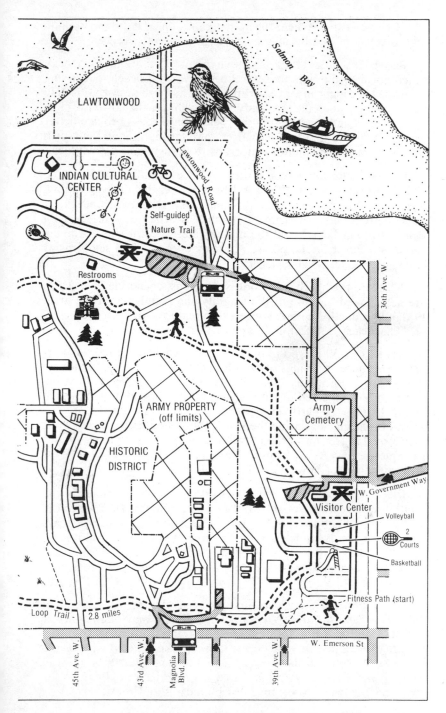

LAWTONWOOD

Salmon Bay

Lawtonwood Road

INDIAN CULTURAL CENTER

Self-guided Nature Trail

36th Ave. W.

Restrooms

ARMY PROPERTY
(off limits)

Army Cemetery

HISTORIC DISTRICT

W. Government Way

Visitor Center

Volleyball

2 Courts

Basketball

Fitness Path (start)

Loop Trail — 2.8 miles

45th Ave. W.

43rd Ave. W.

Magnolia Blvd.

39th Ave. W.

W. Emerson St

Magnolia and Queen Anne 105

of them. You can also hear the hoarse calls of pheasants and perhaps spot a covey of quail scurrying through the scotch broom.

Beach. Discovery Park has two miles of shoreline—a rocky beach north of the lighthouse and a sandy south beach. Prevailing winds have brought in waves primarily from the southwest, eroding the south cliffs to create the sandy beach, while to the north the cliffs are protected and the beach more rocky. Since rocks provide better protection, you'll find a wider variety of intertidal life on the North Beach, from sea anemones and crabs to limpets and periwinkles.

On the South Beach you'll find evidence of clams, sand dollars, and sea worms—plus lots of good barefoot beachcombing, wading, open air, and vistas of Mount Rainier, the Olympics, and Puget Sound. From this westernmost point in Seattle you can see Alki Beach, Vashon Island, and the major waterways for ships bringing cargo into Puget Sound ports. You may even see such sea birds as loons, grebes, terns, and jaegers.

Access to the beach is by foot, shuttle bus, or bicycle only. Dogs are not allowed because of the fragility and popularity of the area. For an introduction to many intertidal creatures, you can get a copy of "The Beach Book" for $1 at the Visitor Center.

Sea Cliffs. While you're on the South Beach, don't miss exploring the beautiful layerings of browns, golds, and grays that make up the Discovery Park cliffs. This is literally a cross-section of Seattle, and a pattern repeated in cliffs all over Puget Sound. On the beach you're looking at earth layers over 20,000 years old, before the arrival of the glacier during the last Ice Age. Successive layers work their way 250 feet up to the present, each layer the sign of a major geological event. Ask a Ranger-Naturalist at the Visitor Center for an explanation of how the cliffs were formed.

Discovery Dunes. Sift your toes through the sand dunes in the South Meadow while you look out over Puget Sound. (But watch the kids here—the cliffs are steep!) Each year more meadow disappears under these sands, which are eroded from the cliffs and blown up here by winds from the southwest. A great deal of erosion has recently been caused by people, too, which is another good reason to stay off the cliffs.

North Bluff. On a clear day you can see the Cascades and Olympics from this area. Views of Puget Sound may offer sights of tankers or the colorful jibs of sloops. Now a picnic area with tables, drinking fountain, and restrooms, it used to be covered with Army barracks, as you will discover if you go beyond the lawns into the wild grasses. There you may find an old basketball court or neglected roadways being recycled by mosses and roots.

SPECIAL FACILITIES

Wolf Tree Nature Trail. Pick up a self-guided pamphlet at the beginning of this half-mile trail and wander with it through marshy areas and woods. Learn about the burls on the bigleaf maple, explore the intricate world of miniature moss forests, watch for witches' brooms above your yead, and see plant worlds turned on their sides. The pamphlet describes twenty-two numbered stations along the way.

Loop Trail. This 2.8-mile trail encircles the heart of the park, wandering through forest, ravines, thickets, small open areas, and a large meadow. It is a haven for hikers and nature students.

Health Path. Keep in shape by jogging and exercising at fifteen stations along this half-mile loop. The path begins south of the Visitor Center.

Picnic and Play Area. Volleyball, softball, football, and baseball fields, and playground equipment for climbing, sliding, and swinging are all here. There are also two tennis courts. The spacious area just east of the Visitor Center is ideal for large group picnics.

NATURE PROGRAMS

To get the most out of Discovery Park, take part in some of the creative nature programs offered by the park's Ranger-Naturalists. Be sure to pick up a seasonal listing of programs at the Visitor Center while you're there, or call 625-4636 to have one mailed to you. To whet your appetite, here is a sampling of one season's programs:

Nature walks for adults. Each walk is guided by a Ranger-Naturalist and usually focuses on some aspect of nature—for example, mosses, lichens, trees, birds, geology, wildflowers, and beach life. Weekend walks are free and usually last an hour and a half.

Nature walks for children. Similar to adult walks, but geared especially for kids, these treks include games and introductions to beach and forest creatures.

Courses and workshops. Moss identification, nature photography, wild edible hunts, vegetable gardening, insect and tree identification, map and compass skills, bird watching, and more. Courses include lectures and field trips for a minimal fee.

Adventure courses for children. Irrestible even for adults! Children use sunshine to capture shadows, make animals that can hide from their enemies, build their own bird nests, find out how "bee bonkers" help bees and plants, and meet an animal that glues its head to a rock and then catches food with its feet.

Family programs. Summertime gatherings with park personnel often include evening campfires with marshmallow roasting and storytelling.

Special events. Fund-raisers for the park, sponsored by the Discovery Park Advisory Council, often feature art shows, lectures, and slide presentations by Northwest artists and naturalists. Keep your eyes open for a variety of exciting things.

Programs for groups. An elementary Teacher's Workshop introduces teachers to the environmental education resources at Discovery Park, and is excellent for adding a new dimension to classroom learning. The park's Ranger-Naturalists will also tailor lectures and nature walks to your group's particular interests. Leaders of large groups are advised to get the "Teachers' and Group Leaders' Guide to Discovery Park," available at the Visitor Center.

Note: Be sure to call the Visitor Center (625-4636) for reservations on all nature walks and for information on course times and fees.

NEARBY ATTRACTIONS

Coast Guard Lighthouse (282-9130). This little building—the oldest in the park and the westernmost in the city—was constructed in 1881, eight years before Washington became a state. Its lamps were first fueled by fish or whale oil. The lighthouse is maintained by three enlisted men and their families, who live in adjacent houses. Visiting hours are from 1 to 4 p.m. Saturdays, Sundays, and holidays. Call to arrange weekday tours.

Metro Sewage Treatment Plant (447-6801). This reminder of civilization on the sandspit east of the lighthouse is the largest of Metro's five sewage treatment plants. Its pipes and huge drumlike tanks (visible as you walk down to the beach) have been providing primary treatment of storm water and domestic sewage since 1966. Metro conducts two-hour tours of the plant during the week for groups of up to thirty. Call at least a week in advance.

Daybreak Star Arts Center (285-4425). This is the Indian Cultural Center, home of most of the educational programs offered by the United Indians of All Tribes Foundation. Here you can see examples of North American Indian art from all over the continent. Hours are Monday through Friday from 9 a.m. to 4:30 p.m. Call for special events and guided tours.

Seattle Mounted Police (625-4638). Discovery Park is the home of the mounted police, which daily patrol various parks in the Seattle area. Call to arrange stable tours, which last about an hour.

U.S. Army and Cemetery (281-3050). A cemetery for military personnel, families, and past civilian employees of the Army, this area is open to the public from 6 a.m. to 6 p.m. daily. Call to arrange tours.

HISTORY

Discovery Park began as a thickly forested bluff jutting out into Puget Sound. The Salmon Bay beaches were inhabited by the Shilshoh people, who lived on an abundant supply of salmon and shellfish. So thick were the yearly salmon runs that at the end of the summer harvest other tribes paddled toward the Shilshoh beaches to share in the bounty

The park is named after Captain George Vancouver's ship, the H.M.S. *Discovery*, which sailed into Puget Sound in May of 1792. Indian fishing and celebrations in the area continued for many years after the American settlement of the bluff, although by 1860 the Indians had been forced to give up the land.

Then began a series of severe changes. From 1866 to 1870, the forests were logged with teams of oxen. Farmers and squatters settled the land, among them Christian Scheuerman and his wife Rebecca and their ten children. Scheuerman's farm included part of the creek that now trickles through the bogs of the self-guided nature trail.

By 1890, Puget Sound had been recognized for its strategic defense value, and the building of the Bremerton Naval Shipyards brought demands for an Army post to protect the area. In a burst of patriotism and civic pride (as well as hopes for increased business), the Seattle Chamber of Commerce raised $35,000, relocated settlers, and arranged for the citizens' generous donation of over 600 acres of Magnolia Bluff to the U.S. Government. This land consolidation was the first important step in the creation of the future Discovery Park.

In 1900, the newly established Army post was named Fort Lawton, in honor of Major General Henry Ware Lawton, known for his capture of Chief Geronimo in 1886. (Lawton was killed in action in the Philippines during the Spanish-American War in 1899.) The new fort, however, was a disappointment to Seattle. While the Chamber of Commerce had visions of a major fortress with coastal batteries and troops streaming in to bolster the local economy, the base smoldered in mediocrity. Other nearby bases grew in importance during World War I, but not Fort Lawton. It seemed to Seattle that the Magnolia Bluff site was going to waste.

Thus, visions of a public park began to take shape—first in a plan by the Olmsted Brothers in 1910; then on the editorial page of the *Seattle Post-Intelligencer* in 1917. Said the *P-I:* "No doubt Uncle Sam, if properly approached will prove as generous as the original donors and will readily assent to the conversion of the reservation into a park."

But Uncle Sam was neither generous nor properly approached. Little more was said about a park until the mid-Depression years, when newly elected U.S. Congressman Warren G. Magnuson was asked by the Army if Seattle would like to buy the Fort Lawton site—for a dollar. Incredibly, the city turned down the offer, fearing maintenance costs would be too heavy to bear.

During World War II, the once quiet roadways and barracks of Fort Lawton rumbled with Army trucks and uniformed troops going to and from the battlefields of the Pacific. The base processed over a million soldiers and some 6,000 prisoners of war before it again sank back into somnolence.

Then in 1964, the Army announced plans to surplus eighty-five percent of Fort Lawton, and suddenly groups began a wild scramble for the land nobody had wanted thirty years before. Instead of a single dollar, Uncle Sam now wanted millions—fifty percent of the fair market value. And while Washington State's representatives were paving the way for an act of congress to clear this hurdle, the Department of Defense began drooling over the idea of sinking shafts into the old fort for an antiballistic missile site.

By 1968, the battle of the ABMs had escalated into full-scale political war. The Citizens for Fort Lawton Park enlisted Washington's entire U.S. congressional delegation and fired off volley after volley of letters and petitions to the nation's capitol. Finally, after a crucial summit conference with Senator Henry M. Jackson, the federal government gave up the missile site.

But the Fort Lawton war was not over. Next, the Navy and the Coast Guard announced plans to take over large chunks of the bluff. This brush fire was snuffed out, again by Senator Jackson. Then, in early 1970, the United Indians of All Tribes stormed Fort Lawton's main gate, demanding the surplused land be returned to native Americans under the provisions of an 1865 treaty. After a month-long seige, the city agreed to set aside nineteen acres in the new park for an Indian cultural and educational center.

Finally, in the summer of 1970, after a long nationwide debate, Congress passed a bill allowing surplused federal property to be returned to the cities at no cost. Another skirmish in the war of Fort Lawton was over. But the base that had seen so little military action had now become the scene of domestic squabbles from every quarter. How should the land be used? *An aquarium! A zoo! A radar station! A hospital! A police academy! A national park! A federal housing project! A golf course!* All of these things were seriously suggested and pushed by various groups.

Despite the onslaught of conflicting pressures, 391 acres of Fort Lawton were dedicated as Discovery Park in October of 1973. Most recently, in 1968, the Army shut down even more of the fort, and another 129 acres were added to the park.

Each year now Discovery Park's grasses grow longer, its forests thicker, its animals and birds more numerous. Each year more mosses, horsetails, and blackberry vines march across the surplused military roadways, providing new homes for woods creatures and reclaiming the wildness of the old Magnolia Bluff. Today, Discovery Park has the potential of becoming the greatest urban nature park in the nation. The only things missing are regular funding to ensure the continuance of its nationally recognized environmental educational program, and legislation to prevent the erosion of its identity as a quiet natural preserve.

Kinnear Park

7th W. and W. Olympic Place
Size: 14 acres
Buses: 1 to upper park; 15 to lower
Major uses: picnics, walking, views

DESCRIPTION

A roughly pie-shaped, two-tiered park, Kinnear is bigger, grassier, and woodsier than the parks on the upper part of the hill, and offers closer views of the city and sound. Have lunch on a tiny patio roof (built over the restrooms!) while watching the view. It is dominated here by the grain elevators of Pier 86, where ships dock to be fed their cargoes through snaking tubes. You can also spot joggers moving antlike along the narrow green of Myrtle Edwards and Elliott Bay parks on the shoreline.

For a different, quieter mood, follow the low cyclone fence southeast for treetop views of the leafy woods. Or descend into Lower Kinnear on a narrow pathway, which leads to a tennis court, another set of restrooms, and walks among glacial boulders and maple trees.

HISTORY

The park is named for its original owner, George Kinnear, one of Seattle's early realtors and civic leaders. Kinnear first came to Seattle on a visit from his native Illinois in 1874. Intrigued by the city's real estate potential, he sold his Illinois farmlands and invested in property on southwest Queen Anne. Among Kinnear's many accomplishments is his promotion of the first wagon road through Snoqualmie Pass. He also organized the Immigration Board and in 1886 helped quell the anti-Chinese riots that broke out after the construction of the railroads. Neighbors of Kinnear, who greatly enjoyed the wooded slopes of his land, asked him to sell some of it to the city, which he did, in 1889—for a dollar.

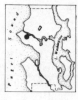

Kiwanis Memorial Park

33rd W. and W. Fort Street
Size: 7.4 acres
Bus: 33
Major use: natural woods

DESCRIPTION

"Is there any way to get down there?" you'll ask as you peer over a steep embankment into the luscious ravine.

Sure, go ahead, if the nettles in the first hundred yards or the bog at the bottom don't deter you. Slippery beaten paths will take you past towering old maples, big juicy mushrooms, and thickets of ferns and blackberry brambles. It's a wild, musty place down there.

The Kiwanis Club gave the park to the city in 1956 as a wooded preserve for neighborhood children. Residents say the city was once thinking about bridging the ravine and lacing it with trails to form an exciting woods corridor connecting Discovery Park with Commodore Park on the canal. (What a great plan!) But it has been put aside, at least for the time being.

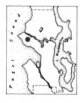

Lawton Park

27th W. and W. Thurman
Size: 7.8 acres
Bus: 24
Major use: neighborhood play area

DESCRIPTION

A wide path leads through this hilly woods and grass patch between plush apartment complexes and Lawton Elementary School. A small ballfield, swings, and a slide are near the school. A dirt path that winds around maple trees leads to three old picnic tables and more primitive paths blazed by children.

The city bought the park in 1952 and named it after the Fort Lawton Army Base, which in turn was named after its first commanding officer, Major General Henry Ware Lawton, in 1900.

Magnolia Park

31st W. and W. Garfield
Size: 16.2 acres
Bus: 24
Major uses: picnics, views

DESCRIPTION
This is a small, cool, leafy picnic park under maple and chestnut trees. Sloping toward Puget Sound at the south end of Magnolia Boulevard, it has ten small picnic tables, a shelter, barbecues, and play equipment. Don't miss this park a half hour before sunset on a clear day if you revel in mountain views and blazing atmospheric displays. To get there, drive south from Discovery Park along Magnolia Boulevard, past exclusive homes with elegant landscapes, grassy viewpoints, and clear vistas of the sound.

HISTORY
Magnolia is actually a misnomer. The name was originally given by Navy geographer George Davidson, who in 1897 mistook the bluff's abundant madronas for magnolias, and people have been calling it Magnolia ever since. Thanks to the Buena Vista Garden Club, whose members made good the error by planting two magnolia trees in 1949 (and the park department which added a few more), the bluff and the park now somewhat, though barely, live up to their names. The tree in question honors a seventeenth-century French botanist named (properly, one assumes) Pierre Magnol. The city bought the park in 1910.

Mayfair Park

2nd N. and W. Raye
Size: 1 acre
Buses: 3, 13
Major use: neighborhood playground

DESCRIPTION
Go three blocks east from the southeast corner of Rodgers Park to find this street-end knoll, cleverly converted into a tiny park. It has a central play area, with a drinking fountain and benches conveniently placed so you can watch kids while they climb, slide, and crawl.

Parsons Gardens

7th W. and W. Highland Drive
Size: 0.4 acre
Buses: 2, 13 to Highland Drive
Major uses: walking, resting

DESCRIPTION
A formal nook behind hedges, this place is suitable for a quick stroll, a moment of quiet seclusion, or even a wedding (call 625-2683 to arrange for one). The park was formerly the family garden of the Reginald H. Parsons, whose children gave the land to the city in 1956 as a memorial to their parents.

NEARBY ATTRACTIONS
Marshall Viewpoint. Right across the street, this tiny green oasis offers three benches, a friendly tree, and a view of the sound. The spot includes a memorial to Betty Bowen, a well-loved matron of the arts. Such prominent Northwest artists as Morris Graves, Margaret Tompkins, Victor Steinbrueck, Guy Anderson, Kenneth Callahan, and Charles Stokes have done some unsigned work, which is cast in the concrete walkway there. See if you can figure out which is whose.

Kerry Viewpoint. (2nd W. and W. Highland Drive) An unsurpassed view of Elliott Bay and the Central City, with an occasional backdrop of Mount Rainier, draws camera buffs to this spot. At sunset they often line the wall just as the city and the sound are beginning to glow with lights. At night it becomes almost a fantasy scene, with brightly lit ferries gliding across the water and the Space Needle shining from its 500-foot pedestal.

Rodgers Park

3rd W. and W. Fulton
Size: 5.3 acres
Buses: 3, 13
Major use: neighborhood play area

DESCRIPTION
The ice age certainly left its mark on this park, built on a steeply sculptured hillside. In the upper (southeast) portion off 1st Avenue

W., you'll find benches, a play area, fire slabs, three tennis courts, and restrooms. Paths then wind down grass-covered knobs and knolls to the Queen Anne Bowl and North Queen Anne Elementary School with adjacent football/soccer field and cinder track.

HISTORY

Queen Anne Hill was not an easy place for the pioneers to settle. The hill was so steep that it remained relatively inaccessible for many years. Even the first trolley car (in 1902) had to be built with a counterbalance to overcome the frustrating pull of gravity. It proved well worth the trouble, though, since the views up top were spectacular.

The portion of the north slope containing Rodgers Park and Queen Anne bowl was homesteaded by Nils Peterson, who made a living excavating gravel from the glacial remains there. Realtor B. F. Day bought the Rodgers Park section and donated it to the city in 1883. The elementary school was built on the north side of Peterson's old gravel pit in 1914, and soon thereafter the pit became a small lake and a favorite play spot for children. It has since been filled and leveled into the present athletic fields.

Rodgers Park was named for David Rodgers, who helped make Seattle famous for shipbuilding.

Smith Cove Park

Port of Seattle, Pier 91
Size: 0.4 acre
Bus: 33 on Thorndyke to 23rd W.
Major use: picnics, views, jogging, biking

DESCRIPTION

Follow the signs from W. Dravus Street south to this Port of Seattle park just west of Pier 91 on Elliott Bay. A 0.7-mile jogging and biking path parallels the road as it winds past warehouses and a sea of new Datsun trucks behind cyclone fencing. Finally it emerges beside the Officers' Club at the Smith Cove bulkhead right beside Pier 91 and Elliott Bay. A small garden of chrysanthemums brightens up the street end here, and a fine concrete promenade with modern picnic tables spreads out for your better enjoyment of views southward to Alki and the bustling port activity. At low tide you can sneak down over the bulkhead boulders to the sandy, driftwood-strewn beach beside the pier for even more secluded picnics. This is a great buffer strip between the industrialized port and Magnolia Hill to the west—well worth a visit and still relatively unknown.

HISTORY
Conveniently, a quick history of the cove has been engraved on an "anchored" plaque at the park, placed there during Maritime Week of 1978 by the Yukon and Propellor Club of Seattle:

> "Henry A. Smith was the pioneer who settled here in 1853. Early shipping began in 1891, when the Northern Pacific Coal Bunker Pier was completed. At that time it was not uncommon to see steam and sailing vessels berthed on either side of the 2,500-foot trestle, loading coal from railroad cars. That came to an end in 1899 when the adjacent Great Northern Piers, Piers 88 and 89 were completed, linking the Transcontinental Railroad to the Orient.

> "In 1912 the Port of Seattle purchased the tide flats presently known as Piers 90 and 91, for $150,000. At a cost of $3,500,000 the 2,350-foot piers were completed in 1921, at which time they were the largest earth-filled piers in the world. The Port of Seattle operated these piers as a public facility until 1962, when they were sold to the U.S. Navy. They remained under Navy control until 1975, when they were purchased by the Port."

Soundview Terrace

11th W. and W. Wheeler
Size: 0.2 acre
Bus: 1
Major use: viewpoint

DESCRIPTION
On your hilltop boulevard tour, turn off 10th W. at W. Wheeler for a quick view of the sound and acres of glittering autos in the Port of Seattle freightyards. This tiny, terraced but unmaintained hillside was donated to the city by Mr. and Mrs. R. M. Kinnear in 1905.

West Ewing Mini Park

3rd W. and W. Ewing
Size: 0.2 acre
Bus: 17
Major uses: canal overlook, picnics

DESCRIPTION
A little grass patch just across the street from Seattle Pacific University on the Lake Washington Ship Canal. An upper concrete overlook with lights has benches for sitting and watching boats and munching lunches. This is a favorite (although often noisy) snacking spot for students and workers from nearby manufacturing plants. The park was dedicated in 1973.

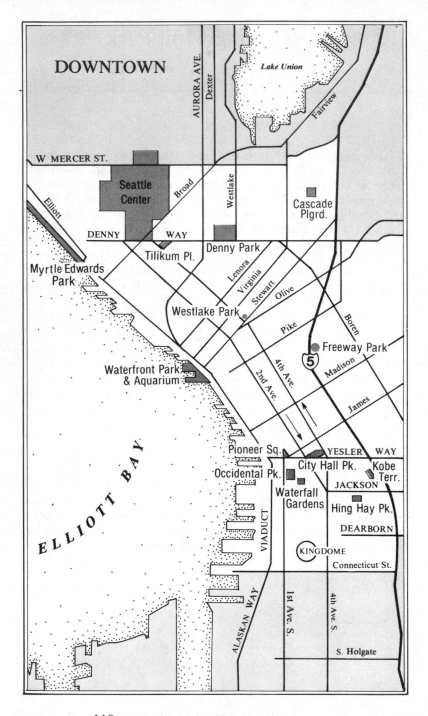

DOWNTOWN

Lake Union

AURORA AVE.

Dexter

Fairview

W MERCER ST.

Seattle
Center

Broad

Westlake

Cascade
Plgrd.

DENNY   WAY

Tilikum Pl.

Denny Park

Elliott

Lenora

Virginia

Stewart

Olive

Myrtle Edwards
Park

Westlake Park

Pike

Boren

Freeway Park

Waterfront Park
& Aquarium

4th Ave.

5

Madison

2nd Ave.

James

E L L I O T T   B A Y

Pioneer Sq.

YESLER   WAY

Occidental Pk.

City Hall Pk.

Kobe
Terr.

JACKSON

Waterfall
Gardens

Hing Hay Pk.

DEARBORN

VIADUCT

KINGDOME

Connecticut St.

ALASKAN WAY

1st Ave. S.

4th Ave. S.

S. Holgate

4

Downtown Parks

I believe a leaf of grass is no less than the journeywork
of the stars ... The smallest sprout shows there is really
no death.

—Walt Whitman

Cascade Playground

Harrison and Pontius N.
Size: 1 acre
Buses: 8, 22, 305
Major uses: community park and playground

DESCRIPTION

"Do you call that playground a park?" asks an inquisitive visitor.

"Yes, definitely," says the Cascade resident. "And we're very possessive of it!"

Cascade Playground has been a focal point of organization in the Cascade Community for years. This three-quarters block of grass—with swings, a wading pool, slide, picnic tables and restrooms—is hemmed in by traffic, warehouses, and laundry establishments, while the community itself is caught between the freeway and downtown businesses. Surrounded by a cyclone fence and a few trees, it stands as an important symbol of life in a fast-disappearing residential area. Despite its small size, Cascade's urban pioneers use the playground/park for many purposes, including occasional church services and community fairs. A better loved park would be hard to find.

Cascade is named after a former school (now a warehouse) that was in the area and was named after the Cascade Mountains east of Seattle. (The cascading rivers of these mountains prompted the English botanist David Douglas to give this range its name.) The city bought the park in 1926.

City Hall Park

3rd and Yesler
Size: 0.7 acre
Bus: 27
Major use: urban resting spot

DESCRIPTION

Bordering on the south side of the King County Public Safety Building, this former battlefield is now a small walking and sitting space filled with grass, trees, benches, small tables, and chairs. A small oak here commemorates the founding of the United Nations, and a plaque with cannonballs recalls the 1856 Battle of Seattle, when Indians led by Chief Leschi attacked the pioneer village in a last effort to save their land. The battle was short lived, however, largely because of the fire power of the gunship *Decatur,* moored in Elliott Bay. During freeway construction in 1964, several more cannonballs were unearthed below Harborview Hospital. City Hall park, in keeping with its military history, was used as a drill ground for troops during World War II.

Denny Park

Dexter N. and Denny Way
Size: 5 acres
Buses: 15, 17, 28E, 306
Major uses: lounging, picnics

DESCRIPTION

A peaceful green island in a sea of traffic, Denny Park lies on the central business district's northern fringe, and is surrounded by major thoroughfares. Broad pathways planted with rhododendrons and azaleas lead to a central circle and benches, where an occasional summertime concert perks harried spirits. Thick-crowned maples, pines, and other trees shield the grass and its sprawling occupants from city noises until it's time to return to the working world.

The central offices of the park department are at the west end of the park, where you will also find restrooms.

NEARBY ATTRACTIONS

If there's not enough going on at Denny Park, try the **Seattle Center** at 5th and Thomas, a few blocks west. (See "Seattle Center" in this section.) This major entertainment hub has something for everyone, from sports, theatre, and the Food Circus to the Space Needle, Science Center, and an amusement park.

You might also want to stop by and pay your respects to Chief Seattle, whose statue stands at **Tilikum Place** (5th and Denny), four blocks west of the park. Architecture buffs or those prone to gawking at fascinating buildings, can walk down to 4th and Vine on the Denny Regrade to see the glassy golden walls of Martin Selig's new office buildings. Some interesting shops and restaurants are beginning to show up in this rediscovered area, too.

HISTORY

Denny Park lies on the south end of pioneer David Denny's old land claim, once one of the hilliest parts of town. The land was first donated to the city as a cemetery by Denny and his wife Louisa in 1864. It was rededicated as a public park—Seattle's first—in 1884. To make it worthy of the name, the bodies and gravestones were removed, and public-minded citizens from Pioneer Square brought beautifying flowers.

However, these early excavations and replantings were only the foreshadowing of greater diggings. For, shortly after the Great Seattle Fire of 1889, City Engineer R. H. Thomson began a long-term project of leveling off some of the city's steepest hills. Denny's hill, known to Seattleites as "Impossible Hill" because of its near inaccessibility, was a prime candidate. Starting from 5th and Pine, steam shovels, tram cars, and conveyer belts chewed away at the hillsides, and barges dumped the dirt and clay into the flats on Elliott Bay. By 1910 the land-eaters were working on the Denny Regrade and threatening Denny Park. But outraged pioneers demanded that it be left alone, and soon it stood as an island at the top of a sixty-foot cliff along 9th Avenue.

By 1930, Denny Park had also been fed into tram cars and dumped into Elliott Bay. Its flat, bare remains were relandscaped by L. Glenn Hall of Cambridge, Massachusetts. More constructive uprootings and transplantings took place in the years that followed. In 1932 a giant sequoia was planted in the park to commemorate Washington State's centennial. The park administration building was constructed there in 1948. And in 1968, eastern gray squirrels were successfully transplanted from the Woodland Park Zoo—an especially noteworthy accomplishment among such downtown turmoil.

Freeway Park

6th and Seneca
Size: 5 acres
Bus: 2
Major uses: views, lounging, picnics

DESCRIPTION

A most amazing construction, Freeway Park has won national acclaim for illustrating the inventive possibilities of combining natural and urban environments. In this freeway "lid" between First Hill and the heart of downtown, concrete canyons resound with thundering waterfalls—some 27,000 gallons of water rush through every minute—drowning out the freeway roar and transforming the park into a state of mind. Pollution-resistant trees and concrete boxes filled with flowers and shrubs intermix with pathways and stairways leading to grassy terraces, fountains, and views of buildings and ten lanes of freeway traffic.

Since its Bicentennial dedication, the park has succeeded surprisingly well. Elderly residents and medical personnel walk down from apartment houses and hospitals on First Hill. Bankers and business people descend elevators to munch on sandwiches and dangle their feet in the fountains. Road-weary travelers leave the rush of traffic for a rejuvenating walk among the restful greenery. And onlookers can watch the freeway traffic through a curtain of falling water.

The park includes several key sections. The **Great Box Garden** is bounded by 6th and 7th avenues and by Spring and Seneca streets. The **Canyon** and its waterfall are between 7th and 8th avenues and Seneca and Union streets. And east of 8th Avenue is a lawn and children's play area. An elevator, with restrooms adjacent, descends to a 630-car parking garage.

THINGS TO KEEP IN MIND

Watch the kids near the canyon. The concrete walls are exciting to climb, but there's not much to prevent a bad tumble.

NEARBY ATTRACTIONS

Food spots are abundant in the downtown area. Soup and sandwiches are good at **The Deli #2** (4th and University, 622-6307). And you can get fancy Japanese fare along with a spectacular view of the freeway fountains at the **Asuka** (6th and Seneca in the Park Place Building, 682-8050).

Tall buildings and works of art. Freeway Park is a great place to start on a walking tour of the downtown area. Call the city's Department of Community Development (625-4534) for their map and brochure entitled "Art and the Urban Experience." It will take you past fascinating sculptures, fountains, decorative screens, and eye-catching architecture. And on the way you'll pass some of the city's biggest and oldest buildings—the forty-three story Seattle-First National Bank Building at 4th and Spring, the Olympic Hotel at 4th and Seneca, the ornate Coliseum Theater at 5th and Pike, and the Rainier Tower on its twelve-story pedestal at 5th and University.

OTHER FREEWAY VIEWPOINTS
Incurable freeway watchers have much to entertain them on Seattle's freeway—13,000 cars an hour, 130,000 a day, and 48,000,000 a year. Small parklike places and viewpoints, all of them owned by the State Highway Department and maintained by the city, are scattered around Interstate 5. All but one are located on the east side of the freeway. From north to south, they are:

N.E. Banner Street (off N.E. 75th). The view is somewhat overgrown with willows at this writing.

N.E. 60th Street (west side of freeway at 6th N.E.). Turn south onto 6th N.E. from N.E. 65th. The view is from barely above the level of the freeway.

Lakeview Place (just north of Belmont Avenue E.). This one includes excellent views of Lake Union and the Space Needle.

Belmont Avenue E. (up the Belmont E. hill and turn right). Fine, high views of Lake Union, Queen Anne Hill, and the Denny Regrade area.

Boren Avenue (both sides of the street).

University Place (at 9th and University).

HISTORY
While trying to subdue the wilderness, the early pioneers were certainly not interested in creating parks. So downtown Seattle grew by leaps and bounds, leaving very little open space. Even farsighted park planners such as the Olmsted Brothers and Virgil Bogue directed their energies to the outer fringes of the city. And no doubt they, too, would have been bowled over by the idea of a concrete park over a roaring freeway. But that was before the age of the automobile.

The first "horseless carriage" puttered down Seattle's streets in 1900, bringing more jeers than cheers from skeptical onlookers who saw it as only a rich man's toy. About sixty years later the Interstate 5 freeway, a veritable riverbed of concrete, was built to accommodate the flow of over 133,000 cars per day—nearly fifty million per year.

Even before the freeway was completed in 1966, such far-sighted people as attorney James Ellis and architect Paul Thiry began urging the city to create more green space at its congested core. As a beginning the city purchased a parking lot at 6th and Seneca. Then developer Richard Hedreen agreed to fuse the idea of a freeway park with his plans for a twenty-one-story office building called Park Place.

Planning and construction problems were enormous: shallow soils, harsh winds, air pollution, legal hassles over air rights, engineering problems with underground parking, and ten lanes of busy highway—enough to short-circuit the minds of even the most ardent of the early visionaries. But gradually the park took shape—first on the drawing board and modeling clay of a young Bulgarian designer named Angela Danadjieva, of San Francisco's Lawrence Halprin Associates; then on the freeway itself.

Construction barely interrupted the flow of the traffic. Twenty-three precast concrete bridge girders weighing up to eighty-four tons—the largest ever carried on the state's highways—were transported and gingerly nudged into place in the earliest hours of morning. Trees that could endure pollution were planted in a lightweight mix of sand, peat moss, and fertilizer. A gigantic pumping element was sunk beneath the park to circulate the water. And where once there was only thin air, today there are 12,375 cubic yards of concrete; 20,000 cubic yards of sand and topsoil; 105 evergreen trees; 279 deciduous trees; 1,980 shrubs; five eighty-foot directional lamp poles; a fifty-foot automatic flagpole; a 630-car parking garage; three drinking fountains; and nineteen trash containers. And all for a little less than fourteen million dollars.

How about *that*, pioneers?

 # Hing Hay Park

S. King and Maynard S.
Size: 0.33 acre
Buses: 1, 7, 14 to Maynard and Jackson
Major use: community square

DESCRIPTION
Hing Hay is the hub of the Asian community, or International District, which spans the blocks east of the Kingdome from 6th Avenue South to 8th Avenue South and from Yesler Way to Weller

Street. Terracelike stairs lead down from Maynard to a red brick square with an ornate Grand Pavilion designed and constructed in Taipei, Taiwan. Artwork on an adjacent building features a dragon in a depiction of Asian-American history in the Northwest. The park is a favorite meeting place for Asian-American family groups and friends.

NEARBY ATTRACTIONS

In the International District you can hardly walk a block without running into something of ethnic interest or delight: excellent eating spots, herbal shops, cultural centers, martial arts emporiums, and even former gambling dens.

Food spots are too numerous to name, but a couple of the most popular spots are right on King Street near the park—**Tai Tung** (655 S. King, 223-9143) and the **King Cafe** (723 S. King, 622-6373). **Uwajimaya,** the international supermarket, is also nearby (6th S. and S. King, 624-6248).

Tours of "Chinatown" are easy to take on your own. But if you want an especially good orientation, call the **Center for Asian Arts** (622 S. Washington, 624-6342) for a $2 tour including a thirty-minute slide show—and a fine restaurant finale. **The Wing Luke Museum** (414 8th S., 623-5124), with its Chinese historical photographs and artifacts, is also within easy walking distance of the park.

HISTORY

The first Chinese pioneers came to Seattle in 1860, lured across the sea by the "mountain of gold" they hoped to find in California. With it, they hoped to return to their homelands and become landowners. Instead of gold, they found only menial jobs, persecution, and misery. Many suffered and died of hardships during the construction of the railroads. After the railroads were built, jobs became scarce for everybody, and Anti-Chinese riots broke out across the western states. Seattle became the scene of such riots in 1886. Many Chinese people were shipped out, some fled to Canada, and others went into hiding in the International District, relying on strong family bonds for survival.

Today the Asian-American is an important part of Seattle's community life. The protective societies, craft halls, and secret rooms that were once vital to survival are no longer necessary, and in their place a vital spirit has blossomed. Hing Hay Park, with its ornate pavilion and outgoing air of conviviality, stands as a symbol of that spirit. It was purchased in 1970 with Forward Thrust money and designed by landscape architect S. K. Sakuma.

Kobe Terrace

7th S. between S. Main and S. Washington
Size: 1.1 acres
Bus: 27 to 6th and Yesler
Major uses: sitting and views

DESCRIPTION

This terraced hillside on the northeast edge of the International District is adorned with Mt. Fuji cherry trees and laced with ground vines and pathways winding alongside the freeway. The trees and a four-ton, 200-year-old Yukimidoro stone lantern on the hilltop were gifts from the people of Seattle's sister city, Kobe, Japan. Since Yukimidoro means "View of the Snow," keep your eyes open for Mount Rainier to the south. The park provides pleasant sitting, viewing, and walking between S. Washington and S. Main, with an eye-level view of the cars flashing along the freeway.

NEARBY ATTRACTIONS

From Kobe Terrace you can easily walk to any part of the International District, with its fine restaurants and cultural and historical spots (see "Hing Hay Park"). The nearest is the **Nippon Kan,** the Japanese Community Center at the top of S. Washington Street. To see this former theatre and meeting hall, call the **Center for Asian Arts** (622 S. Washington, 624-6342) and sign up for their $2 "Chinatown Tour."

HISTORY

Like the Chinese, the Japanese immigrants (Issei) came to the Pacific Northwest seeking a fortune, and instead found mainly oppression and persecution. They worked in forests, canneries, sawmills, and on the railroads. In Seattle, most settled north of Jackson Street. Others went to the Duwamish Valley, where their farms at one time supplied seventy-five percent of the produce for Seattle and Tacoma. Washington State's oyster industry was begun also by two young Issei men who transplanted Japanese oysters in Samish Bay.

Despite these successes, the Japanese suffered many years of social and economic discrimination, from immigration restrictions to the deportation of 110,000 of their number to concentration camps during World War II. They did not receive citizenship rights until 1952, and were never fully compensated for their loss of property during the war.

Again like the Chinese, the Japanese turned inward for protection and survival. Their most important gathering center in Seattle was Nippon Kan, or "Japanese Hall," an old hotel they had converted into an all-purpose community center. For years its stage was the scene of Japanese plays, dances, martial arts contests, flower displays, political debates, movies, and art shows. Simultaneously it served as a center to help people find jobs and housing, and to organize for rebuilding the farms that were burned out during the years of persecution.

The Nippon Kan was abandoned from World War II until 1974, when it was rehabilitated along with the Pioneer Square area. Two years later, during the dedication of Kobe Terrace Park, its halls once more resounded with dancing and kabuki music in celebration of a new and brighter day.

The park itself was part of the Yesler Terrace Housing Project prior to the freeway construction. Formerly known as Yesler Terrace Park, it was redeveloped in 1975 with Forward Thrust funds. The once-fertile Issei farmlands of the Duwamish Valley— now filled with industrial plants instead of green ones—can be seen from the park.

Myrtle Edwards Park

Alaskan Way between W. Bay and W. Thomas
Size: 3.7 acres
Buses: 1 or 2 to 1st and Bay
Major uses: jogging, biking, views, kites

DESCRIPTION
It would be simpler if Myrtle Edwards Park and the Port of Seattle's Elliott Bay Park had the same name, since they run right into each other and hardly anybody bothers with the artificial boundary anyway. The two combined provide a long, relaxing swath of grass with 1.25 miles of snaking bike and footpaths sandwiched between the railroad tracks and Elliott Bay.

The Myrtle Edwards section begins at the Pier 70 parking lot (better have the kids use the Sani-Kans here before you go) and goes north, presenting you with a fresh, open, windy exposure along the bay to W. Thomas Street. Here the Elliott Bay Bikeway continues north past grain elevators to a sea of new cars at Pier 86.

Pathways are well supplied with benches for viewing the islands of the sound, the Olympics, and Mount Rainier over the Seattle cityscape. Most of the beach is bulkheaded with basalt boulders, but there is one small, sandy, driftwood-strewn spot that is suitable for a beach picnic, and lots of open space for flying kites. There is also a massive concrete and granite "sculpture" (you decide) called "Adjacent, Against, Upon."

This park is a beautiful example of what the city could do with more of its shorelines—simply open them up to the public. Myrtle Edwards means regeneration for downtown spirits: try a 2.5-mile jog on your lunch hour, a relaxing walk after work, or mix it in with a weekend visit to the Seattle waterfront.

NEARBY ATTRACTIONS

Pier 70 (Broad Street). This colorful complex of specialty shops and eating spots waits for you in a renovated warehouse at the south end of the park. If you come by car, park either on the pier (for free), in an upper garage, or in the metered lot near Myrtle Edwards.

The Old Spaghetti Factory (Elliott and Broad Streets, 632-3520). This restaurant can be an evening treat for the whole family (especially the kids). Particularly after a day at the waterfront, spaghetti dinners of all kinds are served in an old-time atmosphere, complete with a 1917 trolley car and a cantankerous old organ-piano. They open at 5 p.m. most nights, 4 p.m. on Sundays.

British Columbia Steamship Company (Pier 69, 623-5560). The Canadian ship *Princess Marguerite* makes round trip tours to Victoria daily at 8 a.m. through Labor Day and returns at 8 p.m. No reservations are needed for walk-on passengers. Round trip fare is $19 for adults and $10 for seniors and children eleven and under, with an additional $19 charged each way if you take your car. Call 682-8200 for reservations.

HISTORY

The Seattle shoreline changed shape rapidly in the early part of the century—much of it the result of the Denny Regrade Project, in which the city's steepest hills were leveled and dumped into Elliott Bay. The hills provided convenient fill for the new seawall that eventually stretched all the way from Washington Street in Pioneer Square to Bay Street, at the south end of the present park.

In 1912, the present piers 90 and 91—then the largest commercial piers in the world—were built at the far north end of Elliott Bay Park. There, among other things, delicate raw silk imported from the Orient was carefully loaded onto high-speed trains for quick shipment to East Cost mills.

The idea of a park between Bay Street and the big piers originated in 1956, when the city's comprehensive plan called for preservation of more open space for a growing city. Just twelve years before, the property between Bay and Thomas Streets had sold to a private company for $15,000. At that time, it was still washed by the tide. In 1965, after considerable freeway fill, the southern half alone was resold for $181,000. Soon afterward, all of the property was offered to the park department for $761,000—an increase of 8,000 percent over its previously estimated value. With a Forward Thrust mandate for a new park there in 1968, the city decided to try a condemnation suit in order to buy it more cheaply.

No such luck. The jury decided that the northern half *alone* was worth $718,000, and the city fathers threw up their hands in frustration. However, after lengthy negotiations with the owner of the southern half and a pot of federal and state matching money, they went ahead and bought the works for a whopping total of $1,539,000.

Meanwhile, the Port of Seattle had acquired the land from Pier 88 south to Thomas Street. The Port was initially reluctant to join the city on a park/bikeway project because biking was not an "income-producing activity." But finally it acquiesced, and the two parks were fused into one long, refreshing strip of green.

Occidental Park

Occidental S. and S. Main
Size: 0.6 acre
Buses: 1, 7, 14, 27
Major use: public square

DESCRIPTION
Occidental Park is in the heart of the historic Pioneer Square District, which includes about twelve square blocks, from the waterfront east to 2nd Avenue and from King Street north to Yesler Way. This busy square overflows with business people, pigeons, tourists, shoppers, and wanderers, most of whom coexist surprisingly well. Maple trees, benches, and a modern pergola provide shade and shelter beside fashionable shops and eateries. And the square is frequently the site of concerts and rallies of various sorts.

NEARBY ATTRACTIONS
From Occidental Park you can walk in almost any direction and find a variety of experiences. Start with the **Grand Central Arcade**. If you're hungry, **The Bakery** (214 1st S., 622-3644) here will quell your pangs, as will **Yogibob's** (209 Occidental S., 624-1631). Then you can

descend the stairs to watch glassblowing, or shop for toys, leathers, imports, tapestries, ceramics, and such. Or try a lunch at one of the many sidewalk cafes around the three-block, red-brick mall running through the park.

Just north, at 1st and Yesler, is **Pioneer Square** and **Doc Maynard's Public House** (682-4649) starting point for the Seattle Underground Tour (682-4686). Directly south is the **Kingdome.** Seattle's center for sports and various extravaganzas, with seating for 60,000. Tours are given three times daily. For game schedules and tickets call 628-3311.

To the southeast is the colorful **International District,** with excellent ethnic restaurants and items of historical interest (see "Hing Hay Park"). And to the west is the **Waterfront** with harbor tours, seafood delicacies, and intriguing displays of marine life at the public aquarium. **Nighttime entertainment** is also plentiful nearby, with lots of discos and bars.

HISTORY
Back in the 1850s, when logs began streaming down Skid Road to Henry Yesler's sawmill, this area was part of the heart of a young and rowdy Seattle. It was also the birthplace of the Salvation Army in 1887, and later the site of the Savoy Hotel, which was torn down and replaced with a parking lot in 1965. The present park was built over this half-acre of asphalt in 1971, during the general renovation of the Pioneer Square area (see "Pioneer Square").

Pioneer Square

1st and Yesler
Size: 0.1 acre
Buses: 15, 18, 21, 130, 132
Major use: historic square

DESCRIPTION
Pioneer Square—the heart of old Seattle—is the place to go to experience Seattle's early history. Turn-of-the-century street lamps line the square. A Tlingit totem pole towers up beside a drinking fountain fitted with a bust of Chief Seattle, the Suquamish Indian chief for whom the city was named. And under a renovated pergola, indigents lounge on benches while traffic roars around the little triangle of grass and cobbles that was once the focal point of the new town.

NEARBY ATTRACTIONS

Just off the square is **Doc Maynard's Public House** (682-4649), which offers literate and witty tours of musty Underground Seattle—the Seattle that was destroyed in 1889 and buried under the reconstructed buildings. The tour costs $2 for adults, $1.25 for seniors and children five to twelve, and is free for kids under five. Call 682-4686.

Another interesting spot is the **Pioneer Square Wax Museum** (112 1st S., 624-6486), where you walk among life-size figures of the early pioneers. Admission is $2.50 for adults, $1.75 for students and seniors, and $1.25 for children.

HISTORY

A short history of early Seattle is inscribed on a kiosk in the square, and most of the places it mentions are within easy walking distance.

"In the beginning, before there was a village, a small stream emptied into the Sound where Washington Street now meets the bay. Beyond the shore a spit ran south along First Avenue to King Street, toward the mouth of the Duwamish. A tidal lagoon lay behind it to the east. Indians called it Duwamps, and its sheltered banks attracted the settlers that first landed at Alki in 1852.

"Denny, Boren, and Bell claimed the land from the stream north, and Maynard chose the low spit to the south. Yesler came the following year and started the mill on the stream where the other claims joined. He cleared the steep slopes to skid the logs to his mill and gave the country its original Skid Road: Yesler Way.

"Within twenty-five years, Yesler milled more than forty million board feet of lumber and the village sprawling across the flats boomed with a population of 4,533. Behind the mill a flagpole marked a muddy, sawdust-filled place and the first public meeting ground.

"The Great Fire of 1889 razed the haphazard frame settlement. The town that rose in its place was of brick and stone, and the handsome multi-storied buildings were in the style of the day. Seattle was a destination worthy of the Great Northern Railroad, and in 1893 witnessed its long-awaited arrival. When news of gold struck, Seattle prospered as a gateway to Alaska, and Pioneer Square with its nearby shops, bars and brothels welcomed and catered to the fortune-seekers heading north.

"In 1889, local businessmen returning from Alaska brought back a Tlingit totem pole and gave Puget Sound its first landmark. In 1909 the iron pergola was built as a shelter over an underground restroom [known as 'the finest underground restroom in the United States'], and the square took on the unique identity that has distinguished it to this day. It has served Seattle well from the early pioneer days through the first years of this century as the heart of a thriving town that in time outgrew the area as it spread north."

Seattle Center

5th and Thomas
Size: 74 acres
Buses: 3, 4, 6, 16
Major use: entertainment center

DESCRIPTION

This massive entertainment center just northwest of the central business district is not a city park, but its parklike atmosphere should not go unmentioned. In 1962, it was the site of the Seattle World's Fair, and today it is just as popular as it was then, drawing throngs of people from all over the world.

Packed into its spacious grounds are the prominent Space Needle, with its 500-foot-high observation deck and revolving restaurant; the Pacific Science Center, with its museum of flight, mathematical, and engineering wonders; a multicultural food circus; an international bazaar filled with import shops from all over the world; a coliseum for concerts and sporting events; a high school football stadium; an opera house; a theatre playhouse; an art museum; and an amusement park with many rides. An international fountain spouts multiple streams of water in concert with music and multicolored lights. Various events will draw you back to the Center—as it is justly called—again and again. For event information, call 625-4234.

HISTORY

It is fitting that the Seattle Center is such a popular entertainment site today. Over 1,000 years ago, the grounds on which it stands were known as "Potlatch Meadows," the place where Indians around Puget Sound gathered for their own great celebrations. And around the turn of the century, traveling circuses and carnivals came to entertain Seattleites on these grounds.

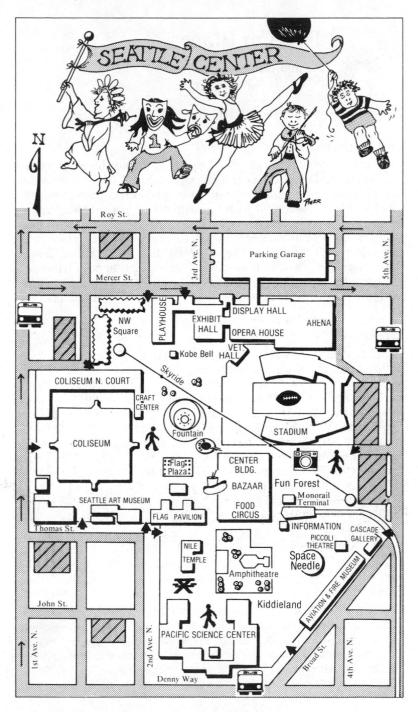

Tilikum Place

5th and Denny
Size: 0.01 acres
Buses: 3, 4, 6, 16
Major use: historic square

DESCRIPTION

The main attraction of this small square in the northwest corner of the central business district is a life-size statue of Chief Seattle, for whom the city was named. Wrapped in a stained copper shawl, the chief stands on a pedestal with one arm raised in symbolic greeting to the first white settlers who landed at Alki Point in 1851. Bear heads at the base of the pedestal spout streams of water into a pool. A plaque commemorates the 1792 sighting of Captain George Vancouver's ship by the Indians, and an inscription pays tribute to the great Indian: "Seattle, Chief of Suquamish. A firm friend of the citizens. For him the city of Seattle was named by its founders."

HISTORY

Chief Seattle's life was caught up in what he himself might have called "a change of worlds"—the clash of cultures brought on by the white settlement of Puget Sound. He was born on Blake Island, probably in 1786, in a cedar longhouse built by his father. Like other young Indian boys of his time, he learned to make bird and animal traps, nets, and fishhooks, and spent joyful days either hunting or honing his strength with wrestling and foot races by the sound. Under the tutelage of Chief Kitsap, he also gained wisdom and gradually developed a great way with words.

At age twenty, Seattle put his powers to their first full test when he devised a plan to ward off an impending attack from the mountain tribes to the west. The day before the attack, he and other braves paddled up the Duwamish River and, in an area where the current flowed swiftly, felled a large fir tree across the channel. Near nightfall five large canoes loaded with twenty warriors apiece came coursing down the river. They crashed into the tree, and the flailing warriors who managed to escape drowning fled back to the hills. Soon thereafter Seattle was chosen head chief of the six Salish tribes.

But long before he became chief, Seattle had experienced hints of a new way of life. In 1792, at age eight, he had stood by an amazed Chief Kitsap's side when the billowing sails of Captain George Vancouver's ship, the H.M.S. *Discovery*, were first sighted on Puget Sound. Not many years later, the missionaries began arriving, and

Seattle himself was baptized Noah Sealth after his favorite Bible character.

Then came the settlers, with dreams of reshaping the land. To Seattle, who had lived his life in communion with nature, the concept of reshaping the land was strange. Even so, he welcomed the first settlers—the Dennys, Bells, and Borens—when their schooner, the *Exact,* landed at Alki in 1851. His first greeting, "*Kla-how-ya!*" or "Welcome," was symbolic of the open friendship he was to show the settlers until he died.

One of the first ways that chief Seattle helped the settlers was by urging "Doc" Maynard to settle down and bring medicine to the area. "Doc" soon became one of the town's foremost citizens—acting at once the part of physician, attorney, justice of the peace, realtor, and civic leader. He also learned the Salish language and became known as a fast friend of the chief, and ultimately an "Indian lover."

The cultural rift grew stronger and the tensions grew more strained as the pioneers leveled forests and spread out into new territory. In 1855, Chief Seattle was one of four regional chiefs and 2,300 native Americans called by Washington Governor Isaac Stevens to sign a treaty ceding their land to the settlers. Since the concept of land ownership was foreign to the Indians, most of them did not understand that they had given away their homeland— 2,236,000 acres—for about three cents an acre.

The following year, when the subtler implications of the treaty became clear, many of the angered Indians gathered to plan an attack on the settlement. They asked for the leadership of the chief, but true to his love for white and Indian alike, Seattle pledged that he would not fight. The battle lasted only a day, and life for the Puget Sound Indian was never the same again.

The old chief was greatly saddened. Perhaps his own words best express the mixture of hope and despair that marked his final years:

"Why should I mourn at the untimely fate of my people? Tribe follows tribe, and nation follows nation, like the waves of the sea. It is the order of nature, and regret is useless. Your time of decay may be distant—but it will surely come. We may be brothers after all . . . At night, when the streets of your cities and villages shall be silent and you think them deserted, they will throng with the returning hosts that once filled and still love this beautiful land. The white man will never be alone. Let him be just and deal kindly with my people, for the dead are not altogether powerless. Dead—I say? There is no death. Only a change of worlds."

Chief Seattle died in 1886, at about age 80—but not before his old friend Doc Maynard had convinced the townsfolk to name the city in his honor. The chief himself was at first aghast at the suggestion, believing according to Indian legend that he would turn over in his grave at every mention of his name. But Maynard finally won him over, and a tax was levied on the settlers in advance for any discomfort he might experience after his death. He was buried at the Port Madison reservation near Suquamish, on the Kitsap Peninsula.

Tilikum Place itself (the name meaning "welcome" or "greeting" in Chinook jargon) is located at the juncture of the original land claims of Denny, Boren, and Bell. The statue, sculpted by James Wehn from the only existing photo of the chief, was unveiled on Founders' Day, November 13, 1912, by Chief Seattle's great-great-granddaughter.

Waterfall Gardens

2nd and S. Main
Size: 0.2 acres
Buses: 20, 31, 107, 123, 142, 147, 150, 174
Major use: urban resting spot

DESCRIPTION

Step off busy downtown streets into this refreshing environment with water crashing over moss-covered boulders and bubbling from fountains and sculptures. Large spherical bulbs light the interior of a large, brick-lined pergola, and benches and concession stand cater to weary pedestrians. Despite such civilized amenities, the effect of the flowing water is to make you feel as though you had suddenly stepped from the city into the Cascade Mountains.

Waterfall Gardens marks the 1907 birthplace of the United Parcel Service. It was completed in 1977 and is maintained by the Annie Casey Foundation, which honors the mother of United Parcel Service founder James Casey.

Waterfront Park/Aquarium

Alaskan Way from Pier 57 to 59
Size: 10.7 acres (2.3 acres tidelands)
Bus: 25
Major uses: picnics, views, fishing, sea life

DESCRIPTION

Follow the smell of fish and chips and salty air to this exciting sea world park on piers a few blocks north of the ferry terminal. Long ramps lead to observation decks; then winding, ship style staircases descend to piers beside renovated warehouses, where sheets of water pour from a block-shaped fountain. Sea life of all kinds is displayed in the adjacent new municipal aquarium.

Pier 57 is a public fishing pier, lined with lamps and benches and made safe for kids with high railings. The warehouse here has been converted into the **Sourdough Bakery and Restaurant** (623-1800), where you can get fresh sourdough bread, rolls, and other delectables. At the end of the pier is a patio, with tables and wide, rustic benches big enough to lie down on—and open views of Elliott Bay, from Alki and Harbor Island to Magnolia Bluff.

The Seattle Aquarium (625-4358) at Pier 59 is the biggest and most exciting marine attraction in the city. Here you walk through corridors lined with fish tanks housing some of the most exotic, brightly-colored, strangely-shaped, wierd-mannered sea creatures you have ever seen.

An underwater viewing dome with circular seating lets you relax as if at the bottom of the sound, surrounded by schools of salmon and other Puget Sound fish. There is under- and over-the-water viewing of sea otters and harbor seals in two-story-deep tanks. A "touch tank" lets kids make closer acquaintance with seashore animals, with monitors there to introduce them. A public auditorium is also available for lectures and school programs.

You may have to wait a little while to get inside the Aquarium, but the time spent inside is well worth the wait. It is truly an education and an adventure. From the beginning explanations of life's origins, attractive and easy-to-read graphics lead you slowly and enticingly on to discovery after discovery. Once-dim concepts of evolution, adaptation, and physiology come alive in the tanks, sparking a sense of wonder and excitement.

Hours and Admission: The Aquarium is open daily from 10 a.m. to dusk (6 p.m. winter, 10 p.m. summer). Admission is $2.50 for adults, $1.25 for teens thirteen to eighteen and seniors over sixty-five, $.75 for children six to twelve, and free for children under six. Group rates and reservations are available on request by calling 625-5030.

And a yearly family membership fee of $25 entitles the whole family to come whenever you like, with two guests.

Another point of interest before you leave the park is the Deep Water Observation Chamber. It is located on the north side of the Aquarium entrance and looks like a cross between a many-eyed sea monster and a corrugated trash can. This blue-and-white-striped drum was used during the 1950s to inspect underwater cables in the San Juan Islands. It could descend with divers inside to depths of up to 1,000 feet. (In 1959, observers peering through its portholes at a wreck 666 feet below the surface helped to convict a misguided captain of purposely sinking his ship to collect insurance.)

NEARBY ATTRACTIONS

The Waterfront Park is a good starting point to get to a number of other intriguing places. For one, you'll eventually want to climb the steep stairs to the **Pike Place Market** and sample its abundance of farm fresh fruits, vegetables, breads, shops, and streetside craft stands. But be sure you also get a good look at what the waterfront has to offer. Here is a quick sampling of some of the more interesting piers and public places north of Yesler Street:

At **Pier 51** you'll find **Ye Olde Curiosity Shop** (601 Alaskan Way). This is *really* a curiosity. Souvenirs and strange things—shrunken heads and ten-pound geoducks, for example—plus Indian and Eskimo artifacts, have been sold here since 1899.

Pier 52 is the home of the **Wasington State Ferries** (464-6400). The gaping ships churn out to Bainbridge Island and Bremerton about every half hour and offer a wonderful trip in any weather. Without car, the fare is $1.20 round trip for adults and $.60 for children. Special five-hour excursion rates are also offered.

Pier 54, at the foot of Spring Street, houses **Firehouse Five,** the center for Seattle's fireboats. Monday mornings you can often see them practicing their pumping here, with huge plumes of water spouting into the bay. You can also tour the small fire fighting museum here.

Pier 56, at the foot of Seneca, is the berth for **Seattle Harbor Tours** (623-1445), which provides waterfront tours in Elliott Bay. Tours go daily, five times a day, from May through October. A one-hour cruise costs $2.50 for adults and $1 for children five to twelve. Two cruises each day in the summer go out to Blake Island for an Indian-style salmon bake at Tillicum Village.

For descriptions of **Piers 69 and 70**, see "Myrtle Edwards Park."

HISTORY

Within thirty years after the pioneers' landing, Seattle's waterfront had been transformed from a quiet bay rimmed with virgin forests into one of the busiest ports in the country. By 1885, the east shore of Elliot Bay had become a maze of trestles, piers, and pilings. Sailing ships and steamers, many of which waited for lumber from Yesler's sawmill, glutted the harbor. Tracks ran along the shoreline (now called Railroad Avenue) and spurs jutted out over the bay.

In the rush for economic supremacy on Puget Sound, a train depot was built near the present site of Pier 52. Shortly thereafter Seattle was chosen as the terminus for the Transcontinental Railroad, touching off a boom period for the city.

The boom was further fueled by the Alaska Gold Rush. In 1896,the steamship "Portland" docked at the present site of the Waterfront Park with what was described in one local paper as "a ton of gold." Almost overnight Seattle became the Gateway to Alaska, and easily made its own millions outfitting and entertaining the gold-hungry hordes.

So frantic was the port activity in Seattle during the boom years that few paid any attention to the physical appearance of the port itself. Wind, waves, salt, and sea borers joined with sawmill pieces and miscellaneous refuse to ravage the pilings and the unprotected shoreline as the boom reached its high tide.Not until 1929 was any serious effort made to clean it up. First the tracks were moved to the east side of Railroad Avenue. Then, in a spectacular works project inspired by the Depression, prefabricated seawall sections were floated in at high tide and positioned during low tide to protect the shoreline. Railroad Avenue was renamed Alaskan Way, and the shoreline began to take on some permanence.

During the 1940s, the entire waterfront was taken over by the military to bolster the war in the Pacific. Port activities on the central waterfront began to slow down as the southern portion, with its abundance of plants and railroad yards continued to flourish. By 1960 the central waterfront had completely lost its original vitality and had begun catering to tourists, shoppers, and restaurant-goers.

Seattle's aquarium was a long time in coming. The city's first marine exhibit came in the form of a dead whale which washed up on the shores of Alki Beach's Luna Park in 1908. It was quickly towed back out, though, when the odor overpowered the public interest.

In 1917, a longer-lived, though somewhat static, exhibit was started in a cold storage plant at the Spokane Street Terminal near the present Pier 27. It began when manager George Jaeger hung up a frozen 331-pound halibut on the hallway wall. Thereafter, fishermen began bringing in strange and unusual catches from around the world, and Jaeger's chilly hallway became famous as "the only frozen fish exhibit in the U.S. and Canada." By 1932, it contained over 100 species, and was open to a warmly dressed public until 1956.

In 1938 seafood restaurateur Ivar Haglund built an aquarium on the end of Pier 54 to help lure hungry visitors into his Acres of Clams Restaurant. Both the clams and the exhibit were good bait. Ivar closed down the aquarium in 1949 to make more dining room for the clam lovers. Then, to fill the gap left by Ivar's departing sea creatures, the Seattle Harbor Tours ticket office next door created "the world's smallest aquarium"—a one-gallon jar of saltwater that bristled with bits of sea life for many years. Its most beloved resident was a large barnacle, affectionately known to his friends as "Old Barney."

Many requests for a municipal aquarium were made over the years, but Seattle did not take them seriously until a businessman-diver named Ted Griffin built a full-fledged aquarium of his own at Pier 56. Its tanks were filled with marine creatures—from starfish to trained seals—just in time to delight audiences during the Seattle World's Fair in 1962. And in 1965, Griffin cinched the urban aquarium craze when he managed to capture a killer whale named Namu. The municipal aquarium opened at Pier 59 in 1977.

Westlake Park

4th and Pine
Size: 0.1 acre
Buses: 1, 2, 3, 4, 6, 15, 16, 18, 19, 24, 33
Major use: shoppers' mall

DESCRIPTION

Right now the future Westlake Park is part of a shoppers' mall—a way station providing benches and pedestrian access to major department stores, restaurants, banks, and shops in the heart of the downtown shopping district. But by 1981, the area between 4th and 5th Avenues directly south of Pine Street is suposed to become a restful natural retreat, as part of a major new mall project. The Westlake Mall north of Pine will include a large indoor plaza on the street level, outdoor sculpture gardens, three floors of retail shops, and a large art museum. Sky bridges from the monorail terminal will connect with three major department stores.

From this centrally located park site, the monorail can take you to the Seattle Center in one-and-a-half minutes—or buses can carry you to all parts of the city.

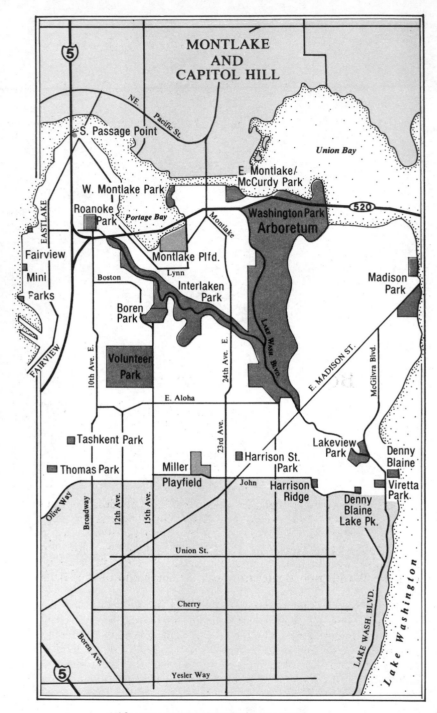

MONTLAKE
AND
CAPITOL HILL

5

N.E. Pacific St.

S. Passage Point

Union Bay

W. Montlake Park

E. Montlake/
McCurdy Park

Roanoke Park

Portage Bay

520

Washington Park
Arboretum

EASTLAKE

Montlake

Fairview

Montlake Plfd.

Mini
Parks

Boston

Lynn

Madison
Park

Interlaken
Park

FAIRVIEW

Boren
Park

Lake Wash. Blvd.

10th Ave. E.

24th Ave. E.

Volunteer
Park

E. MADISON ST.

McGilvra Blvd.

E. Aloha

23rd Ave.

Tashkent Park

Lakeview
Park

Denny
Blaine

Thomas Park

Miller
Playfield

Harrison St.
Park

Olive Way

Broadway

12th Ave.

15th Ave.

John

Harrison
Ridge

Viretta
Park.

Denny Blaine
Lake Pk.

Union St.

Lake Washington

Cherry

Boren Ave.

LAKE WASH. BLVD.

5

Yesler Way

142   ENJOYING SEATTLE'S PARKS

5

Montlake and Capitol Hill Parks

*Those who learn to play well will be more apt to work
with a purpose.*

—Virgil R. Bogue
Plan of Seattle, 1911

Arboretum (See "Washington Park")

Boren/Interlaken Park

Interlaken Boulevard
Size: 59 acres (Boren, 6.8 acres)
Buses: 4, 48 to east end; 25 to west end
Major uses: bicycling, jogging

DESCRIPTION

The Boren/Interlaken complex has been one of Seattle's most popular boulevard tours since the 1890s, when it was the principal bike and buggy path linking Capitol Hill with the boulevards on Lake Washington. The two-mile boulevard loops downward along canyonlike, wooded hillsides and ravines from E. Roanoke southeast to Lake Washington Boulevard, near the south end of the Arboretum.

Bicycling is still the best way to go—or jogging. If you start from E. Roanoke by the freeway interchange, curve southeast over the lakebound interchange and keep to the right. Interlaken enters the woods just below the Seattle Prep School hillside. From there it's mostly easy coasting all the way to the Arboretum. If you are going uphill from 24th Avenue E. (a block uphill from prominent Boyer

Avenue), the switchbacks allow easy pedaling. Either way, you'll pass pleasant hillside homes (some of them hidden away in the woods), absorb the atmosphere of greenness and solitude, and come out refreshed at the other end.

About midway up the boulevard a steeper roadway, Interlaken Drive E., winds uphill to the left, passing the old Forest Ridge Convent (now the Seattle Hebrew Academy), and coming out at the bus stop at E. Galer and 19th Avenue E., just across from Stevens Elementary School. This is a third good access.

For the foot traveler, several trails give closer communion with the lush woods. The principal one starts at the bus stop at 19th E. and E. Galer and branches into several others, all connecting with the main boulevard. If you stay to the far right, one of them will take you all the way down to Howe Street in the Montlake neighborhood.

Another trail toward the west end of the boulevard leads into Boren Park and is marked by a plaque commemorating Louisa Boren, one of the original pioneers who landed at Alki in 1851. If you follow this trail, don't expect to make it out the other side; it gets steeper, muddier, and less well marked as you go. Leave this jungle for the hardy, woodswise kids living on E. Olin Place near the Louisa Boren Viewpoint. From here, Boren Park plunges down like the inside of a bowl, graced as it goes down with morning glories, blackberries, nettles, and hanging vines so thick you can hardly see the sun. Kids can often be found thrashing around down here, following its primitive pathways or charging through still uncharted woods.

HISTORY

A bicycle boom hit Seattle in 1895. It was touched off by the conversion of the high wheel to the low wheel, which made bicycles considerably easier to ride. But still, most of the city's streets were paved with planks, and the cracks between them made biking hazardous. So Assistant City Engineer George F. Cotterill toured the city looking for good bikeways.

The result of his research was twenty-five miles of paths, some of which went from Volunteer Park (then City Park) to Washington Park through what is now Interlaken Boulevard. Cotterill's bike trails formed the basis of the city's boulevard system.

In 1903, the Interlaken stretch was approved by the Olmsted Brothers Landscape Architects as a boulevard route. With its spectacular views of mountains and lakes, it also became a popular walkway for passengers who came out from town via the Broadway trolley along 10th Avenue. With the advent of the auto, the boulevard became a "speedway," and as early as 1906 it was patrolled by police on horseback. Beginning in 1908, a motorcycle was used in apprehending traffic offenders.

In 1913, five acres of the Interlaken complex were set aside to honor eighty-six-year-old Louisa Boren Denny, last surviving member of the pioneer party that landed at Alki in 1851. Typical of the early pioneers, Louisa made her own moccasins, shot game, chopped wood, and raised a managerie of eight children and assorted livestock. She died in 1916.

Denny-Blaine Park

Lk. Wash. Blvd. E. and E. Denny Blaine Place
Size: 2.0 acres
Bus: none nearby
Major use: swimming and sunbathing

DESCRIPTION
Descend a looping driveway at E. Denny Blaine Place to a small, two-tiered beach lawn between private residences. The grassy beach (no lifeguards) is surrounded by an old stone wall, which marked the shoreline before 1917, when the lake level was lowered nine feet by the construction of the Lake Washington Ship Canal. There is enough room for a volleyball net above, and quiet picnics and sunbathing below. Of course, on hot days this beach is as crowded as any other, and, according to local residents, the teen crowd pretty much takes over after sunset.

HISTORY
This beach park is one of many small land parcels donated to the city by realtors Charles L. Denny and Elbert F. Blaine. Unlike most of their contemporaries, Denny and Blaine were firm believers in the "open space" rather than the "amusement park" concept of parks, and as a result their 1901 plat is perforated today with many of these little breathing spaces. Others include Denny-Blaine Lake Park, Howell Park, and Viretta Park.

Charles Denny was the son of pioneers Arthur and Mary Denny. His first act of distinction was his own birth, which delayed the cornerstone ceremonies for the University of Washington in 1861. He went on to become one of Seattle's prominent businessmen. Elbert Blaine, an attorney and park commissioner from 1902 to 1908, is sometimes called the "Father of the Seattle Park System" because of his part in implementing the far-reaching Olmsted Plan. He also started the Columbia Basin Irrigation Project.

Denny-Blaine Lake Park

E. Denny Way and Madrona Place E.
Size: 0.05 acre
Bus: 2
Major use: bus stop

DESCRIPTION

Today this park (across the street from the Epiphany Church) is just a bus-stop shelter with a lily-padded pool and fountain. But back in the old days it was the site of Charles Denny and Elbert Blaine's elaborately designed realty office, which they purposely built along the busy trolley line that led down a "deep, wild canyon" (Madrona Drive) to Lake Washington. As the realtors had planned, many picnickers and sightseers were so taken with the land on the trip out that on the return trip, or soon thereafter, they stopped in to sign on the dotted line. The park and pool were originally called "Fountains of Minerva" in honor of Blaine's wife.

East Montlake and McCurdy Park

E. Hamlin and E. Park Drive E.
Size: 4.8 acres
Buses: 4, 25, 48
Major uses: museum, waterfront trails

DESCRIPTION

Being the site of the Museum of History and Industry and the starting point for miles of waterfront trails makes this park one of the most popular areas in the city. Turn east onto E. Hamlin from Montlake Boulevard, a few blocks south of the Montlake Bridge, or take E. Park Drive from Lake Washington Boulevard across the freeway to the museum parking area.

Museum of History and Industry (324-1125) hours are Tuesday through Friday, 11 a.m. to 5 p.m.; Saturday, 10 a.m. to 5 p.m.; and Sunday noon to 5 p.m. The museum is divided into several fascinating wings. Children particularly enjoy the **Natural History Wing,** with its displays of stuffed animals and birds (including Bobo, Seattle's long-beloved gorilla). In the **Maritime Wing,** they run to the submarine periscope. then gawk at ship models and artifacts. The **Transportation Gallery** goes back to Seattle's beginnings, and displays actual trolley cars and horse-drawn fire engines, then travels through time from the first flimsy Boeing biplanes to cutaway views of the 747 Stratocruiser and models of moon landers.

Old Seattle artifacts are on display here, too—the "primitive" tools and machines that built the city, the pot that started the Great Seattle Fire, burning the city down—as well as diorama displays of the pioneers themselves struggling across the Oregon Trail and sharing their miseries at Alki Point.

One of the special events the museum sponsors is **"Christmas Round the World,"** which gives you a close look at customs and costumes of twenty different countries. You can see the display during the three weeks before Christmas, with hour-long presentations made only on the weekends. In July and August you can watch demonstrations of pioneer skills, or try them yourself. At the beginning of each season during the school year, kids aged seven to twelve can sign up for free history-crafts classes.

If you have a group, arrange for tours two months in advance. The museum is a popular place for school field trips.

NEARBY ATTRACTIONS

Rain or shine, you can't go wrong at Montlake-McCurdy. If it rains, stay inside. If it shines, tour the museum and then take a walk along the **Waterfront Trail.** It starts behind the museum at the east end of the parking lot. One branch goes left and winds around the Lake Washington Ship Canal, with platforms for picnicking, fishing, and watching the bridge rise for oversized sailboat masts. Then the trail continues along the canal a quarter mile to West Montlake Park and the Seattle Yacht Club. Eventually it may continue all the way to the Ballard Locks.

The other trail follows marsh bridges and pontoon pathways to Foster Island, then curves south under the freeway to the Arboretum, and eventually back again along Lake Washington Boulevard to the Museum. This journey is about a mile and a half.

HISTORY

In 1854, pioneer Thomas Mercer named Lake Union, convinced that someday great canals would enlarge its western and eastern arms to unite Puget Sound with Lake Washington. At that time, only a small stream connected Union Bay with Portage Bay, just north of the present museum and park. The stream was large enough for only canoes and small boats, with water dropping so low that at times the Indians and early pioneers had to portage across—hence the name, Portage Bay.

As timber and coal were carted from the woods in greater quantities, a canal was more urgently needed. In 1860, a frustrated landowner named Harvey L. Pike took pick and shovel and spent a week hacking and sweating in an attempt to dig the canal single handedly. It was not until 1885, though that Judge Thomas Burke's Improvement Company finally widened the channel with small locks between Lake Union and Lake Washington. The Wa Chong Company built locks between Lake Union and Salmon Bay.

This first channel, which became known as Portage Canal, was big enough for only small boats and logs. One of its primary beneficiaries was Henry Yesler, who had built another sawmill on the shores of Union Bay in 1888. The present canal, deep enough for ocean-going vessels, was dug in 1916 (see "Commodore Park"). However, a portion of the old canal can still be seen from the windows on the south part of the museum.

The museum itself is the legacy of British-born Morgan J. and Emily Carkeek—particularly Emily, who was an inveterate history buff. After 1884, her talk of forming an historical society began to compete with whist and hearts at Wednesday evening card games at the Carkeek's First Hill mansion. Slowly the mansion became a repository for artifacts and mementoes of early Seattle, and Emily began collecting money to make the museum a reality.

Emily Carkeek never lived to see her dream come true. She died in 1926. Two years later, her husband gave the city a portion of Piper's Canyon (now Carkeek Park), with the understanding that part of it would be used for a museum. But there was not enough money.

Luckily, daughter Guendolen Carkeek had picked up her mother's passion for history. She continued the collecting and stepped up the fundraising campaign as the city's centennial drew near. The History and Industry wing of the museum was finally dedicated in 1952, a hundred years after the founding of Seattle. Since then, the museum has grown to include a Maritime Wing (1958), a Natural History Wing (1961), and the McEachern Theatre (1971). The Maritime Wing includes many of the artifacts of Horace W. McCurdy, a fifth-generation shipbuilder and engineer famed for his construction of the first Lake Washington Floating Bridge in 1940.

The reeds and cattails along the shores of Union Bay began sprouting in 1916, when the lake level was lowered by nine feet as a result of the Lake Washington Ship Canal opening. Much of the original marsh was filled in with garbage and dirt to create the flats that now support the University Village Shopping Center and the lower fields and parking lots of the University of Washington.

The marsh was not recognized as a "valuable natural resource" until 1967, when the UW Arboretum Society and the park department began constructing the Waterfront Trail. Until the mid-1960s the Army Corps of Engineers used part of this marsh area to burn huge rafts of floating snags and other flotsam. Now the debris is taken care of by the sternwheeler *W. T. Preston,* which can often be seen moored near the museum or churning around Lake Washington under white a white cloud of steam.

Fairview Avenue Mini Parks

Fairview Avenue E.
Size: street end plus small piers
Buses: 7, 8, 22, 71, 72, 73, 305
Major uses: picnics, views, fishing

DESCRIPTION
"Caution—Slow to 15 miles—Bicycles, Pedestrians, Ducks." That is the sign houseboat dwellers have been wanting the city to install along this stretch of Fairview Avenue, with its three street-end mini parks. So far the warning has not been installed, but the world along here is obviously a different one—houseboats, waterside shanties, sailboats, seaplanes, and flotillas of waterfowl.

These three little parks are not on the city's official list, but they are worth a visit. All are flowerings of Eastlake and Floating Homes community spirit. They were first put together by local residents with old pilings and planks and later fitted with drinking fountains, benches, and picnic tables by the city. Now they are rustically landscaped with railroad ties, and all three offer waterside seating and interesting views of Lake Union.

One of the best ways to see them is in conjunction with the city's *"Eastlake Walking Tour,"* available from the Seattle Department of Community Development (625-4534). After you have snatched a view from People's Park at the foot of Newton, walk north along Fairview. On your way you'll pass clusters of floating homes among a tangle of wires and masts. Colorful planter boxes line the piers. Walk by on a Tuesday evening in the summertime, or around noon on a winter Saturday, and you may witness one of Lake Union's weekly "Tenas Chuck Duck Dive" sailboat races—an all-comers' contest with every finisher a winner.

NEARBY ATTRACTIONS
You will find ample eats along the way—for example, **Pete's Grocery** a the foot of Lynn Street, or fancy dining at the **Hungry Turtle** (2501

Fairview E., 329-6333), just before you get to Roanoke. For delicious hamburgers, try **Daly's Drive-In** (2317 Eastlake E., 322-1918).

When you're done with the view from E. Roanoke, you can continue your lakeside tour all the way to the University Bridge by going up Roanoke and threading your way back down to Fairview again at Hamlin Street.

HISTORY
The houseboats themselves are of historical interest. The original houseboat dwellers scavenged logs and scrap lumber and tied their shanties to public piers in the early 1900s. Floating-home living received another big boost when upland dwellers were forced to buy underwater property to help finance the upcoming Alaska-Yukon-Pacific Exposition. These people made money by leasing water space to houseboaters, both then and from 1911 to 1971, when workers streamed in to build the Lake Washington Ship Canal. For many years houseboats provided cheap and convenient housing for marine workers, bootleggers, bohemians, and drifters. Today they are quaint, but no longer cheap, as they include some of the most fashionable homes in the city.

A second historical spot is at the foot of Roanoke, where benches now look out onto the unsightly concrete platform of the unfinished Roanoke Reef Condominiums. This is the place where airplane manufacturer William Boeing put together his first rickety planes in 1915.

Boeing's hangar was torn down in 1971 to make way for the 112-unit condominium complex, the construction of which was halted by a neighborhood lawsuit. Already the concrete slab is being used as a moorage. With a few planter boxes and picnic tables, it could even be converted into an attractive public park.

Harrison Ridge Park
32nd E. and E. Denny Way
Size: 1.3 acres
Bus: 38 along Empire Way to E. Denny
Major use: natural woods

DESCRIPTION
"There doesn't seem to be any way to get in there," you think, as you walk along the old concrete retaining wall on 32nd E. And for all

practical purposes, there isn't. But then the park has no "practical" purpose, either. It is a steep stretch of woods slanting up from 32nd E. where E. Denny jogs up into the Denny Blaine neighborhood. The only visible trail dead-ends after beating its way through the best of the blackberry brambles off 35th E. There has been some talk about opening and enhancing the woods with a trail that would connect with other wild patches, and eventually with Lake Washington Boulevard. But for the time being, Harrison Ridge remains virtually impenetrable to all but testy squirrels and undomesticated cats. The park was bought with Forward Thrust funds in 1973.

Harrison Street Mini Park

24th E. and E. Harrison
Size: 0.3 acre
Bus: 48 to E. Harrison
Major use: neighborhood playground

DESCRIPTION
This attractive play area, bordered by grass in a woodsy bowl, sits at the foot of steep Harrison Street on the east side of Capitol Hill. Kids come from all over the neighborhood to clamber up climbing poles, bounce on springboards, sway on swivel tire swings, and scamper up hillside paths. Periodically they refresh themselves at the drinking fountain. The park was bought with Forward Thrust funds in 1970. Just three blocks up the hill is Miller Playfield, with more activities for boundless energies.

Lakeview Park

Lake Wash. Blvd. and McGilvra Blvd. E.
Size: 4.5 acres
Bus: no nearby stops. Bus 11 to Lk. Wash. Blvd. E.
Major uses: play area, views

DESCRIPTION
Slow down, or you'll miss this combined lookout/boulevard/picnic park at Hillside Drive, just where Lake Washington Boulevard E.

begins its switchbacking descent to Lake Washington. The lookout is planted with peonies backed by a stone wall, and has a good view of the lake and the Cascades. Just to the right of the lookout, a trail leads down to meet the next boulevard loop beneath a magnificent coastal redwood tree.

The park proper, a grassy bowl enclosed by woods and brush, is bounded by Dorffel Drive, which curves off and up to the right at a three-way intersection, just before the boulevard heads downward. This is a fine, quiet place for a family picnic beneath a cedar or maple tree. The park continues on down with the boulevard to McGilvra Boulevard.

Lakeview Park was part of the grand Lake Washington Boulevard design proposed by the Olmsted Brothers in 1903. It was developed in 1910 as "a resting spot on the parkway where a sweeping view of Lake Washington and the Cascade Mountains can be obtained from a sightly knoll." It still serves that purpose admirably.

Madison Park and Beach

43rd E. at the foot of E. Madison
Size: 12.1 acres (7.5 acres shorelands)
Bus: 11
Major uses: swimming, picnics, views

DESCRIPTION
Madison Park residents work hard to make their neighborhood quiet, friendly, and relaxed. Their grassy park slopes down to a 400-foot beach, with cement steps on the north and a short sandy portion on the south near a tall apartment building. The beach includes a bathhouse with restrooms, bike rack, raft with one- and three- meter diving boards, roped-in swimming area for children, and well-placed benches for parents to keep an eye on them. Lifeguards are on duty in the summer. A public fishing pier is north of the beach at the foot of Madison.

On the west side of 43rd E., a high and dry portion of the park includes two lighted tennis courts. For more children's activities, follow 43rd north a block to E. Lynn and a sloping play area.

NEARBY ATTRACTIONS
After your park visit, you might want to walk south a block to see old **Pioneer Hall,** a community center and museum constructed in

1910. It is open to the public from 1 to 4 p.m. on the second Sunday of each month.

You may also want to inspect some of the many inviting shops and eateries nearby. The **Crepe de Paris** (1927 43rd E., 329-6620) concocts delicious crepes in the classic French style. For a quick cup of coffee and luscious pastries Tuesday through Saturday, stop in at Stoll's 30-year-old **Madison Park Bakery** (4214 E. Madison, 322-3238). Sample some of the wide variety of cheeses at the **Cheese Shop** (4122 E. Madison, 323-6110), or try an omelette at **Eggs Cetera** (4220 E. Madison, 324-4140), a block down the street.

For interesting views of old architecture, get the city's "Madison Park Walking Tour" brochure by calling 625-4534.

HISTORY

The original Madison Park was the gala creation of pioneer judge John J. McGilvra, who once practised law in Chicago with Abraham Lincoln, and was later appointed by President Lincoln as U.S. Attorney for Washington Territory.

McGilvra staked his homestead claim on Lake Washington just south of Union Bay. There, in the 1880s, he and his wife Elizabeth built an estate and cut a rough wagon road straight through the wilderness to Pioneer Square. Soon stagecoaches rumbled over the rutted thoroughfare. Picnickers on their way to the lakeshore gawked at bear and deer and beautiful raw land. And McGilvra went into the real estate business.

When the cable car came of age, McGilvra and other realtors formed the Madison Street Cable Railway Company and began scheming to lure prospective buyers. They developed the lakeshore with a boathouse, piers, a promenade, a paddlewheel steamer, floating bandstands, beer and gambling halls, baseball and football fields, and a greenhouse abounding with exotic plants. Their park soon became the most popular beach in the city. Cable cars ran to it all year long, departing from Pioneer Square every two minutes on summer Sundays. Hundreds disembarked at the foot of Madison to board steamers for cruises on Lake Washington. Hundreds more lined the shore to listen to bands on rafts blaring out John Phillip Sousa's marches. And sometimes thousands packed the beaches to watch over-the-water vaudeville acts, cheering with delight when the villain was tossed overboard.

McGilvra's flair for business and entertainment did not end here. For those who wanted to make it more than just a Sunday outing, he built wooden platforms near the beach where they could set up tents—for a price—and stay the entire summer if they wished. (Many did, and the "Tent City" area south of Blaine street flourished for years.) Also, instead of selling his own lakeshore land,

McGilvra invited prospective buyers to build cottages and then charged them a yearly tithe for the use of his property. This procedure earned him the reputation of being perhaps the only feudal lord in the country.

McGilvra died in 1903. Later, as the automobile became popular, the Cable Railway Company went into debt and the popularity of the park declined. The exotic plants were transferred to Volunteer Park. The famed Mosquito Fleet that had offered paddlewheel lake cruises was replaced by a ferry system, which itself became obsolete in 1940 with the construction of the Lake Washington Floating Bridge.

One relic of the early days that has remained relatively unchanged is Pioneer Hall on Blaine Street. This hall was built in 1910 with the $20,000 bequest of Sarah Denny, daughter of pioneer Arthur Denny. It was added to the National Register of Historic Places in 1971.

Roanoke Park

10th E. and E. Roanoke
Size: 2.2 acres
Bus: 9
Major use: neighborhood play area

DESCRIPTION
This is a small grassy park on Roanoke Street where the freeway branches east to the Evergreen Point Bridge. Because of all the traffic, it is anything but quiet, but even so it is a welcome relief from all the actvity around it. Neighborhood people especially enjoy dropping by for seasonal glimpses of its domestic flowering trees, or sitting with a picnic lunch while kids romp in the play area.

HISTORY
The park was originally acquired in 1908 for hikers and bikers who took the looping boulevard run down the hill to Washington Park and Lake Washington. Its original owners, David T. Denny and Henry Fuhrman, named it after the first English settlement in America, Roanoke, Virginia.

South Passage Point

Fuhrman E. and Fairview E.
Size: 0.1 acre
Buses: 7, 8, 9, 22, 25
Major uses: waterside lounging, picnics

DESCRIPTION

Take a quick right off the south end of the University Bridge to find this welcome patch of grass by the water. It is nestled between the pillars of the Freeway Bridge on the passage between Portage Bay and Lake Union, directly across from its sister park, North Passage Point. People often come here for quick breathers, or to wade, sunbathe, and watch boats in a quiet spot beside willow trees. Two tables are provided for picnickers, who can sometimes smell barbecued salmon from Ivar's Salmon House across the channel.

NEARBY ATTRACTIONS

Blackberries abound in late summer along the stretch of Fairview just south of the park. And if the berries aren't in season, you can always foot it on up to Eastlake for a fresh strawberry sundae (with berries flown in from Australia!) at the **Cricket Restaurant** (2947 Eastlake E., 322-2226), gargantuan cakes and cookies at the **Great American Food and Beverage Company** (3119 Eastlake E., 325-8855), or a variety of giant hamburgers at the **Red Robin** (3272 Fuhrman E., 323-0917) by the University Bridge.

Tashkent Park

Boylston E. between E. Republican and E. Mercer
Size: 0.5 acre
Bus: 61
Major use: neighborhood resting spot

DESCRIPTION

Tashkent is a welcome backyard for a great many residents on the west side of Capitol Hill. Almost daily this grassy half-block—with red-brick patio, pergola, and lighted pathway connecting Boylston and Belmont avenues—draws apartment dwellers and business people for restful lunches and relief from the day's tensions.

HISTORY
Tashkent is one of many mini parks bought with Forward Thrust Bond money in an attempt to provide highly populated neighborhoods with more green space. This Capitol Hill park was originally called Belmont Mini Park while being developed. It was renamed Tashkent in 1973 after the fourth largest city in the Soviet Union. Once called the "City of Stone," Tashkent has a 2,000-year history and in 1220 was part of the domain of Genghis Khan. Today it has the largest cotton mill in the world. The Russian mayor of Seattle's "sister city" helped dedicate the park in 1973.

Thomas Mini Park

Bellevue E. and E. Thomas
Size: 0.3 acres
Bus: 14
Major use: neighborhood resting spot

DESCRIPTION
Here's a wee bit o' green hillside under a 100-year-old chestnut tree on the west side of Capitol Hill. Drinking fountain, two benches, and a tiny table make it another welcome backyard in the midst of apartment houses. Walk (carefully) out into Thomas Street for a good hillside view of the Space Needle and the sound. The park was bought in 1970 with Forward Thrust Bond money.

Viretta Park

39th and E. John
Size: 1.8 acres
Bus: none nearby
Major use: boulevard views

DESCRIPTION
A grassy lookout below steep slopes and brush, this park is suitable for a quick stop and a look at the lake while on your boulevard tour. It could also be a delectable stop around mid-August when the

blackberries are ripe. Stairs lead up to 39th and John from the boulevard.

The park was a gift from landowners Charles Denny and Elbert Blaine in 1901. It was named after Denny's wife, Viretta, a distant relative of Andrew Jackson.

Volunteer Park

15th E. and E. Prospect
Size: 44.5 acres
Buses: 9, 10
Major uses: art, flowers, views, picnics

DESCRIPTION

Volunteer Park is distinctly a people's park—a fountain of activity and renewal near the heart of busy Capitol Hill. Bordered by residences on three sides and a cemetery on the fourth, the park draws people from all around for all kinds of reasons: to tour the Seattle Art Museum and the Conservatory, to climb the water tower, and to lounge and play on the open grasses. The park is periodically the scene of bicycle races, rock concerts, ribald open air theatre productions, and kite-flying contests. Monuments, statues, and sculptures have been erected here to commemorate everything and everyone imaginable, from stately William Seward to the Eager Beaver Junior Gardeners and the sinking of the *Maine*. And along with its regular visitors, Volunteer is filled with regular residents— pigeons, crows, and squirrels—who make their homes among trees and eaves and who find that "the livin' is easy" on human handouts.

Enter this four-block-square park by car from either the northeast corner off 15th E., or from 14th E. on the south. Better yet, go on foot, since parking is limited and you can easily find your destination with minimal walking.

The Seattle Art Museum (447-4710) is centrally located, facing the water reservoir and views of the Space Needle through a marble sculpture called "Black Sun," by Isamu Noguchi. (Some call it the "doughnut.") The museum entrance—graced with marble sculptures of rams, camels, a tiger, and warriors, all of which used to guard the tombs of fifteenth- and sixteenth-century Chinese noblemen—offers permanent exhibits of Asian and European classical art, as well as exclusive shows and traveling exhibits from all over the world.

Art museum hours are from noon to 5 p.m. Sundays, 10 a.m. to 5 p.m. Tuesday through Saturday, and from 7 to 10 p.m. Thursday

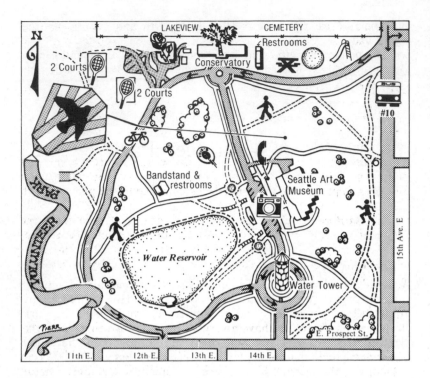

evenings. Admission is $1 for adults, $.50 for students and seniors, and free on Thursdays.

The Conservatory (625-4043) at the north end of the park is three large greenhouses filled with such exotic plants as orchids, orange begonia, velvet gloxinia, jewel box, and sensitivity plant.

The Conservatory is open daily from 9 a.m. to 5 p.m., including holidays. There is no admission charge. Group tours can be arranged by calling first.

The Water Tower is at the south side of the park just beyond the 14th Avenue entrance. Its 106 steps spiral around the old water tank to an observation deck seventy-five feet above the park. With Capitol Hill under that, you have a 360-degree bird's eye view of the park gardens and the city from a level not much below that of the Space Needle.

A bandstand with twenty-amp outlets and restrooms in the back is on the sloping northwest lawn. During summer concerts and open-air stage productions put on by the Empty Space Theatre (for free), the grass here becomes a magnet for human and canine crowds and Frisbees.

Tennis courts (two upper and two lower) and a backboard are located in the northwest corner of the park.

A play area, which dominates the northeast corner, features a large wading pool, a fort, and a geodesic climbing dome. Occasional benches and picnic tables are located here and throughout the park.

NEARBY ATTRACTIONS

During the summer you can usually find a portable snack bar in front of the Art Museum. For more substantial meals, go south on 15th E. a few blocks. There you will find a variety of cafes, restaurants, and groceries.

Lakeview Cemetery. This famous graveyard, where plaques and tombs mark the final resting spots of many of Seattle's early pioneers, is just north of the northeast entrance to the park on 15th E.

Louisa Boren Lookout. A superb view of Lake Union and Lake Washington from E. Olin Place, just east of the cemetery entrance.

For further explorations of the area (and especially for architectural delights), order a copy of the city's "Capitol Hill Walking Tour" by calling 625-4534.

HISTORY

Volunteer Park did not have a very auspicious beginning. Its forty-odd acres were originally bought by the city for $2,000 from a sawmill engineer named J. M. Colman (see "Colman Park"). From 1876 to 1887, it was called Washelli Cemetery. Its future began looking a little brighter when the gravestones were removed and it took on the new name of Lake View Park.

By 1892, the city had cleared enough timber to plant a nursery and greenhouse, but the new park was by no means popular. In fact, that same year, Park Superintendent E. O. Schwagerl announced that he hoped to exchange it for a better one (Seward) on Lake Washington. Both he and the park commissioners petitioned the city council for the trade, complaining that City Park, as it was now called, was too isolated, too expensive to maintain, and "exceedingly high and dry." Luckily, the council rejected their plan.

The turn of the century established a firmer identity for the park, and for the neighborhood itself. In 1889 it was one of the sites offered to the legislature for the new state capitol. In 1901, the mound on which the park is situated was named after Capitol Hill of Denver, Colorado. That same year, the park's name was changed to Volunteer to honor the veterans of the Spanish-American War, which was still under way. The water department built a reservoir, which made the area a little less "high and dry," and paths, lawns, flower beds, settees, and swings began attracting more people.

By this time, Capitol Hill had become a haven for Seattle's richest citizens. Many of them were drawn to the north end of 14th

Avenue, which led to the park's south entrance. There they built twenty-room mansions with leaded Italian glass windows and hitching posts for horse-drawn carriages. The street became known as "Millionaires' Row.'

Volunteer Park's lasting identity and design was developed by the Olmsted Brothers in 1904. During the next eight years, the park was shaped to conform to their sweeping plan: formal gardens, circling drives, lily ponds, central concourse with vine-covered pergola and music pavilion, and finally (in 1912) the conservatory.

Construction of the water tower in 1906 added considerably to the park's popularity, as did the frequent concerts during and after the Alaska-Yukon-Pacific Exposition. Landscapers planted heavily on the east side of the park to keep children from running into the trolley tracks on 15th Avenue. A hedge was planted to replace the walkway around the lily ponds.

The pergola and music pavilion was replaced in 1932 by the massive Seattle Art Museum. This building and its original art collection were gifts from Mrs. Eugene Fuller and her son, Dr. Richard Fuller, who became its director.

Over the years, Volunteer Park and Capitol Hill have mellowed. As one old-timer recently put it, "Around the turn of the century you used to have to wear a tophat to walk down Broadway." The neighborhood is much more homogeneous these days. It doesn't matter how much money you have, and it certainly doesn't matter what you wear in the park!

Washington Park/Arboretum

E. Madison and Lake Washington Boulevard E.
Size: 172.5 acres
Buses: 11 to south end; 4, 48 to west side
Major uses: nature, walking, jogging, fishing

DESCRIPTION

Washington Park is a beautiful woodland stretching from the south shore of Union Bay to E. Madison Street. Lying along the west side of the Broadmoor Golf Club, it is shaped like a giant squid, with boulevards and pathways along the contours of its body, and freeway tentacles entwining marshy islands and canals at its head. The body of the park is the home of the University of Washington Arboretum, with its labeled plantings of over 4,000 different species of trees, shrubs, vines, flowers, and herbs.

The marsh and island area, with pathways running through forests of cattails, trees, and concrete freeway pillars, is the most amazing mixture of civilization and wilderness in the city. It is at once a haven for wildlife, nature students, hikers, swimmers, canoers, fishermen, and cars.

The Arboretum's miles of graveled pathways are also favorites for hikers, joggers and dogs (on leashes, please), as well as bird-watchers and photographers. Picnic tables are few, but the trees and open grass offer thousands of private places to put down blankets and baskets. Restrooms are available only at the Visitor Center and Madison Playfield.

OFFICES AND PROGRAMS

To familiarize yourself with the Arboretum, start with the offices near the south entrance:

The Visitor Center (543-8800) is open from 8 a.m. to 5 p.m. weekdays all year, and Sundays from 10 a.m.to 5 p.m. during April and May. Here you can get information and buy selected books and pamphlets.

The Arboretum Foundation Office (325-4510) is open from 9 a.m. to 4:30 p.m. weekdays only. Information, postcards, books, and pamphlets relating to the Arboretum, and a horticultural reference library are inside. For information on educational programs, tours, and foundation membership, call during business hours.

The Northwest Ornamental Horticultural Society (325-4510), a nonprofit organization affiliated with the Arboretum, holds monthly program meetings featuring subjects such as garden shaping, pruning, seeds, bulbs, soil, and native plants. Meetings are open to the public. Get a schedule by calling during business hours.

Public classes offered through the Arboretum are listed quarterly in *Spectrum* magazine, available free by calling 543-5290.

A QUICK TOUR OF THE ARBORETUM

The plant exhibits. Azalea Way and Arboretum Drive are the park's two main thoroughfares, which branch out into a myriad of other trails. Some go through glens of maples and magnolias; others through plantings of hollies and multicolored rhododendrons; still others through groves of pines, ashes, and giant sequoias.

You will find rare specimens here, too—for example, the meta-sequoia, a prehistoric redwood once thought to be extinct; and the bristlecone pine, which lives for 4,000 years. There are plants here from nearly every temperate region of the world—cypress from California, eucalyptus from Tasmania and Australia, oriental sweet-

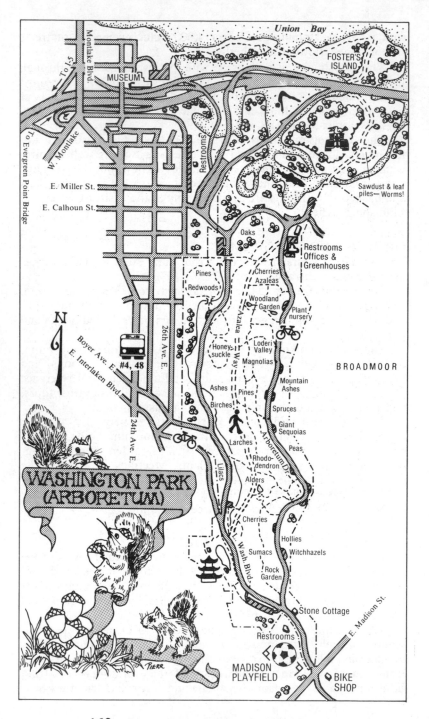

Union Bay

FOSTER'S ISLAND

To I-5

Montlake Blvd.

W. Montlake

MUSEUM

To Evergreen Point Bridge

E. Miller St.

E. Calhoun St.

Restrooms

Sawdust & leaf piles— Worms!

Oaks

Restrooms Offices & Greenhouses

Pines Redwoods

Cherries Azaleas

Woodland Garden

Plant nursery

N

Boyer Ave. E.

E. Interlaken Blvd.

#4, 48

Honey-suckle

Loderi Valley

Azalea Way

Magnolias

BROADMOOR

26th Ave. E.

Ashes Birches

Pines

Mountain Ashes

Spruces

Giant Sequoias

24th Ave. E.

Larches

Arboretum Dr.

Peas

WASHINGTON PARK (ARBORETUM)

Lilacs

Rhodo-dendron

Alders

Cherries

Hollies

Witchhazels

L. Wash. Blvd.

Sumacs

Rock Garden

E. Madison St.

Stone Cottage

PIERR

Restrooms

MADISON PLAYFIELD

BIKE SHOP

gum and sycamore from Turkey, and the delicate silk tree from Asia.

Japanese Tea Garden. Turn off Lake Washington Boulevard near the south end of the park to see the tea garden, with ornamental plants adorning rockeries and water trickling into glassy pools. The original teahouse burned down in 1973, but the garden is still a beauty. Hours from late spring through early fall are 10 a.m. to 7 p.m. every day, and on weekends only during the winter.

Waterfront Trail. At the north end of the Arboretum you can tour the marshlands by taking a one-and-a-half mile loop trail along the Waterfront Trail. A good place to start is from the parking lot behind the Museum of History and Industry. From here, follow bridges and floating pathways through a forest of cattails to **Foster's Island.** The waters along the way are sprinkled with lily pads and tiny duckweed disks, and the air is alive with all kinds of birds. Bridges and platforms along the way provide spots for fishing, picnicking, and watching waterfowl. You will also see fine views of Union Bay, the university campus, and cars roaring onto the Evergreen Point Bridge.

The Marsh Channels. On Foster's Island the trail goes under the freeway through wooded glens to more marsh channels near the Broadmoor Golf Club. From here you can curve back to Lake Washington Boulevard and the museum. But don't miss the fascinating channels by the freeway ramps. Here, cars stream high over the water past the butt ends of concrete interchanges. A kayak slalom course dangles among concrete pillars. Cliff swallows paste gourdlike nests to the undersides of the freeway. Climbers sometimes sling ropes from ramps and hang baboonlike in the air. Divers leap from ramp edges while the water and grass around them abound with swimmers, sunbathers, boaters, and fishermen.

Join them, if you like, by either walking across the grass from the parking area by Lake Washington Boulevard, or by renting a canoe for $1.50 an hour at the University of Washington Waterfront Activities Center behind the football stadium.

If you like to fish, the marsh channels are teeming with bass, perch, crappies, chub, catfish, trout, and crawfish from early spring through fall. You say you forgot the bait? No matter. Several piles of leaves and sawdust on Foster's Island provide good digging for worms (see map for location).

Spring and summer are the most popular times to tour the marsh, but certainly not the only times. Take your camera, binoculars, or hand lens out some early fall morning when dewdrops hang from spider webs, or in the winter when the grass and bulrushes are bleached and frosted with ice crystals.

THINGS TO REMEMBER
The Arboretum gounds are open from 8 a.m. to sunset. There is no admission fee. There is no food in the park—unless you're content with squirrels' fare, in which case the trees will supply you with plenty. For more palatable items, walk west a few blocks to 24th E. near the north end of the park. **Stop 'n' Go** (2401 E. McGraw) has groceries round-the-clock, and a few blocks farther north the **Super Foods Grocery** on E. Roanoke has a wider selection. Beer and sandwiches are abundant at **Jilly's East Tavern** (2307 24th E., 322-1930), and **Kelly's Bar-B-Q** (2305 24th E., 322-3300) is nearby, too.

HISTORY
Washington Park was originally a rough, forested ravine with a stream runing along its length into Union Bay. Its timber was particularly attractive to the Puget Mill Company, which logged off the best trees before 1900. The company then gave sixty-two of its northernmost acres to the city in exchange for $35,000 worth of water-main work on a nearby real estate development.

Meanwhile, pioneer judge John J. McGilvra had established his wilderness estate on Lake Washington, just south of Union Bay. He put in a road to Elliott Bay, and soon Madison Street began clanging with trolleys. Madison became the southern boundary of Washington Park after the city bought the rest of the ravine.

In 1903 Seattle began planning the Alaska-Yukon-Pacific Exposition to celebrate its cityhood and the gold rush that had brought it riches. The Olmsted Brothers of Brookline, Massachusetts, were hired to design a boulevard through Washington Park as a major entryway to the exposition. The result was Lake Washington Boulevard, which follows the contours of the land and stream bed from Madison Street to the university. It quickly became the city's most popular thoroughfare.

Washington Park had space for other thoroughfares, too. At the time of the exposition, in 1909, the automobile was still only a curiosity. That year, horse owners developed a raceway for harness horses along what is now Azalea Way. For the next ten years, cheering spectators were periodically treated to the sight of steeds with flaring nostrils pounding along the dusty parkway, with wild-eyed drivers cracking whips beind them.

Change came rapidly as the years went by. Horses were replaced by automobiles. A surge of interest in golf around 1915 led to the subdivision of the park's east boundary and the creation of the exclusive Broadmoor Golf Club. In 1916, the Lake Washington Ship Canal lowered the lake level by nine feet, creating the Union Bay marshlands. Dredging and filling operations expanded the shoreline still farther.

The Arboretum itself was the inspiration of a determined history professor named Edmond S. Meany. Meany ran for the state legislature in 1881 with the sole mission of wrangling land for the university campus. Having succeeded in this, he established a school of forestry. In his own home garden he planted tree seeds sent to him from all over the world. Then, with student help and hand-carried bucketfuls of water, he transplanted them onto the campus and began a seed exchange program with foreign universities.

For many years construction on a rapidly expanding campus threatened to uproot Meany's dream. But in 1924, by a happy coincidence, the city began moving several of its nurseries to the northeast portion of Washington Park. University president Henry Suzallo proposed joint use of the park as a city nursery and Arboretum classroom for the university's growing forestry and botany departments. Ten years later, in 1934, a formal agreement between the city and the university set aside the Arboretum to be jointly operated, under management of the university. The Arboretum Foundation was founded the following year.

State and federal work relief programs during the Depression began to develop the park according to the recommendations of the Olmsted Brothers, the Arboretum Foundation, and the Seattle Garden Society; and the first planting took place in May of 1937. In 1938, an unseccessful attempt was made to "transplant" 600 fireflies into the Arboretum from the East Coast. Two years later, 300 Japanese cherry trees and 200 eastern dogwoods were planted along Azalea Way, followed the next year by 1,500 rhododendron plants in Rhododendron Glen. Today about 900 plants are added to the Arboretum's greenery every year, most of them raised from seedlings in the nursery. The ultimate goal of the Arboretum is to test-grow and reproduce every type of woody plant that the area can support.

The natural growth of the Arboretum has often been threatened by competing developments. One of the most recent came in 1963, when fifty-four acres of plantings were uprooted and relocated to make way for construction of the Evergreen Point Bridge across Lake Washington. The proposed R. H. Thomson Freeway, which was to connect with the bridge over the Arboretum, was halted by citizen lawsuits, resulting in several ramps that dead-end over the marsh channels. As if to reemphasize the park's usefulness as a nature sanctuary, the Waterfront Trail was built as a joint university-federal-city project in 1971.

The Japanese Tea Garden was a natural outgrowth of the Alaska-Yukon-Pacific Exposition, which emphasized the economic interdependence of the Pacific Rim countries. Several teahouses were established in Seattle prior to the one in the Arboretum—one in Madison Park just after the world's fair of 1909, and another at 5th and University in 1930. The Arboretum Foundation began pushing its tea garden plans as early as 1937, but the present one was not built until 1960. Its authentic design was a gift from Japanese cities and included a magnificent teahouse, which burned down in 1973.

West Montlake Park

E. Shelby and W. Park Drive E.
Size: 2.0 acres
Buses: 4, 25, 48
Major uses: waterside views and walks

DESCRIPTION
Turn west onto E. Shelby Street just south of the Montlake Bridge to this stretch of flat grass bordering the Seattle Yacht Club and Montlake area homes. Magnificent poplar trees line the bulkhead and a few sturdy benches look out onto Portage Bay.

NEARBY ATTRACTIONS
From the park you can follow the **Waterfront Trail** east along the Lake Washington Ship Canal to fishing spots and the **Museum of History and Industry**. This is also a particularly exciting place to be on the yachting season's opening day, the first Saturday in May, when eight-oared sculls race through the **Montlake Cut** and yachts and sailboats clog the channel for as far as the eye can see. The University of Washington crew races are also held here on Saturdays from March through May. Call 543-2210 for schedules.

HISTORY
West Montlake was part of the Montlake Park land claim filed in 1908, about the time the city was gearing up for the Alaska-Yukon-Pacific Exposition on the university grounds to the north of the canal. The construction of the Lake Washington Ship Canal in 1917 made this enclave an especially good spot for yacht clubs and boat moorages. A former casino at this site was bought and converted into the Seattle Yacht Club, and in 1929 the U.S. Bureau of Fisheries constructed its laboratories nearby. The Waterfront Trail was constructed in 1971. (For more history, see "East Montlake and McCurdy Park.")

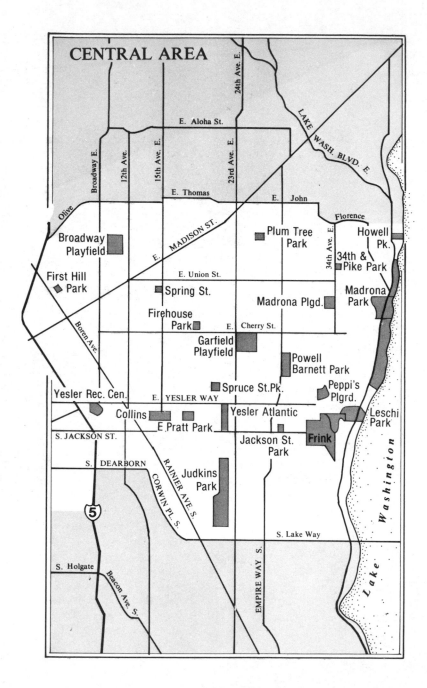

CENTRAL AREA

Broadway Playfield

First Hill Park

Plum Tree Park

Howell Pk.

34th & Pike Park

Madrona Park

Spring St.

Madrona Plgd.

Firehouse Park

Garfield Playfield

Powell Barnett Park

Peppi's Plgrd.

Yesler Rec. Cen.

Spruce St. Pk.

Collins

E. Pratt Park

Yesler Atlantic

Leschi Park

Jackson St. Park

Frink

Judkins Park

Lake Washington

6
Central Area Parks

Either go far into the wilderness where no has been, or else find some undiscovered place under everybody's nose.

—Aldo Leopold

Edwin T. Pratt Park

18th S. and S. Washington
Size: 5.5 acres
Bus: 27
Major uses: playground, ceramic arts

DESCRIPTION
This play and picnic ground and fine arts center fits beautifully alongside a modern apartment complex just southeast of the Langston Hughes Cultural Center. Picnic tables and benches on asphalt give a narrow view of the Olympics from beside the ten-story Kawabe Memorial House, a fashionable retirement home. The Wonder Bread factory borders the park on S. Main.

Residents of the retirement home love to walk and sit in this park, their "backyard." But it's certainly not intended only for their enjoyment. The exciting play area nearly empties the apartment complex of kids in the evenings. Older kids flock to the nearby basketball pavilion in fair weather and foul. And the Fine Arts Center (625-4572) offers Central Area residents classes in all kinds of ceramic arts, from pottery and metal sculpture to glass blowing and jewelry making.

East of the apartment complex, a large grassy area has six picnic tables, each with a barbecue stand and shady trees, plus lots of room to run around in an open field.

NEARBY ATTRACTIONS
The Langston Hughes Cultural Arts Center (17th S. and E. Yesler Way, 329-0115), a former synagogue, is a multipurpose facility that offers courses for all ages in a multiplicity of arts and crafts, from

African drums and dance to cooking, flower arranging, and karate. The center also includes a theatre and a day care center.

HISTORY

The beginnings of the Central Area are attributable to an enterprising black named William Grose. Grose came to Seattle in 1859, six years after sailing to Japan with the famous Commodore Peary. Having distinguished himself in the Navy, he was invited by Washington Governor Isaac Stevens to manage the town's second hotel, located on the south side of Mill Street (now Yesler Way). Under Grose's management, "Our House" prospered and became a favorite meeting place for Seattle businessmen. Grose prospered, too, joining the Chamber of Commerce and eventually accumulating enough money to make a sizeable loan to pioneer lumberman Henry Yesler.

In repayment for the loan, Yesler gave Grose a large section of property south of Madison Street and east of First Hill. Blacks and other ethnic groups found themselves particularly welcome in this "Central Area" (but not anywhere else), and it became the core of Seattle's minority population.

Europeans also settled in this area, many of them fleeing the intolerable tenement conditions on the East Coast. Among them were Jewish immigrants, who built the city's first synagogue at 8th and Seneca Street. In 1914, the Seattle Bikur Cholim Congregation built a magnificent synagogue at the corner of 17th and Yesler; the building was converted into the Langston Hughes Cultural Arts Center in 1917.

The Fine Arts Center was originally a one-man bakery owned by Soren N. Sorensen in 1920. In 1926, it was bought and remodeled by the Continental Baking Company, then later was used as a garage by the Wonder Bread Baking Company. Today it is a center for ceramic arts, and its ovens bake bowls instead of bread.

The park site was first bought by the city in 1958 as part of the grounds for the Washington Junior High School, a block to the east. In 1966, it was chosen as the site for a park and low income housing project—a federal-state-local effort called Operation Breakthrough. The Bryant Manor Apartments and playground on the park's northwest corner were the focus of the project.

In 1976, the park was named after Edwin T. Pratt, a community leader who lived in the area. His efforts led to the founding of many self-help and equal rights programs, including the Central Area Motivation Program and the Seattle Opportunities Industrialization Center. Pratt was assassinated in the doorway of his home in 1969.

Firehouse Mini Park

18th between E. Columbia and E. Cherry
Size: 0.3 acre
Bus: 2
Major use: playground

DESCRIPTION

"Help! Rescue me!" pleads a little girl pretending to be trapped on the second story of a gaily colored tree house. This double-decker with fire pole is the favorite in this tiny park, but there are other things packed in here, too: a boxed-in play area, drinking fountain, benches, and a maple-shaded promenade leading to a heptagonal wading pool. This park's small trees also make it a good cooling off place for pedestrians overheated by walking among large buildings.

The park was purchased in 1970 with Forward Thrust funds. It is located on the south side of the renovated firehouse that now holds the offices of the Central Area Motivation Program. The Central Area Welfare Office is just across the street, and south of Cherry are the clustered buildings of Providence Medical Center. About a block north is the **Church of the Immaculate Conception,** Seattle's oldest Catholic Church (built in 1904). Its stained glass windows were made in Germany, and Jesuit frescoes adorn the interior.

First Hill Mini Park

University and Minor
Size: 0.2 acre
Bus: 2 to Minor and Seneca
Major use: urban resting spot

DESCRIPTION

This is one of Seattle's newest parks (finished in the fall of 1978), and a more deserving area for its breathing space could hardly be found. It takes up only a sixth of a block in an area so crowded with hospitals it has become known as "Pill Hill." Already, harried pedestrians are making good use of its few benches, flowers and blades of grass.

NEARBY ATTRACTIONS

The many hospitals on the hill may be attractions for some, but a much better one is the old **Joshua Green Mansion** (1204 Minor) next door. This pioneer businessman's twenty-eight-room home, with crystal chandeliers and turn-of-the-century interiors, is now open for tours Monday through Friday at 11 a.m., 1 p.m., and 3 p.m., and can even be rented for parties. Call 624-0474 for arrangements.

Frink Park

Lake Washington Boulevard S. and S. Jackson
Size: 19.6 acres
Bus: 27
Major use: natural woods drive

DESCRIPTION

Follow Blaine Boulevard up behind Leschi Park and through a tunnel, and take a winding spin through this primitive ravine park. It's so thickly overgrown with old trees and spiraling vines that it looks like a tropical forest. The boulevard winds over bridges and past steep hillside staircases, straightening out into Lake Washington Boulevard as it leaves the park. A small parking spot is located at the foot of Frink Place, which leads up a steep hill to Yesler Way and the Leschi Elementary School.

HISTORY

This park was donated to the city in 1907 by John M. Frink, who lived in a mansion at 31st and Jackson Street. Frink was a schoolteacher, park board member, Washington State senator, and founder of the Washington Iron Works. His park was spruced up for the 1909 Alaska-Yukon-Pacific Exposition with a bridge over the ravine, dams with pools, paths, benches, and rustic footbridges. It offered magnificent views and secluded retreats to early travelers along the boulevard.

Howell Park

E. Howell off Lake Washington Boulevard E.
Size: 1.2 acres
Bus: none nearby
Major use: small beach

DESCRIPTION
If you come by car, you might as well pass this one by, because there is no place to park. If coming by foot, turn left onto Howell Street, which quickly turns into two *private driveways*. The trail to the beach starts between the driveways, just to the right of a cyclone fence, and leads down through woods to a beach lawn.

HISTORY
Howell Park was one of several small chunks of property donated to the city by realtors Elbert Blaine and Charles Denny. Denny and his wife, Viretta, first called this one "Children's Park," but the name was changed so that the public would not confuse it with a playground. Both the street and the park are named after Captain Jefferson D. Howell, the brother-in-law of Confederate President Jefferson Davis. Howell was killed when his ship sank off Neah Bay in 1875.

Jackson Street Mini Park

28th S. and S. Jackson
Size: 0.5 acre
Buses: 14, or 38 to S. Jackson and Empire Way
Major use: neighborhood playground

DESCRIPTION
This little park on bustling Jackson Street attracts children to its basketball hoop, slide, sky fort, balance beam, and drinking fountain. The park is bordered on one side by the Cedar Tree Tavern, and on the other by the Tabernacle Missionary Baptist Church. Often quiet during the day, it is crowded with five-to-thirteen-year-olds every summer evening. An undulating concrete wall, brightly painted with fish and fantasy figures, keeps them from overflowing onto the street.

In 1853 Doc Maynard named Jackson Street in honor of President Andrew Jackson. The park was bought with Forward Thrust funds in 1969.

 # Judkins Park and Playfield

Between S. Lane and Day from 21st to 22nd S.
Size: 5.4 acres
Bus: 48
Major uses: playfields, picnics, athletics

DESCRIPTION

Judkins is a multi-purpose park corridor in the Central Area, just north of the approach to the old Lake Washington Floating Bridge. Its six-block stip of green enlivens the Rainier Valley with picnic, play, and sports areas—and with grass, grass, and more lovely grass.

The park is roughly divided into two sections, north and south. For access to the south part, turn west off 23rd S. at Day Street and drive to the parking lot. Asphalt paths lead to modern picnic and play areas, a shelter, barbecues, basketball hoops, a pentagonal lookout area with benches, and restrooms. North of S. Norman Street you will find another shelter house, two spacious ballfields, play equipment, lots of open green fields, and restrooms. More parking space can be found on the east and north sides.

Both an abundance of facilities and attractive landscaping here draw residents from all over the Central Area and Rainier Valley all year long. The park is kept well lighted at night by a veritable forest of lamps.

HISTORY

This park was a long time in coming, but it was worth the wait. In pioneer days, the site of Judkins Park was a ravine thirty-five to forty feet deep in places. After 1910, when the area had become well settled and was predominantly an Italian community, the city began filling the ravine with garbage to create more play space. But the accumulating trash created more of a stink than a play space, and after 1930, dirt was dumped on top to dilute the accumulating odors. Even so, area residents continued to turn their noses up at the fermenting playground as odiferous gases continued to escape from the unstable fill.

The Lake Washington Bridge approach at the south end of the park site was built in 1940. Six years later, a scattered patchwork of private and public land—thirty acres in all—was set aside as a potential Civil Defense airport site and designated temporarily for park and recreation purposes. It was named Scavotto's Playground, after the city councilman who had made it a reality.

But when bulldozers began contouring it into a park, they only unearthed more decaying garbage. This disappointment was followed by more dirt fill and grading. Two of the thirty acres were finally made into a ballfield in 1952 and named Judkins Playground from the adjacent street named after pioneer realtor Norman B. Judkins.

But then there were more delays; further land consolidation and park plans were put off by the proposal for a second Lake Washington Bridge paralleling the first. Then half of the acreage was given to the school board for construction of Washington Junior High School joint-use playfield in 1959.

Finally, in 1973, with Forward Thrust dollars and considerable lobbying from Central Area groups, the park began to take on a more substantial shape. Modern playgrounds and playfields were eventually fused in a six-block strip that now serves as the Central Area's most attractive multiple-use park.

Leschi Park

Lakeside S. and Leschi Place
Size: 15.2 acres
Bus: 27
Major uses: walking, gardens, lake views

DESCRIPTION

Located across the street from the Hindquarter Restaurant and the Yacht Basin buildings, Leschi Park is a well-manicured, rolling hillside of grass planted with exotic trees and gardens of roses. Pathways follow an undulating terrain to restrooms above. A path to the right leads to a tennis court, and one to the left goes on up to a playground with slides and a sand box. A grassy spot under willows on the east side of Lakeside S. looks out on acres of sailboats and and old-time ferry.

NEARBY ATTRACTIONS

If you've gotten hungry along your boulevard tour, you can find food at the **Leschi Mart** (103 Lakeside S., 322-0700) or at the fancy **Hindquarter Restaurant** (102 Lakeside S., 329-2255).

The Yacht Basin just north includes public boat moorages, a fishing pier, and the **Corinthian Yacht Club** (122 Lakeside S., 322-7877), where you can sign up for sailing classes.

HISTORY

Geologists have discovered that Leschi's sloping hills and steep shoreline are the remains of an ancient landslide that created a steep cliff into Lake Washington. The park was a former campsite of Leschi, chief of the Nisqually tribe.

Chief Leschi himself is famed for his part in the Battle of Seattle. The Indians, angered by the 1854 treaty that took away their land, attacked the settlement on January 26, 1856. Two settlers and countless Indians were killed. Later, by order of Territorial Governor Isaac Stevens, Leschi was arrested, chained in public view for months until weak and emaciated, and then hanged.

In 1889, Leschi's campsite became an amusement park at the end of the Lake Washington Cable Railway's trolley line from Pioneer Square along Yesler Way. Like other real estate schemes of the day, the park was intended to lure customers out to buy land. Attractions included a bandstand, boathouse with canoe and rowboat rentals, a casino, a dock for sidewheel steamers, vaudeville acts, zoo animals, and magnificent gardens.

The zoo and garden were created and lovingly tended for years by Seattle's first head-gardener, Jacob Umlauff, who was born in Hamburg, Germany, in 1871. Umlauff planted the stately giant sequoia that now stands in the park. He also cared for the Madison Park Zoo and Conservatory, and later for the Volunteer Park Conservatory until 1941. He died in 1954.

In 1903, the Seattle Electric Company, feeling the pinch of the 1893 Depression, donated Leschi's zoo animals to the city, which elicited the following commentary from a local paper: "These animals have proven quite a drawing card at the park, and the company has made considerable money hauling people out to look at them. It has, however, taken considerable of the profits to feed them. Hereafter, the animals will be maintained at one of the parks [Woodland], and the company will make just as much money hauling people out to see them, but the city will have to rustle for their grub."

The company sold the park itself to the city in 1909, the year of the Alaska-Yukon-Pacific Exposition. For fear of landslides, Lake Washington Boulevard (which was constructed partly as a tourist attraction for the fair) was routed away from the shoreline here and wound up into the hills. Lakeside Avenue, along the shoreline, was not constructed until 1925.

There have been changes beyond the shoreline, too. The steamboats quit their runs shortly after the lake level was lowered in 1917 by the opening of the Lake Washington Ship Canal. And the ferries, which once carted passengers and vehicles across to Mercer Island and Kirkland, went out of business after construction of the Lake Washington Floating Bridge in 1940. The Corinthian Yacht Club moorage was added after 1949, and more moorage space was put in north of the park after 1960.

Madrona Park and Beach

Lake Washington Boulevard and Madrona Drive
Size: 16.3 acres
Bus: 2
Major uses: swimming, picnics, views, dance

DESCRIPTION
On the north end of this park, a wide, grassy strip leads to a bulkheaded beach. Joggers lope by on a beaten waterside path and speedboats and sailboats skim over the lake. Conveniences include a picnic shelter, restrooms, and five sturdy picnic tables. The upper part of the park west of Lake Washington Boulevard is a steep, natural hillside growing thick with trees and vines.

Just south of the park proper is Madrona Beach, home of the **Madrona Dance Studio** (625-4303). The studio is open from 9 a.m. to 9 p.m. Monday through Friday all year, and also on Saturdays from 9 a.m. to 3 p.m. during the school year. Dance classes for children and adults include every kind of body gyration imaginable: modern ballet, jazz, primitive, yoga, tai chi, tumbling, gymnastics, disco, and more. The park department and Dance Advisory Council also present performances by dance companies from all over the country at Meany Hall. Tickets are usually sold out well in advance, so call early.

In front of the studio, a sandy, bulkheaded beach borders Lake Washington. Facilities include restrooms, a raft with a one-meter diving board, and benches. Lifeguards are on duty in the summer. A large parking lot just south of the bathhouse parks ninety-four cars, and is a popular place at any time of the year to sit and munch on a sandwich while viewing the lake.

NEARBY ATTRACTIONS
Along the shore just south of Madrona Beach, a cinder pathway leads under weeping willows to a fishing pier and to the **Leschi Boat Moorage.**

Lake Washington Boulevard runs out here, turning into Lakeside Avenue, and opening up into a triangular area bordering **Leschi Park.** You can find the boulevard again by jogging right on Blaine Boulevard, which heads uphill through a small tunnel behind Leschi Park. Then it winds through the undeveloped woods of Frink Park to a straight, uninspiring three-fourths mile of Lake Washington Boulevard, which switches back down to the beach again at Colman Park. A viewpoint overlooks the floating bridge on this stretch, but it is unmaintained and overgrown with brush. It's more enjoyable (and simpler) to stay on Lakeside Avenue as you go south.

HISTORY
Madrona Park was named for the many madrona trees that were (and in some places still are) leaning out over the lake. It was first a private "trolley park," developed by the Seattle Electric Company, which ran a scenic trolley line from the top of the hill to the beach through the "deep, wild canyon" that is now Madrona Way. Enticements to prospective real estate investors included rustic shelters, swings, a boathouse on the lakefront, and even a hotel.

The park was sold to the city in 1908, and afterwards was operated as a public beach. A frame bathhouse built in 1926 was replaced with a brick structure in 1928. With an increasing emphasis on the cultural arts, the bathhouse was converted into a dance studio in 1971.

Peppi's Playground
32nd S. and Spruce
Size: 2.7 acres
Bus: 27
Major uses: school and neighborhood playground

DESCRIPTION
At the easternmost end of Yesler Way, Lake Dell Avenue winds around Leschi Elementary School and this well-located playground,

to continue its plunge into Alder Street and the shore of Lake Washington. Peppi's is definitely a playground, full of unique playthings—a box-shaped climber made of vertical and diagonally bolted twelve-by-twelves, a wedge-shaped slide, a hemispherical sand box, and a geodesic climbing dome. Children pass through an Exit/ Entrance on a wall painted with people and fantastic creatures to emerge beside a wading pool and a nearby drinking fountain.

Despite the playground emphasis, there is room on the landscaped grass for a picnic (two tables), or to gather your wits after a rough day.

Peppi's Playground was built in 1970 to make up for the lack of playground space in nearby Frink Park. It was named by the Leschi school children after Peppi Braxton, a first grader who was killed in an auto accident in 1971.

Plum Tree Park

26th between E. Howell and E. Olive
Size: 0.3 acre
Buses: 2, 48, 38 (all within three blocks)
Major use: neighborhood playground

DESCRIPTION

This little neighborhood park was designed with telephone pole stubs! Arranged in neat rows, the varying stub lengths form stairways, seats, and climbers that spiral through a sandy play area and provide decorative touches around the periphery. An alleyway basketball hoop draws neighborhood athletes, while young skateboarders slalom around the grassy patch on an undulating asphalt pathway. Several benches are also provided, and small children and resident squirrels often climb the stub by the drinking fountain to gulp the flowing water.

The park, originally called 26th Street Mini Park, was acquired in 1970 with Forward Thrust bond money.

Powell Barnett Park

E. Jefferson and Empire Way
Size: 4.4 acres
Bus: 38
Major uses: playground, picnics, walking

DESCRIPTION

You'll know when you get to Powell Barnett. Traveling along Empire Way a few blocks east of Garfield High School, be careful not to drive off the road when you see its castlelike restrooms brilliantly painted with horses, mountains, butterflies, blooming flowers, and other displays both celestial and earthy.

On a hot summer's day, the hub of activity is a kidney-shaped wading pool at the park's southeast corner. Here, kids gather in droves to splash and zip down a slide made slick by a geyser of water spouting from its top. Parents keep watch from a grassy embankment. On cooler days, the children congregate in the sandy play area uniquely contoured with sandstone bricks. Here, they distribute themselves onto jumping boards, bars, and balance poles, or lose themselves in an elevated labyrinth of pole stubs.

North of the play and picnic area (with four tables), the park stretches out wide and open all the way to E. Jefferson. A winding pathway with occasional benches encircles the meadow grasses. The paths are off limits to bikers.

The park is named in honor of Powell Barnett, the organizer and first president of the Leschi Improvement Council. This former coal miner, construction foreman, and sousaphone player was a great force behind integration in Seattle.

Spring Street Mini Park

15th and E. Spring
Size: 0.3 acre
Bus: 2
Major uses: sitting, tiny tot playground

DESCRIPTION

Young maples decorate this small Central Area lawn and parking strip two blocks south of Madison Street. A pathway from Spring Street curves down past benches to a large, concrete-sided sandbox that contains the crawlings of the tiny ones. The park was bought in 1969 with Forward Thrust Bond funds.

Spruce Street Mini Park

21st and E. Spruce
Size: 0.7 acre
Bus: 48 to 23rd and Spruce
Major uses: neighborhood playground, relaxing

DESCRIPTION

Turn east off 23rd a block south of Garfield High School and go two blocks to find this meeting place of the generations. A modern play area, a circle of benches, and a shallow bowl of grass and trees attract people of all ages. Kids sometimes pour down here in packs to eat sack lunches and roll garbage cans down the asphalt pathways. But fortunately the area is cleaned up each day by nearby residents (and sometimes twice after unusually heavy holocausts) so that everyone can continue to enjoy it.

The park was bought in 1969 with Forward Thrust Bond funds.

34th and Pike Mini Park

34th and E. Pike
Size: 0.7 acre
Buses: 2, 3
Major uses: sitting and relaxing

DESCRIPTION

In the middle of the Madrona neighborhood, you'll find a square block of grass, assorted small trees, a few benches, and concrete paths. This mini park is located one block north of the Madrona Foodliner and just across the street from an Exxon gas station. It provides a welcome buffer between 34th E. and quiet residences to the east. It was bought in 1973 with Forward Thrust funds and developed in 1975.

Yesler-Atlantic Pathway

22nd from E. Yesler to S. Jackson
Size: 2 acres
Buses: 27, 14
Major uses: picnics, walking, relaxing

DESCRIPTION

Bright red railings mark the north entrance of this pleasingly land-scaped and lighted park corridor in the Central Area. Starting down the concrete rampway, you are greeted first by a small amphitheatre with a bandstand. Summer concerts here send cheery notes up through the windows of adjacent apartment houses and into a grassy picnic area, which has two tables. This spot is very popular around lunchtime, drawing crowds from nearby institutions such as the Langston Hughes Cultural Arts Center and the Seattle Oppor-tunities and Industrial Relations Center (SOIC) at its south end. On a blustery day, you can hide under the roof of a spacious shelter to fry hamburgers or warm yourself by a fire.

From the amphitheatre, the pathway leads under a chestnut tree, past restrooms, to a red brick square and promenade shelter with 100 feet of benches. Then it passes another open square and the austere SOIC building to merge with the traffic of S. Jackson Street across from Gai's Bakery.

Because of its unique and attractive design, the Pathway has gained a tremendous popularity in the Central Area and is a prime spot for picnics, leisurely strolls, and group gatherings. The Pathway property was bought in 1972 with Forward Thrust funds.

NEARBY ATTRACTIONS:

Many enjoy their walk through the Pathway on their way to the more activity-oriented fields and playgrounds of **Judkins Park,** just two blocks south. And five blocks to the west, at 17th and Yesler, is the **Langston Hughes Cultural Arts Center** (329-0115), with arts and crafts courses for all ages.

Note: For further enjoyment of Central Seattle, get ahold of the city's "Mann-Minor Walking Tour," available by calling the Department of Community Development at 625-4534. The tour connects several of the above-mentioned parks with interesting views and architecture, both old and new.

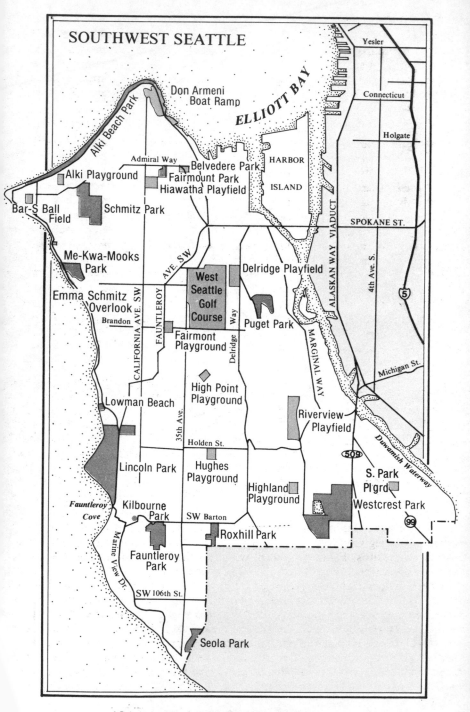

SOUTHWEST SEATTLE

ELLIOTT BAY

Don Armeni
Boat Ramp

Yesler

Connecticut

Holgate

Admiral Way

Alki Playground

Belvedere Park
Fairmount Park
Hiawatha Playfield

HARBOR
ISLAND

Bar-S Ball
Field

Schmitz Park

SPOKANE ST.

Me-Kwa-Mooks
Park

Delridge Playfield

West
Seattle
Golf
Course

Puget Park

Emma Schmitz
Overlook

Brandon

Fairmont
Playground

High Point
Playground

Lowman Beach

Riverview
Playfield

Lincoln Park

Holden St.

Hughes
Playground

Highland
Playground

Michigan St.

S. Park
Plgrd

Fauntleroy
Cove

Kilbourne
Park

SW Barton

Roxhill Park

Westcrest Park

Fauntleroy
Park

SW 106th St.

Seola Park

CALIFORNIA AVE. SW
FAUNTLEROY AVE. SW
35th Ave.
Delridge Way
MARGINAL WAY
ALASKAN WAY VIADUCT
4th Ave. S.
Marine View Dr.
Duwamish Waterway

509

99

5

184 ENJOYING SEATTLE'S PARKS

7
Southwest Seattle Parks

There is a love of wild nature in everybody . . . As long
as I live, I'll get as near the heart of the world as I can.

—John Muir

Alki Beach Park

Alki Avenue S.W.
Size: 154 acres
Bus: 37
Major uses: sunbathing, swimming, walking, biking

DESCRIPTION

Alki is a two-and-one-half-mile beach strip that runs along the edge
of West Seattle, from Alki Point to Duwamish Head in Elliott Bay.
With parallel path, sidewalk, bikeway, and street thoroughfares, it is
a park of movement with different moods at different times: cool and
calm in fall, storm-lashed in winter, crowded in spring and summer.

On warm mornings you can see people taking quiet walks in the
fresh salt air, perhaps with binoculars for sighting sea birds. Parents
bring children to make castles in the sand; dogs bound into the surf
for sticks. Then, as the morning wears on, sunbathers head for the
beach, and the quiet strand surrenders to the stream of joggers,
bicycles, cruising motorcycles, and hotrods. By mid-afternoon, Alki
is a teeming Coney Island, clogged with bodies, blaring radios, and
acres of autos. From then until well into the night, the beach is a
teenage haven.

If you pick the right time, you'll have plenty of fun. At the south
(Alki Point) end of the beach are picnic tables, a bathhouse, a stove
shelter, and restrooms. Here also is a monument to the first Seattle
pioneers who landed at Alki in 1851.

Next comes the sandy beach, where you can swim (in forty-six to
fifty-six-degree water), sunbathe, dig clams, build a beach fire, and
collect shells or driftwood. Some people even saw and split firewood
here, or make shakes from cedar stumps.

Then comes the bulkheaded beach that leads to Duwamish Head at the north end of the strand. It is flanked by quaint cottages beneath the bluff and affords exciting views of Puget Sound, the Olympics, and the steamships, ferries, freighters, tankers, and tugs that plow in and out of Elliott Bay. The fishing is good here for cod and flounder.

One of the best views on this last stretch is from a little seawalled square that was once the site of one of early Seattle's amusement parks (Luna Park). Here you'll find a drinking fountain and an ancient, two-and-a-half-ton anchor dredged up by the Nor'west Divers that has been rusted by the corrosive action of the salt water to reveal beautiful forged iron patterns.

South of Alki Point, at 69th S.W. and Beach Drive S., is a somewhat junky beach strip. The upper part is strewn with sawdust chips and the beach is laden with chunks of concrete.

NEARBY ATTRACTIONS

Food and drink. There are plenty of eating places along the south beach and in the Alki community. Along the southern four blocks of the strand you'll find everything from an IGA food store to fast-food havens like Taco Time and Spud Fish and Chips to fancier spots like La Croisette d'Alki (937-0086, reservations only).

Alki Point Light Station (3201 Alki S.W., 932-5800). Guide yourself and the kids through this exciting place on weekends and holidays from 1 to 4 p.m. A coast Guard attendant will answer questions you may have about how the equipment works.

Alki Playground (58th S.W. and S.W. Stevens). Two little league fields and a play area are located a few blocks east of the lighthouse.

Alki Bikes and Boats (2722 Alki S.W., 938-3322). Stop in here for bike and small-boat rentals to better enjoy the strand.

Driftwood carving. Talk to Glen Raught at the **Alki Boutique** (2648 59th S.W., 938-4855). Glen is an old salt who's lived here for fifteen years and has taught driftwood carving courses through the park department. He'll tailor his classes to meet the demand.

Don Armeni Boat Ramp (Harbor S.W. off S.W. Maryland). At this public facility you can launch your boat or yacht and go out for a day of cruising or salmon fishing, leaving your trailer in the parking lot while you're gone.

Salmon fishing If you're going after the big ones, or even if you just want an enjoyable cruise, you can rent rods, reels, bait, boats, and motors for reasonable fees and get expert angling advice at the **Seacrest Marina** (1660 Harbor S.W., 932-1050), near the Don Armeni Boat Ramp.

Skin Diving. You can frequently see scuba and skin divers bobbing among the pilings near the Don Armeni Boat Ramp or along the Alki Beach strip south or the point. If you want to try it yourself, you'll find everything you need at **Seattle Skindiving Supply** (1661 Harbor S.W., 937-2550), just across the street from the Seacrest Marina.

Fantastic Views. Be sure to turn up shady California Way S.W. from Harbor Avenue for telescopic views of the Seattle cityscape from Hamilton Viewpoint (California S.W. and S.W. Donald). A dime will get you three minutes of closeups of the Space Needle, the Cascades, and the Seattle Waterfront. And don't miss **Belvedere Viewpoint**. Drive up S.W. Admiral Way and turn off to a small roadside parking strip for a closeup of the **Duwamish River** and industrial **Harbor Island** with its tanks, crates, tugs, ships, barges, and cranes. It's hard to believe that the Indians used to string nets here for schools of returning salmon!

HISTORY

For centuries before the arrival of the white man, Alki was the domain of the Indians. Near what is now Alki Point, there was a little village called Me-Kwa-Mooks, where other tribes would often visit to feast on clams or to share in the stringing of nets across the Duwamish River when salmon ran to their spawning grounds. Alki was also one of the favorite campsites of Chief Seattle, for whom the city was eventually named.

In November, 1851, the young pioneers David Denny and Henry Van Asselt began building the log cabin (at what is now 63rd S.W.) that would house Seattle's first settlers. Chief Seattle himself was on hand to see the schooner *Exact* sail into Elliott Bay, letting off the members of the Denny, Low, Boren, and Bell families who formed the nucleus of the new town. The settlers were fired with the prospect of a great new city, so they named the spot New York-Alki ("Alki" being Chinook for "by and by"). After that first stormy winter, though, and after taking soundings with clothesline and horseshoes, they abandoned the beach for the more protected and deeper inner harbor of Elliott Bay.

But the lure of the beach did not die. As Seattle grew, it became the site (in 1889) of an amusement center, Luna Park, which was modeled after New York's Coney Island. With its rides, bands, and saltwater tidepool, Luna Park was a realtor's dream, luring central city settlers out to buy land in West Seattle. In 1889, it became the terminus for the West Seattle ferry. Soon after, a cable car curved up the bluff to enhance Sunday outings and increase real estate sales of land with elevated views of the sound. Then, in 1902, trolleys began racing across the Duwamish flats to connect Pioneer Square with Alki Beach and a fast-growing West Seattle.

The Luna Park craze hit its high point when L. G. Mecklem soared into the sky from the shores of Alki in a heated air balloon and wafted across the Duwamish River to Georgetown. Two years later, the city purchased the beach strip between 58th and 65th streets, creating the first municipal saltwater beach on the West Coast. Luna Park burned down in 1931, but its spirit rose again in 1934, when a salt water natatorium—complete with a turkish bath, a pipe organ, roller skating, gambling, dining, and dancing—was built farther down the beach, between 58th and Marine Avenue.

All that is gone today, replaced by a recreation center and a plethora of shops and quick eateries that cater to the summer hordes. But the piling stubs of both the amusement centers are still visible at low tide, and it takes only a quick visit at the high tide on a hot summer's day to realize that the Coney Island spirit still remains.

Camp Long

35th S.W. and S.W. Dawson
Size: 68 acres
Bus: 21
Major use: outdoor skills for organized groups

DESCRIPTION

Camp Long is not a standard public park because it is open only to organized groups. But its facilities and programs deserve a special mention. The camp covers sixty-eight acres of forested country tacked onto the west side of the West Seattle Municipal Golf Course. It includes camping areas, forest trails, a climbing rock, cabins that sleep twelve (for $10 a night), and wilderness skills programs geared to the seasons.

Courses include such things as backpacking, snowshoeing, cross country skiing, wilderness survival, using a map and compass, gathering wild edibles, and even bicycle maintenance. Most of them feature field trips into the Cascades or Olympics to practice new skills. Special programs include five-day summer outings in the Cascades and Olympics and an adventure camp for boys and girls.

If your group is interested in rambling through the great outdoors beyond the city limits, this is the place to prepare yourself. Call 935-0370 for registration and a complete listing of programs.

Fairmount Park

Fairmount S.W. and S.W. Lander
Size: 3.4 acres
Bus: 15
Major use: natural woods

DESCRIPTION
Fairmount is a short roadside ravine leading beneath the Admiral Way Bridge. It is a pleasant woodsy respite for joggers making a loop trip around Alki, but it's not really big enough to stop and explore.

HISTORY
Before the settlers arrived, Fairmount Park was a favorite Indian campsite during the berry picking season. It was part of an immense ravine, which in 1907 was named Fairmount Gulch after a 4,000-acre model park in Philadelphia. Grand visions at one time included plans for constructing the West Seattle Stadium in this area, but sliding hillsides and empty city coffers put a stop to it. These few acres were donated as a natural ravine in 1913.

Fauntleroy Park

38th S.W. and S.W. Barton
Size: 19.7 acres
Bus: 34
Major use: natural woods

DESCRIPTION
No public access, no maintained trails, no signs, no restrooms—this park is just thirty acres of woods. But what woods! All the city needs to do is open it up and it will be one of the most entrancing wild places in town. A forest of mixed conifers, alder, and maples drops gently down to a ravine and a rushing creek.

Today, Fauntleroy Park is enjoyed and protected by its surrounding residents on dead end streets. Sometimes they are entertained by flickers rattling on rooftops, by the chatter of crows, and by visitations of raccoons peering through living room windows. Some day Fauntleroy Park may be another small window for all of us to look into the Northwest's wild past.

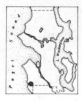

Kilbourne Park

S.W. Brace Point Drive and California S.W.
Size: 0.3 acres
Bus: 34
Major use: natural woods

DESCRIPTION

This is a little greenbelt and children's wild haunt beside Fauntleroy Elementary School. Slide down a steep nontrail to a questionable Fauntleroy Creek—and then try to get back up again.

The park was donated to the city in 1951 by electrical engineer E. C. Kilbourne, an early settler in the area. It never became the amphitheatre and camp site he envisioned, however.

Lincoln Park

Fauntleroy S.W. and S.W. Webster
Size: 130 acres
Bus: 18
Major uses: picnics, athletics, trails, views

DESCRIPTION

Lincoln Park is West Seattle's major multi-purpose park—a nose-shaped bluff on Puget Sound just north of the Fauntleroy Ferry Terminal. Switchbacks on the north and gentle trails to the south connect a mile of seawalled, rocky beaches to a bluff of grassy forests and meadows with play and picnic areas galore.

Amazingly diverse for its size, Lincoln includes 4.6 miles of walking paths, 3.9 miles of bike paths, five picnic shelters, eleven acres of playfields with three ballfields, a football field, six lighted and two unlighted tennis courts, ten horseshoe pitching courts, a wading pool, numerous rings, swings, slides, and climbing contraptions, beachside barbecues, and an outdoor saltwater heated swimming pool and bathhouse.

But for all the emphasis on activity, Lincoln also has its quiet side. This is provided by a bewildering network of paths through groves of madrona, Douglas fir, cedar, and redwoods, and benches from which you can see the Sound and the snowy Olympics.

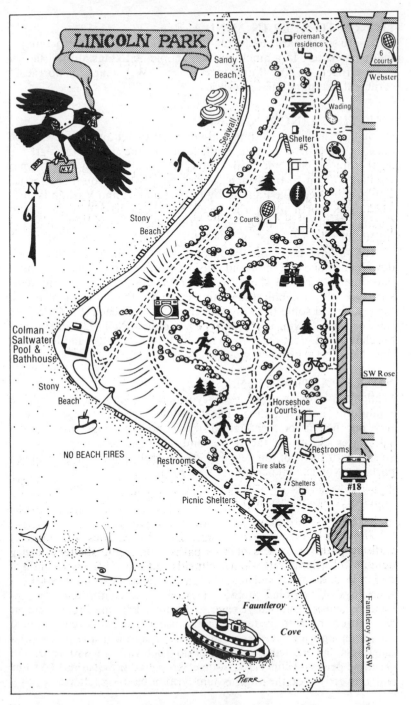

LINCOLN PARK

Sandy Beach

Foreman's residence

6 courts

Webster

Wading

Shelter #5

N

Stony Beach

2 Courts

Colman Saltwater Pool & Bathhouse

Stony Beach

SW Rose

Horseshoe Courts

Restrooms

NO BEACH FIRES

Restrooms

Fire slabs

Shelters

BUS #18

Picnic Shelters

2

Fauntleroy Cove

Fauntleroy Ave. SW

PIERR

THINGS TO KEEP IN MIND

There are snack bars at Lincoln Park, but it's a long way to a major shopping center. In a pinch you can get picnic fixings at the Lincoln Park Grocery (7301 Bainbridge Place S.W.) near the northeast corner of the park off Fauntleroy.

ENJOYING LINCOLN PARK

If you don't have much time and you want to get an overview of the park, a forty-five minute walk can do the job. Start at the northernmost end and walk along the bluff railing that slopes gradually down to the beach to the south, where you'll see ferries chugging between the Fauntleroy Ferry Landing and Vashon Island. Then walk north along the beach bulkhead past madronas and Colman Pool to the other end of the beach, where switchbacking trails will take you back up the bluff to your starting point.

If you have more time, you may want to plunk a picnic lunch down in any one of a thousand grassy spots, or perhaps have a family barbecue in a rented shelter (try number five, a spacious, modern structure with a cobblestone chimney and a thick cluster of picnic tables). Spend some time digging clams at the beach if it's a minus tide, or take a swim in the saltwater **Colman Pool** (935-1903). The beach is also a great place to roam and turn over rocks and look into tidepools.

NEARBY ATTRACTIONS

While you are near the park, you might want to stop at the Fauntleroy Ferry Landing. The fifty-foot stretch of beach here is tiny, but there is room enough to sit (on enormous logs), listen to the salt water lap up on the shore, and sift your toes through sands strewn with shells of mussels and clams, crab pincers, and carapace parts. Or you can launch a kayak or rowboat, or watch the comings and goings of the car-carrying ships. You can even take the trip yourself. Ferries leave about every half hour.

HISTORY

Lincoln Park was called Fauntleroy Park until 1922, when the city bought it. The popularity of the name Fauntleroy in this area springs from the passions of Lieutenant George Davidson, who was taking soundings off the bluff in 1857. Davidson had temporarily left his fiance, Ellinor Fauntleroy, back in Illinois. Presumably to cement his relationship with the family in his absence, he had already named his surveying brig after her father. Now, in a fit of romanticism and loneliness, he named the cove for his beloved, and some of the Olympic peaks—Ellinor, Constance, Rose, and the Brothers (Arthur and Edward)—for the various family members.

The first settlers in south Seattle lived in what is now the White Center area, and made their living cutting trees for masts as the city became famous for shipbuilding. Development of the Lincoln Park area began in 1904, when John F. Adams built a summer resort on the cove. He was followed shortly by Laurence Colman, the son of a Scottish sawmill engineer, for whom Colman Park on Lake Washington is named.

At the time Colman built the first permanent home on the cove, the area was accessible only by boat or by long, arduous travel through the woods. But Colman was aided in his real estate efforts by electrical engineer E. C. Kilbourne, who eagerly extended his trolley system across the Duwamish tideflats to West Seattle, then south to the cove through the forest along what is now Fauntleroy Way. These trolley runs were often adventurous affairs, sometimes interrupted by bear and deer using the right of way as their own forest thoroughfares.

The park was put together piecemeal over the years as West Seattle developed: a shelter in 1925; parking areas in 1928; a playground in 1930; seawalls, trails, fireplaces, and horseshoe pits during the Depression; and major additions just after World War II, as people streamed into the area to work in the burgeoning Boeing aircraft plant in the Duwamish Valley.

The heated, saltwater Colman Pool began as a tide-fed swimming hole in 1929, and was periodically hosed out by the fire department to rid it of accumulating mud and debris. It became so popular that residents began asking for a concrete bottom and sides—much to the chagrin of the city, which wanted to abandon it entirely. The pool took final concrete form in 1941, when Kenneth Colman, son of Laurence, donated $150,000 to have it built in honor of his father.

Lowman Beach

Beach Drive S.W. and 48th S.W.
Size: 4.2 acres (2.6 acres tidelands)
Bus: 37
Major uses: sunbathing, play area

DESCRIPTION
"Omigosh, look at 'em all!" screams a little boy, turning over a rock. And a squadron of crabs scuttles across the beach.

Lowman Beach is small, but like beaches everywhere, it has some surprises. Suitable for beachcombing and clam digging, it includes about 300 feet of rocky, saltwater shoreline a few blocks north of Lincoln Park. Above the beach is an acre of grass with tennis court, swings, restrooms, and drinking fountain. Views of the Olympics, Alki Point, and Williams Point spread out in three directions.

HISTORY
Lowman Beach was a gift to the city in 1909 by the Yesler Logging Company. It was called Lincoln Beach until 1925, when the name was changed to avoid confusion with the larger Lincoln Park to the south. The name was given in honor of James D. Lowman, who first came to Seattle as a teacher in 1887. In later years, he became wharf master for Henry Yesler, then went into the bookstore and printing business, and finally founded the Lowman and Hanford stationers and printing company. Lowman also served two years as park commissioner, from 1896 to 1898.

Me-Kwa-Mooks Park

Beach Drive S.W. and S.W. Oregon
Size: 34 acres (16 acres tidelands)
Bus: 37
Major uses: picnics, walking, views

DESCRIPTION
Up until 1977, this former pioneer hillside estate was completely overgrown. Those who were inclined to dive into the nettles and ivy might have found a few old beams and parts of rock walls and stairways, whose decaying remains hinted at the former grandeur of the place. Now the park department is ambitiously restoring parts of it for public enjoyment. They are putting in pathways that will allow everyone (including the handicapped) to saunter over the old grounds. With some extensive pruning, they have even unveiled some of the overgrown bamboo, cork, and Japanese cherry trees originally planted there by horticulturist Ferdinand Schmitz. The lower lawn, with three new tables just inside the hedge, is a fine place for a picnic, and a new 600-foot landscaped, bulkheaded promenade along the beach invites walking, viewing, and beachcombing.

NEARBY ATTRACTIONS
Just south of the park, along the beach, is **Emma Schmitz Overlook,** an extension of the new promenade. It is also a good spot to rest or

take a cool drink from the fountain as you jog or bicycle along the shores of Puget Sound.

HISTORY

Me-Kwa-Mooks is the name given by the Indians to the landform that includes Alki Point and Duwamish Head. In the Nisqually dialect, it means "shaped like a bear's head," a fairly accurate geographical description. Alki Point itself was called Sma-Qua-Mox and Ma-Que-Buck, and an ancestral village called Me-Kwa-Mooks was located on the flats between Alki and Duwamish Head long before the arrival of the white man.

The park site to the south was the pioneer home of Ferdinand and Emma Schmitz (see "Schmitz Park"), who came to Seattle in 1887. They bought this beautiful hillside in 1907 and built a twelve-room, stucco-and shingle home that had three porches overlooking the sound. Schmitz, an enthusiastic gardener with an added flair for landscaping, also planted an orchard and flower gardens, and even built a pool, which he stocked with fish for gourmet dinners. To the beach he added a 500-foot seawall with an eighty-foot pier, complete with boathouse and picnic shelter at the end. In later years, the Schmitzes even added a beach guest house and a chicken coop to the complex. They named their homestead "Sans Souci," a French term meaning "without care."

In 1945, Emma Schmitz gave the city eleven of the beach acres, the strip now called Emma Schmitz Overlook. The buildings on the upper hillside were demolished after they were damaged during the 1964 earthquake, and the area was neglected until the city bought it in 1971. The restoration project, which is just ending now, began in 1976.

Puget Park

18th S.W. and S.W. Dawson
Size: 17.6 acres
Bus: 48
Major use: natural woods

DESCRIPTION

Some wooded parks are hard to get into. Puget Park, between the Duwamish River and the West Seattle Municipal Golf Course, is one of them. Try from the north and you will be deterred by a barbed wire fence and the University of Washington's radio telescope installation. Try from the south and it's dead-ends and "No Trespassing—Beware of Dog" signs. If you're still inclined to experience this better-left-alone woods, slide down the steep western hillside beside the bus stop to an abandoned rabbit hutch and other miscellaneous junk, thread your way along a muddy pathway infested with spider webs and slugs, and then thrash through tall grasses to 16th S.W. and S.W. Edmunds Street. There, if you have made the journey in August, you may be rewarded with a few blackberries for your pains. If not, you will be rewarded with the same trip back.

HISTORY
Puget Park was the 1912 gift of the Puget Mill Company, which logged off most of the timber before parting with the land. It was actually a quite beautiful wooded park at one time, but after the logging, there was no ambitious plan to convert it into a useful public facility. For many years, it limped along with minimal maintenance. The Boy Scouts were given permission to build trails and camps there. And in 1964, the Yates Stables began establishing bridle trails for horseback rides and filling the ravine with waste material until stopped by community protest. The park still waits for a suitable dream.

The park and the old sawmill owe their names to Lieutenant Peter Puget, who was originally honored by Captain George Vancouver in the naming of Puget Sound in 1792.

Roxhill Park

29th S.W. and S.W. Barton
Size: 10.8 acres
Bus: 34
Major uses: playground, picnics, relaxing

DESCRIPTION
Roxhill is a flat, open lawn laced with cinder pathways and liberally supplied with sturdy benches. You'll find it off busy Barton Street just south of the Westwood Village Shopping Center, in an area of single family homes. It includes ten large picnic tables, two ballfields, a small play area, and three horseshoe pits. Roxhill Elementary School, just to the southwest, has additional swings, a

slide, and a basketball court. The park was bought by the city in 1955 and named by the Roxhill Community Club.

Schmitz Park

S.W. Stevens and S.W. Admiral Way
Size: 50.4 acres
Bus: 15
Major uses: hiking, picnics, nature study

DESCRIPTION
Schmitz Park is one of the city's last remaining chunks of virgin forest. Just east of Alki in West Seatle, it is a ravine cathedral towering with gigantic Douglas firs and western red cedars that escaped the axes and saws of the pioneer loggers. No playgrounds, park benches, or picnic tables here. Just raw, wild paths and trails winding through thick ferns and berry bushes; mammoth tree trunks; stumps supporting salal, red huckleberry, and their own forests of mosses and fungi; and log bridges over rushing creeks.

It is easy to understand—gazing about in this grand, wild place, marveling at tree trunks eight feet across, and straining the eyes to reach the topmost branches—how the early pioneers could have been awed by the Northwest. This place is so wild that once, as I sat beside the trail engrossed in my notes, I heard what I thought was the growl of a bear and was only slightly relieved to look up into the eyes of slobbering St. Bernard. Walking through this park is like taking a short stroll on the forest trails of the lower Cascade Mountains, without even having to leave the city.

NEARBY ATTRACTIONS
For more action, follow Schmitz Boulevard (at the northwest entrance) west three blocks to **Alki Playground** and then another two blocks north to **Alki Beach.**

HISTORY
Schmitz Park was donated to the city in pieces between 1908 and 1912. The most generous chunk came from a German immigrant/pioneer/banker/realtor named Ferdinand Schmitz, who served on the park commission during those years. It was Schmitz's idea, as he saw how rapidly the great forest was disappearing, to preserve part of it in its natural state.

Even Schmitz's land had not been completely untouched by logging, though. Some huge stumps in the park still show deep notches hacked high above the ground for the "spring-boards" on which axemen would stand to avoid having to chop through the lower root crown, the thickest and hardest part of the tree. After 1908, however, the new park rapidly gained popularity as a quiet complement to the West Seattle park complex, including Alki Beach and its adjacent playground and amusement park. Family Sunday outings by ferry and cable car from the central city to West Seattle often included picnics in this quiet sanctuary. Except for the paved entrance and a parking lot at the northwest corner, the park has remained essentially unchanged ever since.

Seola Park

Seola Beach Drive S.W. and S.W. 112th Place
Size: 8.5 acres
Bus: 21 to S.W. 106th
Major use: natural woods

DESCRIPTION

This natural ravine may not be worth going out of your way to visit, but if you insist, at least try not to get lost. From 35th S.W. turn east onto S.W. 106th and go three blocks to Seola Beach Drive S.W., then south along the park's madrona-studded hillside (on your right). Deciduous woods predominate in the middle, turning into another madrona grove at the far south end just before you reach a small sewer pumping plant and the stony beaches of Puget Sound.

HISTORY

The settlers who first came to the White Center area became loggers, cutting the fine timber here to supply building material and masts for the Skinner and Eddy Corporation at Pier 39. Loggers here developed two primary skid roads, one of them located at 20th and Roxbury. The area was named Seola—Spanish for "to know the wave"—after a naming contest in 1910. The town itself was named White Center eight years later. The park property was bought by the city with Forward Thrust Bond funds in 1972.

Westcrest Park

S.W. Barton and Henderson Place S.W.
Size: 93.2 acres
Bus: 34
Major uses: picnics, hiking, playground

DESCRIPTION

This park, until recently called Highland Greenbelt Park, is raw and young, a curious patchwork of lawns, ravines, and woods interwoven with dirt paths and roadways overlooking the industrialized Duwamish Valley. Until 1972, the property belonged to the water department. The present park is wrapped around the West Seattle Reservoir, with treatment tanks nearby.

During the last several years, Forward Thrust funds have built eight sturdy picnic tables, four barbecue pits, a nature trail, and a lighted viewpoint, with vistas east and west to the Cascades and Olympics and north to the city's towering buildings. But much of the park is still dominated by scotch broom, madrona trees, and thickets. These areas are used primarily for children as adventuring places. Unofficial pathways plunge into thick salal, trailing past the remnants of small forts and earthworks in coniferous woods.

As money becomes available, the park department plans to continue developing Westcrest, adding tennis courts, a health trail, path extensions, and a children's play area.

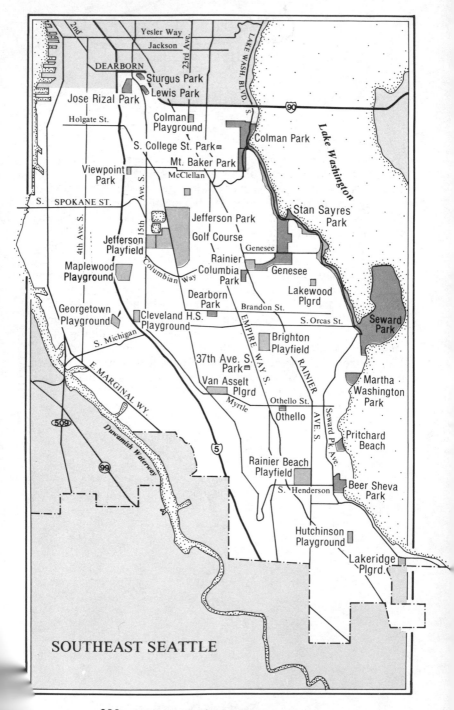

SOUTHEAST SEATTLE

8
Southeast Seattle Parks

*Seattle, though a rapidly growing city, is keeping pace
in the matter of things beautiful.*

—Board of Park Commissioners, 1909

Beer Sheva
(Atlantic City) Park

S. Henderson and Seward Park S.
Size: 25.6 acres
Buses: 31, 39
Major uses: boating, swimming, picnics, views

DESCRIPTION

The recent renaming of this park after Beer Sheva, Seattle's sister
city in Israel, caused such commotion that the "Atlantic City" signs
will stay. The park is located just east of Rainier Beach High School
on the southwest shore of Lake Washington. A three-piered, four-
ramped boat launch with lots of parking makes this one a popular
spot for boaters. A grassy beach for sunbathers and swimmers
includes restrooms, a drinking fountain, and benches for viewing
Mercer Island and the foothills of the Cascades. This is also a
favorite spot for feeding ducks, which usually float in large flocks
near the shore waiting for handouts.

To the north of the boat ramp and beach, an open field of grass
under cottonwoods and conifers turns into a fine picnic area. Here
you'll find another restroom, a drinking fountain, and a picnic shelter
with two small barbecues—but no picnic tables, due to repeated
vandalism.

Beer Sheva was acquired by community court action as Alantic
City Park in 1907. At that time, it was part of the pioneer
community of Rainier Beach, at the end of the longest interurba
trolley line in the state.

NEARBY ATTRACTIONS

For wintertime swimming when the lake gets too nippy, or for athletics such as track and basketball, the **Rainier Beach Community Center** is conveniently located a couple of long blocks west on S. Henderson Street. The park department plant and tree nursery is just to the north, and north of that is the **Pritchard Island Bathing Beach,** which has excellent views of Seward Park and Mercer Island.

Colman Park

36th S. and Lakeside S.
Size: 27.3 acres
Bus: 27
Major uses: picnics, swimming

DESCRIPTION

This is another beach park, located just south of the old Lake Washington Floating Bridge. The beach itself is adjacent to Mount Baker Bathing Beach, but it is still a part of Colman park. Enter from the north either from Lakeside Avenue or by switchbacking over the bridges and horseshoe-curved hillside road along Lake Washington Boulevard. A trail from the horseshoe curve loops out and down into the woods and back again.

The beach features grass, big drooping willows, three picnic tables, a bathhouse, a raft with a one-meter diving board, and a small, sandy swim area with lifeguards in summer. The nearby pier is closed to swimmers, but if you just want to fish, the guard will open the gate for you. And if you've brought along your Frisbee, football, soccer ball, or volleyball, the grass to the north makes a friendly playing ground.

NEARBY ATTRACTIONS

From Colman Park, Lake Washington Boulevard curves smoothly southward past madronas and lakeside homes to **Seward Park**. It is paralleled by a wide asphalt path, which is excellent for jogging and bicycling (three miles from here to Seward Park), with inspiring views of Lake Washington and Mercer Island. About half a mile south of Colman, the boulevard passes another public fishing pier, then curves past the northern meadow of **Genesee Park** to the hydroplane pits and boat launches of **Stan Sayres Memorial Park.**

SPECIAL EVENTS
Colman Park is a favorite place to watch the annual **Seafair hydroplane races** during the first week in August. It is also the starting point for **Bicycle Sunday,** where, on one Sunday of each month, hordes of pedalers gather to spin along the boulevard to Seward Park; traffic is routed elsewhere from 9 a.m. to 5 p.m. on those days.

HISTORY
Colman Park was the birthplace of Seattle's commercial water system. In 1886, the Spring Hill Water Company built the city's first steam-operated pumphouse at the present site of the Mount Baker Bathing Beach and began supplying fresh spring water to Seattle's residents by pumping it through hollow log pipes. The pumphouse's most heroic effort was made during the Great Seattle Fire of 1889, when it steamed around the clock in a vain effort to douse the flames engulfing the distant Pioneer Square.

Once the pump's main element went on the blink, and not even the East Coast experts were able to find the problem. It was finally repaired by a local engineer named James M. Colman, who later bought the property and deeded it to the city in 1907. Colman had a varied career in Seattle as a sawyer, realtor, builder, and philanthropist. He left a long list of civic credits, including the construction of the County Courthouse and the old Colman Ferry Terminal, which has been replaced by the Washington State Ferry Terminal.

Columbia Park

Rainier S. and S. Alaska
Size: 2.4 acres
Buses: 7, 31, 39, 48, 62
Major uses: sitting, relaxing

DESCRIPTION
Along busy Rainier Avenue, Columbia Park offers open grass and two magnificent maple trees beside the Columbia Branch of the Seattle Public Library. The park serves as a buffer against the fuming traffic, and provides a great place to pore over newly borrowed books. The Fifth Church of Christ Scientist is located on the west side. The park was annexed to the city in 1907.

Dearborn Park

30th S. and S. Brandon
Size: 4.6 acres
Buses: 31, 42 to S. Brandon
Major uses: walking, natural woods

DESCRIPTION
This soon-to-be-developed rectangle of woods sits on Beacon Hill just north of the Dearborn Park Elementary School and just east of a clovered, dandelioned swath of grass towering with City Light's power lines. Children have obviously enjoyed forging pathways through the leafy, ferny wilds here. More civilized influences have been at work, too, as the trail bike tracks testify. For a sure, straight shot through the woods, two graveled, lighted paths lead north to the other end from the school parking lot. A play area and softball field are nearby.

HISTORY
In pioneer days, this park patch was located in the little town of Somerville, which was founded by homesteader Charles Waters of Somerville, Massachusetts. Likewise, the park itself was called Somerville Park until it was annexed to Seattle with the rest of the town in 1907. Its present name honors its donors, Mr. and Mrs. George F. Dearborn.

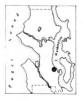

Genesee Park and Playfield

45th S. and S. Genesee
Size: 37 acres
Bus: 39
Major uses: picnics, play area, athletics

DESCRIPTION
Genesee is a broad, rough meadow stretching about five city blocks north from Genesee Street to Sayres Memorial Park on Lake Washington Boulevard. The north meadow (great for kite flying) has been freshly landscaped by the park department, and the southeast corner has been upgraded with a fine complex of new facilities. Included are a picnic shelter with eight tables, restrooms, and an

exciting play area with spring platforms, fire pole, pulley slide, chain bridge, and geodesic climbing dome. Two older tennis courts are next to the play area.

Eventually, a recreational complex will be added in the area south of Genesee. Linked to the park via an overpass, this playfield section' will stretch westward all the way to Rainier Playfield, offering more sports fields, picnic areas, and a fitness path.

NEARBY ATTRACTIONS
From Genesee it's only a short walk to Lake Washington Boulevard, with access to benches, boat ramps, fishing piers and lakeshore jogging and biking.

HISTORY
Stand in the Genesee Park meadow looking north to Lake Washington and imagine the lake level rising nine feet. Then imagine the meadow itself sinking up to fifty feet in places. This makes it a little easier to understand how things looked in the 1860s. In those days, Wetmore Cove at the north end of the present park was actually a slough that stretched southward, completely engulfing the present fields, and extending on to Rainier Avenue and the little town of Columbia City.

Residents of Columbia City once hoped to make their town into an important seaport by dredging the slough to allow the passage of ships. However, the slough began to be filled in from the south beginning about 1870, along with the construction of Rainier Avenue and the trolley that clanged from Pioneer Square to Rainier Beach. All hopes of a seaport sank into oblivion when the level of Lake Washington was lowered nine feet in 1917. The departing waters left only marshlands and little islands, with hardly enough water to sail a toy boat.

The far end of the slough, including Columbia Park and Rainier Playfield, was completely filled in about 1920, and in 1947 the city began a "sanitary fill" between Genesee and Lake Washington Boulevard. This fill was composed mostly of garbage and was anything but sanitary. It attracted flocks of seagulls and hordes of rats for almost two decades. After 1957, it also attracted hordes of hydroplane fans, who parked their cars there (helping to compact the garbage) and went off to watch the annual Gold Cup races from the new Stan Sayres hydro pits.

Seattle voters approved the area as a park in 1960, but development did not begin until after 1968, when the park became a Forward Thrust project. Today, after more than a hundred years of gradual metamorphosis, Genesee takes its place as one of Seattle's youngest parks—and one of the growing number of parks which rest on foundations of recycled garbage.

Jose Rizal Park

S. Judkins and 12th Avenue S.
Size: 8.4 acres
Buses: 1, 60
Major uses: views, picnics

DESCRIPTION

This natural park is located on the west side of Beacon Hill, across from the Public Health Service Hospital. It will soon be a spectacular viewpoint though it is now overgrown with blackberries, horsetails, thistles, thick woods, and grasses. If you walk to the bottom of the long parking lot here, you can catch a glimpse of the future spectacle: the roaring loops of Interstate 5 and the butt ends of unfinished freeway ramps; a sweeping view from the Kingdome north along Elliott Bay to the towers of the central city; and, on a good day, the Olympic Mountains.

The more adventurous picnicker or sightseer may want to brave the thistly trail leading down to matted grasses and closer views on the hillside. Others will want to wait until the city has it properly pruned and spruced up, sometime in the fall of 1979. Facilities will include a picnic shelter and viewpoint at the top of the hill, two trail systems, and a central amphitheatre.

HISTORY

Beacon Hill, the site of the new Jose Rizal Park, is a fascinating mixture of natural and human engineering. The major contour of the hill, composed of sand and clay layers capped with a rocky rubble, was formed by the passing of a glacier over the Seattle area about 15,000 years ago. When the pioneers came, the salt waters of Elliott Bay still spread daily over the tideflats at the mouth of the Duwamish River and even washed up to sixteen feet high against the flanks of the hill. There was also a steep saddle between Beacon Hill and First Hill, which forced both trolleys and foot travelers to switchback up and over on their way to South Seattle and Renton.

Then began the human engineering. In the 1890s, the ridge saddle was leveled—with picks, shovels, and horsedrawn dragging scoops —and dumped onto the tideflats. By 1912, the saddle between Beacon and First Hills had been completely cut away, and trolleys could make a straight shot southward into the Rainier Valley. Another dredging and filling project straightened out the curves near the mouth of the Duwamish River and formed Harbor Island. The former tidal flats quickly filled with railroad cars and fuming industries.

Then came still more construction: the 12th Avenue Bridge (now called Jose Rizal Bridge) between the two hills, and the 3,300-bed Marine Hospital (now the Public Health Service Hospital) in 1933. Finally, the freeway construction during the 1960s created the park meadow overlooking downtown and Elliott Bay. And the Kingdome, a $60 million domed stadium 250 feet high and 660 feet in diameter, was built in 1974.

Much of the park's modern history is the creation of Seattle's Filipino Community. The first Filipinos came to Seattle in 1900, after the Spanish-American War made the Philippines an American Protectorate. Like other minorities here, they saw the U.S. as a land of opportunity, but soon discovered that they must band together to avoid persecution and to preserve their culture. They "melted" into the International District east of Pioneer Square at first, their meager numbers restricted even more after 1934, when they were declared aliens. Over the years, one of their favorite gathering and picnic places was "Pinoy Hill" in Seward Park.

The meadow slope west of the hospital was transferred to the park department in 1971. Three years later, at the urging of the Filipino Community, the park was named after Dr. Jose Rizal, a Filipino patriot of remarkable talents.

Rizal was born in 1861. In his short, 35-year life, he made lasting contributions to medicine, psychology, literature, anthropology, art, drama, philosophy, botany, zoology, engineering, agriculture, and—above all—political and social reform. Partly because of his patriotic writings, he was accused of complicity in the Filipino insurrection of 1896, and was executed.

At this writing, the park is in its final stages of development and is slated for dedication in the fall of 1979.

Lewis Park

Between 15th S. and S. Sturgus S.
Size: 1.4 acres
Bus: 1
Major use: natural woods

DESCRIPTION

Lewis Park is a steep, woodsy area on the southeast side of Beacon Hill just below the Public Health Service Hospital. It seems to serve no practical purpose other than to provide a dumping place for grass clippings. Yet in the green itself there is a reminder of wild and natural things, and it is enough to know that at any time you can step away from the rush of cars along 15th S. to glimpse and momentarily feel part of a quieter world. The park was given as a gift to the city by W. H. Lewis in 1910.

Martha Washington Park

57th S. and S. Warsaw
Size: 9.8 acres
Buses: 31, 39 to S. Holly
Major uses: picnics, lakeside views

DESCRIPTION

Swing down into the grounds of this once-grand estate, with its circular driveway, stately old buildings, and spacious lakeside grounds planted with ancient trees and part of an old orchard. Some of the buildings are boarded up now and neglected, but the northernmost structure is brightened during the day with kids from the Cornerstone Academy, a small Montessori school.

Behind the buildings, a spacious lawn with old trees and brush slopes leads down to the lake, which laps up against a rock breakwater. Spread a picnic lunch in this quiet place and cast your eyes outward to Renton, Mercer Island, and the neck of the Seward Park Peninsula to the north. And when you get a chance, take a closer look at the old monarchs overlooking the lake—particularly the grand old oak and the monstrous madrona whose hollowed-out trunk and rope-ladder staircase invite children to high adventures. Judging from its eight-foot girth, scarred bark, and contorted branches, it has spent many centuries in this spot, twisting its way outward and upward.

The park department has not decided yet what it will do with Martha Washington Park. The grounds are overgrown and neglected, but it probably would not take much pruning to restore their grandeur. In the meantime, don't miss it. It's a little off the beaten track, but more rewarding for that very reason.

NEARBY ATTRACTIONS

For park activities of all kinds—from picnics and swimming to biking and wilderness hiking—go to **Seward Park,** just a few blocks to the north.

HISTORY

The grounds of the present Martha Washington Park were first owned by pioneer homesteader E. A. Clark, who was Seattle's third schoolteacher. After a short time, he sold the land to another pioneer, David Graham, in 1855. Graham in turn swapped the land for his brother Walt's acreage ten years later. Walter Graham's claim at that time included not only the present park site, but also all of the Seward Park Peninsula, which at that time was called "Graham's Peninsula." An avid horticulturist, Graham planted orchards in the upland area, but stayed away from Seward Park because of poison oak.

Another of Graham's claims to fame is that he married one of the Mercer Girls, a cargo of maidens shipped north to Seattle by Asa Mercer to help meet the demand for pioneer housewives. Mercer himself bought the Martha Washington site from Graham, but a year later gave it to a Massachusetts farmer named John Wilson—in payment for a loan when he went bankrupt after shipping his second cargo of maidens. Wilson built a farmhouse here, which was torn down in 1919.

The land was bought from Wilson in 1889 by a young attorney named Everett Smith, who for a time was a clerk for Judge Thomas Burke. Smith served twenty-two years on the Superior Court, and during that time built a youth camp on the site with the help of the YMCA. Children reveled in the open space—especially in the late summer when apple, plum cherry, and pear pickings from the orchard were at their best. And they loved to climb the hollow stairway the judge carved out in the old madrona tree.

In 1920, Judge Smith sold this property to the School District, and the following year a classroom-and-dorm building was constructed there for the Martha Washington School for Girls. In 1957, the State of Washington took over the school, and the grounds were finally sold to the city in 1972.

Mount Baker Park

S. McClellan and Mt. Rainier Drive S.
Size: 11.5 acres
Bus: 10
Major use: boulevard walking

DESCRIPTION

Mount Baker Park is a gentle ravine boulevard sloping down to Colman Park and the Mount Baker Bathing Beach on Lake

Washington. Find it from the north by turning right onto Lake Park Drive just above the beach. Or from the east by following tree-lined Mount Baker Boulevard from Rainier Avenue past Franklin High School to Lake Park Drive.

Although it's mainly a thoroughfare, it beckons you to slow down. Some local residents picnic and play tennis here (on two courts), or set the kids loose in a small playground in the southwest corner. Others stroll down a wide pathway—under maples, mountain ash, and chestnut trees—to Lake Washington Boulevard and the beach. Restrooms are located partway down the path. The northernmost end of the park is the starting point for Bicycle Sunday.

HISTORY

Pioneer David Denny, the same Denny who donated the five-acre patch for Seattle's first public park in 1884, first owned the Mount Baker area. At that time, it was a quiet woods beside a stream trickling down into Lake Washington. Denny never meant it to be a fancy amusement park like Madison or Leschi, and even after it was sold to engineer James Colman (see "Colman Park") and then to the Hunter Tract Improvement Company, the plan intended for it was exclusively residential.

The Olmsted Brothers, whose early park influence is so prevalent in the Lake Washington Boulevard area, were hired to design the Mount Baker Park Subdivision, and in 1908 this little section was donated to the city. Gradually, the exclusivity began to seep away. By the late 1920s, the park had become an important public attraction, partly because of its proximity to the beach. And after 1950, when Stan Sayres located his headquarters for the unlimited hydroplane races at the beach just below, it was flooded annually with fans, who returned in quieter times for pleasant walks.

Othello Park

43rd S. and S. Othello
Size: 6.5 acres
Buses: 42, 107
Major uses: picnics, neighborhood playground

DESCRIPTION

Othello is a nicely designed, spacious spot near Holly Park, and is bordered by a Prairie Market and a community church. Both kids and adults like to wind along pathways in the upper grassy part and picnic on small round tables that look like giant mushrooms surrounded by telephone pole stub stools. Children especially love to zip down the hill on a long slide to the lower open grasses and more paths, picnic tables, and a modern play area. There they spin on bars, clamber on poles, bridges, and tires, and shoot baskets at four hoops. Bike rack, restrooms, and drinking fountain are located near the play area.

Pritchard Island Beach

55th S. and S. Grattan
Size: 8.8 acres (3.9 acres shorelands)
Buses: 31, 39
Major uses: swimming, views

DESCRIPTION

In the Rainier Beach area, north of Beer Sheva Park, turn off S. Grattan into another grassy beach. Several large cottonwoods flutter in the breeze as swimmers head for the raft, where they spring into the air from high and low diving boards. Others just sit on the beach admiring the view of Seward Park to the north and Mercer Island to the east. You'll find this a fine, quiet complement to the Atlantic City beach to the south, since there is no boat ramp ruckus here. Lifeguards are on duty in the summer.

HISTORY

Before Lake Washington was lowered nine feet by the opening of the Ship Canal, there used to be an island south of the beach where the land now bulges out into the bay. The marshland between the island and the shore was called Dunlap Slough, for Joseph Dunlap, who settled there in 1870. The island itself first belonged to A. B. Youngs, who sold it to an Englishman named Alfred J. Pritchard—hence the name, Pritchard's Island. Pritchard spanned the slough with a footbridge and developed the island into an attractive forest estate.

Before the Alaska-Yukon-Pacific Exposition, the Olmsted Brothers recommended that the island and its environs be acquired to enhance the new Lake Washington Boulevard. By 1910, the year after the Exposition, the area had become so popular that a petition was flooded with names calling for construction of a bathing beach. The opening of the Ship Canal in 1917 drained Dunlap Slough, leaving more land for park nursery development and connecting Pritchard's Island to the mainland.

The bathhouse at Pritchard Beach also has some marginal historical significance. It was built on the former homesite of Victor J. Meyers, a musician who ran for mayor as a joke in 1932. He lost that race, but later won five successive terms as Washington State's Lieutenant Governor and one term as Secretary of State.

Sayres Memorial Park

Lake Washington Boulevard S. and 46th S.
Size: 15 acres (including shorelands)
Bus: 39 to Genesee, then north several blocks
Major uses: boat launch, hydro races

DESCRIPTION
Sayres Memorial Park is a small asphalted peninsula with hydroplane pits, boat launching ramps and piers, a water ski pier, a central racing office, restrooms, and a public telephone. This place is crammed with people around the first week of August, when the unlimited hydros are roaring around the adjacent three-mile course to qualify for the big final, the Seafair or Gold Cup race on Sunday.

On the day of the big race, the beach for miles in either direction is flooded with spectators, captivated by the roar of engines and the spray of roostertails as the jet-propelled craft zoom along the lake's surface at speeds well over 100 miles per hour. During other times of the year, the park is a quiet but popular boat launching center. And sometimes the wind is just right for kite flying, too.

NEARBY ATTRACTIONS
Genesee Park and Playfield is located on the other side of Lake Washington Boulevard. And about three-fourths of a mile south on the boulevard, you'll pass the marshy, mast-infested **Lakewood Boat Moorage.** The gate may be locked, but if you talk into the intercom, either the security guard or manager will probably let you in for a walk along the docks, which are flanked with bright planter boxes, lily pads, and a raft "For Ducks Only." In the last three years, they have fixed up the place considerably. It includes a marine store (specializing in hard-to-find marine hardware) and gift shop, with coffee and snacks for sale. Soon they hope to offer paddle-boat rides on the lake, but for the time being, just the unique view of the **Seward Park Peninsula** to the south is worth the stop.

HISTORY

Sayres Park sits on a low, flat finger of land that once was submerged beneath Lake Washington. In pioneer days, this area was the mouth of Wetmore Slough, which extended southwestward all the way to Columbia City, nearly a mile away. The slough was named for Seymore Wetmore, who founded a tanning and shoe-making business here in 1855 with his partner, M. D. Woodin. (For lack of business in Seattle, Woodin later moved north and founded the town of Woodinville.)

In 1909, the slough became the endpoint for the new Lake Washington Boulevard, which looped here and turned northward again. Three years later the slough was bridged with a trestle, leaving a hump in the middle for the passage of boats to Columbia City.

The 1917 opening of the Lake Washington Ship Canal lowered the lake nine feet, drying up Columbia City's dreams of becoming a seaport and leaving a swampy valley in place of the slough. In later years, the slough was filled in (see "Genesee Park" History), and in 1937 a works project replaced the old boulevard trestle with dirt.

Meanwhile, the popular Mount Baker Bathing Beach to the north was getting crowded. It became especially congested after Stan Sayres transplanted the Gold Cup hydroplane races from Detroit to Seattle in 1950 and set up headquarters at the Mount Baker Boathouse. By 1954, Sayres had won five consecutive Gold Cup events with his phenomenal three-point design hydros—Slo Mo Shun IV and V—and set a new speed record of 178.5 miles per hour. In 1955, Joe Schoenith took the cup back to Detroit, and the following year Slo Mo Shun IV flipped and sank in the Detroit river. Sayres died of a heart attack that fall.

The year after Sayres' death the Wetmore Cove site was dredged and converted into the present Sayres Memorial Park.

Seward Park

Lake Washington Boulevard S. and S. Juneau
Size: 277.8 acres (70.2 acres shorelands)
Bus: 39
Major uses: picnics, swimming, hiking, biking

DESCRIPTION

Seward Park is located on Bailey Peninsula, a prominent, forested finger of land poking out into Lake Washington just west of Merce▪

Island. Thanks to the foresight of a few early planners and pioneers, much of this glacier-carved finger has been left just as it was over a hundred years ago. Wooded slopes and picnic meadows spread out below spacious parking lots on the gently inclined south end, while "upland" pathways lace through acres of magnificent forest. Completely encircled by lakeside roads and runways, this is southeast Seattle's major multi-purpose park—unquestionably one of the most beautiful in the city.

A QUICK TOUR OF SEWARD PARK
Enter the park by turning onto S. Juneau Street from Lake Washington Boulevard and circle around to the left, where you will find the **Art Studio Annex,** a public telephone, restrooms, and a portable concession stand in summer. From here you can make a quick acquaintance loop by taking the right fork of the road uphill to the upper parking and picnic areas.

If you're a bicycler or a jogger, you will probably want to start your peninsular rounds on the asphalt path heading east from Picnic Shelter #1. The other alternative is to go straight ahead to the small parking lot facing the swimming beach on Andrews Bay. Like most of the other boulevard beaches, this one includes a raft with a diving board, a swimming area for tots, and lifeguards in the summer.

Part of the adjacent bathhouse includes restrooms, beach facilities, and a first aid station. However, the major portion has become the home of the **Seward Park Art Studio** (723-5780). Here, for moderate prices, professional instructors teach a variety of visual arts, including drawing, sculpture, jewelry making, leaded glass and textile design, and a variety of arts for children of ages three to thirteen. In their off hours, instructors make their own clay creations, which they display and sell to the public, notably around Christmas time. The studio is open from 9 a.m. to 5 p.m. Call for information and brochures.

The neck of the peninsula includes a wide, flat lawn that beckons sunbathers and Frisbee throwers. At its south end, near the park entrance, you will find the Japanese Garden and Torii Gate of Welcome and an eight-ton Japanese stone lantern, a gift from the city of Yokohama in gratitude for American assistance after the earthquake of 1923. Two tennis courts are on the other side of the boulevard.

The southern uplands are amply supplied with parking lots, giving access to beautifully wooded hillsides and picnic meadows, picnic shelters, restrooms, and a central amphitheatre (with sloping grass seating for up to 3,000), which can be rented for outdoor plays and small concerts.

The shoreline road and pathways are popular runways and bike-ways (off limits to cars). Joggers, particularly, find the 2.5-mile

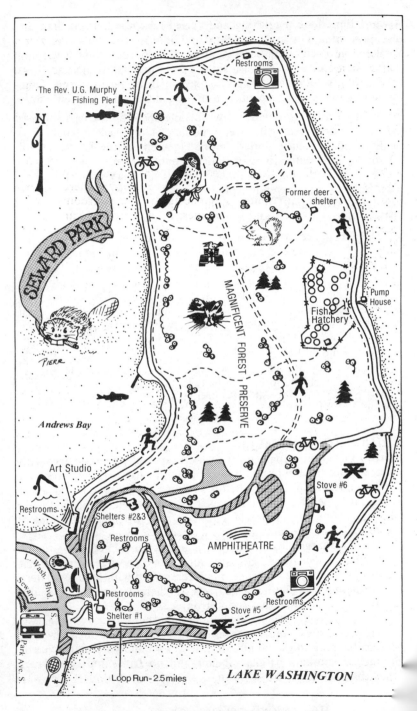

The Rev. U.G. Murphy
Fishing Pier

N

SEWARD PARK

PIERR

Andrews Bay

Art Studio

Restrooms

L. Wash. Blvd.

Seward

Park Ave. S.

Restrooms

Shelters #2&3

Restrooms

Restrooms

Shelter #1

Loop Run - 2.5 miles

AMPHITHEATRE

Stove #5

Restrooms

Restrooms

MAGNIFICENT FOREST PRESERVE

Former deer
shelter

Pump
House

Fish
Hatchery

Stove #6

LAKE WASHINGTON

Seward Park loop a relaxing and varied run, less harried than the often crowded Green Lake path and almost the same distance. Walkers, too, enjoy sauntering along the shoreline and sweeping their vision along the western side of Mercer Island, then north to the floating bridge and Lake Washington Boulevard as they round the northern tip of the peninsula and head back to Andrews Bay.

Another attraction which slows people down on the east shore is the **Fish Hatchery** and its twenty pools of trophy-sized trout. This facility, most recently under the management of the University of Washington, is slated to be open to the public from 9 a.m. to 5 p.m. Aside from producing some 50,000 giant trout every year to stock in local lakes, the university plans to put up displays of Pacific Northwest trout and Lake Washington ecology, and to give summer lectures on trout and salmon behavior.

The forest preserve is one of the most glorious aspects of the entire park. A wide central trail leads lengthwise through the center of the park, with vein-like paths branching down forested hillsides to the east and west. Here is the Northwest almost as the pioneers found it: centuries-old Douglas fir and western red cedar, maples, hemlocks, salmonberry, thimbleberry, and ocean spray. Here you can find spider webs glistening with dewdrops and ants marching along their minute forest pathways. Sparrows and thrushes call from thickets, while nuthatches and woodpeckers probe trunks for insects and chickadees tumble in treetops. This also the home of the Douglas squirrel, the mountain beaver, the raccoon, and the white-footed mouse—an unspoiled ecosystem for the studying and enjoying.

THINGS TO REMEMBER
Seward Park is unsurpassed for picnics, especially gigantic ones with children. But be sure to pick your spot with care, particularly if you have a large group. Picnic Shelter #1, near a brightly colored set of swings, includes five small barbecue pits and two picnic tables. Picnic Shelters #2 and #3 on Pinoy Hill are large log structures (not entirely rainproof), and probably the most attractive picnic sites for large groups. Two large circular barbecues in Shelter #2 and two twenty-foot tables in Shelter #3 are surrounded by another twenty-some tables and a few odd barbecue pits interspersed with fir trees. There is also a modern play area nearby, which makes it an especially handy spot for school and scout groups.

For a quieter feeling, Shelter #4, another big area with two central barbecues, looks out onto the sloping east meadow and Mercer Island homes and hillsides. Stoves #5 and #6 are uncovered, chimneyed smokers with no shelter and no frills, and few places ther than the grass to sit down.

HISTORY

As Seattle grew outward from the shores of Elliott Bay, the distant Bailey Peninsula remained in its wilderness state. Indian fishing and hunting parties undoubtedly visited it before the arrival of white settlers, for it abounded with wildlife.

In the 1880s, a Frenchman supposedly built the first homestead in the vicinity of the present amphitheatre. In 1886, the peninsula was bought by Walter Graham (see "Martha Washington Park History"), who sold it soon afterward to a man named Philip Ritz. Ritz in turn sold the peninsula to realtor William E. Bailey in 1890. Owing to Bailey's prominence as owner of the *Press-Time* newspaper (now the *Seattle Times*), it became known as Bailey's Peninsula.

But the peninsula was still too far from town to be of much profit to Bailey, and in 1892 Seattle Park Superintendent E. O. Schwagerl proposed that the city buy it as part of its first Comprehensive Plan. Many argued that the peninsula was too far from town, but Schwagerl knew better. Luckily, his opinion was backed by the Olmsted Brothers as they developed a plan for Seattle's parks in 1903. In 1911, the city bought the peninsula for $322,000 and named it after William H. Seward, the Secretary of State who was responsible for America's purchase of Alaska in 1867. (Ironically, the statue of Seward stands in Volunteer Park.)

Development of the park was slow at first. The Olmsteds recommended only improvements that would fit in well with the natural setting. The city built a pier for steamers and began filling in the marshy neck to prevent the peninsula from becoming an island during seasonal rises in the lake level. In 1917, the lowering of Lake Washington by construction of the Ship Canal exposed the wide, grassy meadow that now leads to the swimming beach.

In 1919, more boat docking and a plank roadway from Seattle increased the popularity of the park, and larger numbers of people began congregating there. Over the years, it has become a favorite picnic site for scout troops and ethnic groups. For example, Seattle Filipinos, who have picnicked in the park for many years, named Pinoy Hill; and the Campfire Girls, who have also had countless gatherings here, have built a symbolic campfire circle near the south shore.

The bathhouse was constructed in 1927 to allow increasing throngs of bathers to change clothes and shower in privacy. The fish-rearing ponds were built in 1935 as part of an effort to make Lake Washington a "fisherman's paradise." But as the human throngs increased, wildlife began to wane. In 1941, the mink that had inhabited the park (and loved to feed on fingerling trout) were trapped by the Game Department, as were the last few deer that had swum over from Mercer Island to munch at the park's feeding facility.

The park became people oriented. In 1953, a Greek-style amphitheatre was hollowed out on the south hillside and for years was the scene of lavish orchestra, chorus, and dance productions under the direction of Gustave Stern. Concerts were so successful that they caused enormous bottlenecks on the one-way street, and today the theatre is used more casually.

Despite the civilizing influences at Seward Park, a large part of the peninsula remains wild and relatively untouched. The northern upland forests have been consciously left alone over the years for the enjoyment of future generations.

 # Sturgus Park

S. Charles and Sturgus S.
Size: 1.3 acres
Buses: 7, 142 on Rainier S.
Major use: natural woods

DESCRIPTION

Sturgus Park is a wooded hillside that sprouts up below the girders of the Jose Rizal Bridge at the foot of Beacon Hill. Its trees and vines climb toward the hillside just west of the Goodwill buildings, adding leaves to the visual feast that northbound drivers have of Puget Sound and the city. The park was bought by the city in 1904, and named for John Sturgus, a realtor of the 1890s.

 # South College Street Park

S. College and 29th S.
Size: 0.4 acre
Bus: 14 to 31st and S. College
Major use: neighborhood playground

DESCRIPTION

A few blocks up the hill from Sick's Stadium and southeast of the city's new tennis center, this park is just a parched piece of grass—no play area, no ballfield, no picnic tables, no frills. Even so, this half block of open space, with its few dilapidated benches, a drinking fountain, and a trash can in each corner, is a much-loved picnic and play spot for the community of small homes surrounding it. Children bike and skateboard around it, taking the hoods off the garbage cans to use as bases for softball games. The park was bought by the city with Forward Thrust Bond money in 1970.

NEARBY ATTRACTIONS
The hillside just northeast of Sick's Stadium is packed with blackberry bushes. Try a mouthwatering drive along 28th Avenue S. sometime in August. The **Seattle Tennis Center** (324-2980) is also nearby, at 2000 Empire Way S.

37th Avenue S. Mini Park

37th S. and S. Holly
Size: 0.6 acre
Buses: 42, 107
Major use: neighborhood playground

DESCRIPTION
This small play area in Holly Park brightens up a dead-end road. Six hoops are often popping with basketballs. Little ones clamber and slide nearby, and those who want a rest sit on benches a short distance away. This property was transferred to the park department in 1973.

INDEX

Bold Face indicates map entry.